AF564429

Advertising Management

Advertising Management

Dr. Atul Mathur
Louis Taunton

RANDOM PUBLICATIONS
NEW DELHI - 110 002 (INDIA)

Advertising Management

ISBN 978-93-51113-00-3

Published in 2014 in India by

RANDOM PUBLICATIONS

4376-A/4B, Gali Murari Lal, Ansari Road
New Delhi-110 002
Phone: +9111-43580356, 23289044
E-mail: randomexports@gmail.com; sales@randompublications.com;
info@randompublications.com
Reprint : 2021

Type Setting by: Friends Media, Delhi-110089
Digitally Printed at : Replika Press Pvt. Ltd.

Acknowledgement

It is a matter of great honor for me to place on record my gratitudes towards those who were of great help during the completion of this book.

Firstly I would like to pay my regards and reverence at the holy feet of Radhasoami Dayal, who showered all his grace, mercy and blessings on me during the completion of this book. To my revered father professor Dr. Agam Prasad Mathur popularly known as Dadaji, I express my sincere thanks and regards, it is he who has nurtured me and has made me whatever I am today. I bow before him and pray to almighty that he keeps showering his love and affection on me always.

For my wife Smt. Deepa Mathur I have no words to express my deep sense of gratitude for the unconditional support and encouragement, to my children Ms. Sureeti, Ms. Suhani and Saras, I am thankful for their constant support and suggestions. For my grandson Deep I wish to convey all my love and affection.

To the publisher of this book Mr. Sushil Mehra and Mr. Atul Mehra and to Mr. Rahul Singhal, I have no words to express my thanks as it would not have possible without them to publish this book.

Last but not the least I wish to dedicate this book to my brother late Dr. Achint Kumar, for it is he who always had been a guiding force behind me, I miss you a lot dada.

Dr. Atul Mathur

Preface

Advertising management is the process of overseeing campaigns that seek to inform and attract consumers regarding a particular good or service. This process begins with the first stages of the market research that helps to create the advertising strategy, moves on to the development of the general outline for the campaign, the creation of a specific plan of action and the launching of the completed project. Without effective advertising management, ad campaigns and public relations efforts tend to founder and produce little or no results.

Effective advertising always begins by engaging in competent advertising research. The research helps to identify the sectors of the consumer market that are most likely to positively respond to a given product. In order to identify these niche markets within the larger group of consumers, researchers will not only seek to understand what appeals to these buyers but why those goods and services have that inherent appeal. The data collected from the research can then be used to enhance the marketability of products, addressing everything from function to packaging.

The next phase of the advertising management process has to do with deciding exactly how to apply the data collected during the research stage. Here the basis for deciding on what forms of advertising are most appropriate begins to take shape. Depending on the specifics of the products and the nature of the niche markets that the campaign will seek to connect with, advertising services such as print media, and radio, television, or the Internet may be deemed the most appropriate options. Once the niche markets are identified and the determination of which types of advertising media are most appropriate for the campaign, advertising management focuses on the creation of the specifics of the overall campaign. This may involve such elements as the development of print ads for use in magazines and newspapers, audio campaigns for radio advertising, or commercials appropriate for television broadcast or streaming across the Internet. Because any given campaign may use several advertising options in one campaign, the process of advertising management also involves making sure all strategies complement one another and present a unified public image to consumers. To function in advertising management, it is necessary to possess the proper training. Advertising training is often a combination of formal education and experience derived from working under the direction of more seasoned professionals who have learned over time how to identify and interact with consumers in order to secure the data needed to structure a campaign. While creativity and inspiration are always vital elements in any advertising campaign, the ability to organize and view the greater picture are essential to managing the process and launching a campaign that will successfully reach the right consumers and generate the desired amount of revenue over the lifetime of the campaign.

The present book deals with all the important dimensions of this subject. It is a valuable reference source for all those concerned with this subject.

I thank all members of my team who have helped in the preparation of the book. My special thanks go to "Random Publications" who have published the book.

—Louis Taunton

Contents

1

Introduction

Advertising is the means of informing as well as influencing the general public to buy products or services through visual or oral messages. A product or service is advertised to create an awareness in the minds of potential buyers. Some of the commonly used media for advertising are TV, radio, websites, newspapers, magazines, billboards, hoardings etc. As a result of economic liberalization and the changing social trends advertising industry has shown rapid growth in the last decade.

Advertising is one of the aspects of mass communication. Advertising is actually brand-building through effective communication and is essentially a service industry. It helps to create demand, promote marketing system and boost economic growth. Thus advertising forms the basis of marketing.

Advertising plays a significant role in today's highly competitive world. A career in advertisement is quite glamourous and at the same time challenging with more and more agencies opening up every day. Whether it's brands, companies, personalities or even voluntary or religious organizations, all of them use some form of advertising in order to be able to communicate with the target audience. The salary structure in advertising is quite high and if you have the knack for it one can reach the top. It is an ideal profession for a creative individual who can handle work-pressure.

Today, new areas are emerging within advertising like event management, image management, internet marketing etc. Event management wherein events are marketed, Image management wherein a particular profile of an individual or an organisation is projected. Internet marketing has also brought about a lot of changes in advertising as Internet means that one is catering to a select group of audience rather than a mass audience.

Remuneration: Job positions and earnings in an agency vary with its size and turnover. Accredited agencies have a large set up while small agencies may have just a handful of employees looking after all the various jobs. The earnings range from 7,000 for production mangers to 8,000 for copy writers up to 35,000 for General Managers plus perks.

Eligibility & Course Areas: Educational: Most advertising agencies recruit candidates with a formal management or advertising/ mass communication qualification. Preference is given for MBA's for posts in the market research, client servicing and media planning departments. In the creative department, on the other hand, a general BA with a command of the language of communication plus knowledge of designing packages like Photoshop, coral draw or fine arts is the requirement.

There are also specialised courses in advertising/mass communication at diploma level and post graduate level for which basic qualification is graduation. However, advertising is also offered as a subject for the graduate degree course in mass communication studies at certain institutions for which minimum qualification is 10+2. In addition there are also certificate courses for which 10+2 is enough.

Personal attributes: Basic qualities like creativity and flair for writing or ability to translate ideas into a visual format are required for making a successful career in this field. They should have insight into the interests of people from all walks of life, ability to work as part of team, mental and physical toughness to be able to withstand high pressure and criticism, must be sociable and have calm temperament. Market and media researchers should have an analytical and logical brain. Those in creative field should possess artistic abilities to make the ad appealing to the masses.

Job Prospects & Career Options

Job Prospects : Career opportunities in advertising include openings in private advertising agencies; advertising department in private or public sector companies; in advertising sections of newspapers, journals, magazines; commercial section of radio or television; market research organisations etc. One can also do freelancing.

Career Options: Advertising field offers a range of lucrative, interesting careers. The job in this field is categorised into two, executive and creative. Executive side include Client Servicing, Market Research and Media Research. Creative side consist of copywriters, scriptwriters, visualisers, photographers and typographers.

The executive department understand client needs, find new business and retain existing business, selects the appropriate media, analyses timing and placement of advertisements and negotiate the financial aspects of the deal. Creative department creates the advertisement copy. They verbalises and visualises the specific need of the client. As ad films are also a part of film making career options of film are related to this field.

Executive Department

Client Servicing: The Client Servicing department is the link between the client and the agency. It is an important part of any advertising firm like what the heart is to the body. This department is responsible for meeting prospective clients and getting business for the company. It involves a study of the client, the product and the market; an analysis of consumer behaviour and marketing; a knowledge of all available media and their cost effectiveness and a strategic plan to be presented to the client. Those in client servicing must therefore interact with clients, gather information, oversee research where necessary, gauge consumer attitudes and based on this, work along with the various departments of the agency to formulate the most appropriate and effective advertising strategy within the specified budget.

To be an effective client-servicing person, the candidate has to have a thorough knowledge of the client's business and also know his weak points so that, through advertising and communications, the gap can be minimised.

An accounts executive who works in the client servicing department takes care of all the monitory dealings. He should know the most effective way to advertise clients product or service *i.e.* the media and their cost effectiveness. Account executives should also have an idea about market research and target audiences.

Market Research: Every good ad plans, start with research. This is the department which surveys the market and analyses and studies consumer behaviour about a product or service. They are involved with collection of data- information about the consumer, the market, existing competition and so on. The research studies provide basic information to the manufacturer, for planning a new product.

If you are a MBA or hold a degree in statistics/operations research, you can go for market researching jobs.

Media Planning/Research: Responsibility of media planning department starts at the point when the ad is complete. Media Department is responsible for the planning, scheduling, booking and purchase of space and time (in newspapers, magazines, radio and TV and outdoor hoardings). The media department must therefore devise the most effective use for an advertising budget to effectively and economically transmit a campaign message to the target audience. This department consists of the following:

Media Planners who decide the different media where the ads would be featured in order to get maximum viewership.

Media Buyer has to negotiate to buy space in the Press, or time on electronic media at the best rates for which he has to understand the buying as well as selling trends.

Creative Department : The Creative department designs and conceptualizes the advertisement. This consist of copywriting department and art department. Copywriting department works on text for the ad and themes for campaign. Art department visualises the campaign.

Copywriters: The Copywriter evolves a theme for the campaign and provides the text for advertisements. He is responsible for making the ad look attractive and delivering the message to the point. They work out the campaign slogan, jingles, scripts and promotional literature of the product or service as well as proposals, concept notes and film treatments. They are also expected to edit all textual matter for factual, syntax and typesetting discrepancies before it goes into production. Some times specialists called Typographers are appointed for making the format of textual matter who give advise on fonts, lettering etc. Copywriters need to have a flair for writing backed up by the knowledge of advertising and oral communication skills, to become successful. They also need to have skill in analysing clients' needs and research skills for finding out about the products and services they are helping to sell. Problem-solving and time-management skills are important.

Visualisers: The Visualisers work on the visual concepts and decide how the ad shall eventually look. They do the overall layout of message including graphics, sketching etc.

Must be Artistic: A degree/diploma in commercial arts or fine arts as well as the knowledge of designing software like Photoshop, Pagemaker, Corel Draw etc. are often the required qualifications.

Photographers: Photographers should have an idea about angles and lighting effects. Good technical ability and knowledge of cameras and lenses is essential.

Advertising is a major career in Western countries. It is a new and fast growing career in all developing countries including India. The special importance of advertising as a profession is that it has room for so many different kinds of talents.

Once advertising simply meant a good- looking model and a clever head line. Business today is new and complex. The old methods will no longer work. Today more and more products are competing in the market. A whole new set of problems has been created by foreign brands. An entirely new concept of advertising is replacing the old. Clients have become very concerned about the brand image of their products.

Advertising plays a critical role in marketing a product. The success and survival of a product depend to a large extent on its advertising. Advertising is very powerful and it is very costly too. A full page ad in a newspaper like the Times of India may cost Rs.14 lakhs and a 30 second display on Doordarshan's national net work may be about 4.5 lakhs. Advertising is a big business. There is much more to advertising than a cute picture or a catchy slogan. It may take months of hard work for a professional team to set forth the right advertising strategy for a product.

Career Options: Advertising as a profession is a general term, which includes numerous professions. There are several kinds of advertising jobs in a wide variety of areas. Career options are plenty with Advertising Agencies. In advertising agencies, you will find creative people, researchers, production specialists, media experts, management people, account planners and so on. These various functions call for different types of talents, skills and training. Similarly, job opportunities are there with the advertising departments of Companies, with the media, in Public Relations, TV Software Production etc.

Advertising Agencies: You can find a job as a Copy Writer, Art Director/Visualiser, Account Executive/Account Manager, or as Account Planner

Market Research: You can have a career in Market Research. Researchers work on questionnaire design, interviews, sampling techniques and statistical analysis to arrive at meaningful results. Large companies have market research departments. But the job of a researcher in an advertising agency is somewhat different. Here the research is aimed at formulating advertising strategies, evaluating the effectiveness of advertisements etc.

The Media: The media includes the press, the TV, radio, exhibitions and anything, which can be used to carry an advertising message. It may be the side of a bus or a flying balloon. Media professionals ensure that the advertisement gets the best coverage at the lowest cost. Newspapers, magazines, TV and radio sell advertising space or time. This is a growing area for talented professionals.

Govt. Departments: Central and state governments have departments for advertising and publicity.

Working Freelance: It is quite common for advertising people to do freelance work for several agencies. You can work freelance full time or part time and can earn good money

Own Agency: Many advertising professionals start their own agencies. It does not require much capital to start a non-INS accredited agency. Small agencies like these are now spreading all over India and doing quite well.

Advertising Jobs

India is considered to be a great source for creativity; its people are sought after by everyone abroad and they command a lot of respect in the International Advertising Community. The country is now on the international map. The global impact of the Indian aptitude with respect to the advertising Industry is not only being noticed but appreciated worldwide.

The advertising in India is quite superior and the local talent boasts of high production values with interesting ideas and concepts, thus, making it a desirable hub for International Recruiters.

The Advertising Career: There are numerous career options available in the advertising world. In a typical Ad-agency, there are various job options, like, an advertising manager, who administers creative, in-house accounts and Media services departments. Then there is an account executive who manages the account services department in advertising agencies, determines the need for advertising and maintains the accounts of clients. Another vital department in the advertising world is 'The creative services department' which is responsible for developing the subject matter and presentation of the advertisements. There is a creative director who oversees the copy chief, art director, copywriters and associated staff. Then there exists a media department which is headed by a media director who organize planning groups that select the communication media, like, radio, television, newspapers, magazines, Internet, or outdoor signs in order to disseminate the ads.

Other Advertising Career Opportunities: There are many professions, trades and art forms that are closely connected with the advertising industry. You may find one of them suits your talents best, or, they could open the door to a career in an agency.

These include career options as, Printer, Photographer, Illustrator, Commercials Director, Public Relations, Direct Marketing, Designer, Sales Promotion, Set Designer, Make-up Artist, Commercials Producer, Model, voice-over, Sound Engineer, Typographer, Stylist, Brand/ Product Manager, Market Research Analyst.

Job Scenario: The world has woken up to the fact that India is a big market. We have seen every possible global brand available in India. With respect to the advertising industry, it is maximizing this new opportunity. An opportunity to work on global brands is helping the local talents think and stay ahead with the rest of the world. In this knowledge driven industry, its the Indian Advertising Industry's ideas and accepted wisdom, which has shaped winning strategies and scripted many success stories.

The job applicants face a more stable environment but a highly competitive market. Projections for the coming years suggest an average growth of over 30% for marketing research analysts, advertising managers and visual artists. Nevertheless, the International Recruiters will continue to be highly selective. The most motivated, energetic, well-organized candidates with top-notch analytic and communication skills will land the best jobs.

The Recruiters look for the following attributes:

The Must Have's

- Creativity, high motivation, resistant to stress, flexibility and decisiveness.
- Ability to communicate persuasively, both orally and in writing.
- (with other managers, staff and the public)

- Tact and good judgment.
- Exceptional ability to establish and maintain effective personal relationships.
- (with supervisory and professional staff members and client firms)

Eligibility: Though there exists a wide assortment of educational backgrounds which are applicable for accessing the avenues of advertising, but most of the employers favour candidates with a broad liberal arts background plus experience in related occupations. A bachelor's degree in sociology, psychology, literature, journalism, or philosophy, among other subjects, is more acceptable. However, requirements vary, depending upon the kind of job.

For management positions in advertising, some recruiters also look for a Postgraduate Degree in advertising or journalism. The course of study should include marketing, consumer behaviour, market research, sales, communication methods, technology and visual arts.

Like other industries, advertising industry worldwide has toed the line where they look for Indian workforce for outsourcing bulk of their work.

Advertising and Marketing Communications

There is perhaps, no other business that so greatly influences our daily lives. Our choices regarding the type of cars we drive, the beer we drink, or the clothes we wear, are largely influenced by advertising.

The Work: As a career, advertising offers a unique blend of opportunities. In few other industries will you find a more eclectic group of individuals — all under one roof! The main areas of operation are client servicing, media planning, creative and research.

Client Servicing: The front face of the agency, Client Servicing, represents the agency to the client and the client within the agency. After receiving a detailed brief from the client, the Account Executive and Account Planner chalk out a strategy based on the brand's positioning, its USP and its communication objective. While the better agencies require an MBA, some others will be satisfied with a Degree/ Diploma in marketing or mass communication.

Accounts Planning: This is a senior-level position in the Servicing Department. It involves evolving the overall strategic plan including the budget, selecting the right media and zeroing-in on the communication message after interacting with the client and internally with the creative team, the media planning department and if necessary, the market research agency. The various elements of the communication package are integrated into a logical whole in the context of the brand and its desired positioning in the market.

Media Planning: Media Planners help ad agencies choose the best outlet or medium to reach the customer they want. They plan, schedule, book and purchase space in the print media (newspapers, magazines) or outdoors (billboards, kiosks and bus panels) and time (TV & radio, internet). The media planning exercise may also involve conducting some targeted brand or need-specific research to assess recall and viewership/readership of a campaign.

Typically, media planners have a background in Maths and Statistics, an MBA (from MICA or a good B-school) or an MBE and are good with computers and number-crunching using sophisticated software.

The Creative Department: The creative department's task is to harness the right words, the most appropriate and arresting visuals — anything and everything that will grab the attention and prompt a sale.

The creative team in an agency can be further divided into two sections: Copy and Creative.

Copy Department: After the AE briefs the creative team, the Copywriter gets down to the task of putting across the message in words — headline, followed by the body copy in the case of a press ad, a dialogue or jingle for a radio spot, or a detailed story board in the case of a TV commercial.

A good copywriter must be able to think laterally and originally each time, to corelate masses of data and research findings so as to present the conclusions in language that is lucid and convincing. Besides a way with words, you need infinite patience to chisel and craft words into a subtly compelling sales pitch, until you've got it just right. And above all, you need to be highly creative and versatile. However unlike poetry or short story writing, copywriting is not creativity for creativity's sake. The famous ad guru, David Ogilvy, puts it very succinctly, "If it doesn't sell, it isn't creative."

Most copywriters start out as copy trainees after taking a copy test administered by the agency and proceed to write their way to the advertising hall of fame.

The Art Department: Takes care of the overall "look and feel" of the campaign starting with a "scribble" or rough sketch which accommodates the various components *i.e.* headline, visual, picture, text, logo, etc. in a balanced format within the given space.

Selecting the size and type of the font (lettering), the photographic treatment and the overall treatment of the TV commercial is the purview of the visualisers and art directors who man (and woman) the art department.

While a high level of originality and creative talent form the mainstay, a BFA or degree in applied art or graphic design with knowledge of computer graphics/multimedia is mandatory.

Market Research: The Research department tries to measure the effectiveness of the ad campaign. It Is research that provides the media planner and creatives a scientific and measurable basis to sharp-focus their strategy. These professionals are from a variety of disciplines, but share a common comfort level with mathematical or statistical modelling, sampling techniques and psychographics.

What it Takes?: Advertising demands a high level of creativity, imagination and innovative thinking from every person working in this profession. Writers and artists need to develop a portfolio of their best work. This might include work from art school, or as a result of freelance assignments. Although no specific academic degree is required by most agencies, a commercial or graphic arts course from a reputed college of art coupled with some knowledge of multimedia and computer graphics is essential for those pitching for a spot in the art department. Account Executives on the other hand, usually have a business degree in marketing, or mass communication or specifically in advertising.

What you'll Make?: In this industry rewards are directly commensurate with the initiative you display, the effort you put in and the results you achieve. If you are ambitious and hard working, you can quickly move up the ladder. Starting with Rs.3,500 or thereabouts as a fresh wet-behind-the-ears trainee, you can easily gross ten times as much five years down the line if you've got what it takes.

Where to Train?: Very few colleges offer specialisation in advertising at the bachelor's level. However, elements of advertising such as media planning and client servicing are covered in Mass Communication courses offered at both the undergraduate and postgraduate level.

- Indian Institute of Mass Communication, Aruna Asaf Ali Marg, JNU, New Campus, New Delhi 110067 (UT)

- MS University of Baroda, Fatehganj, Vadodara 390002. (Guj)
- Mudra Institute of Communications (MICA), Shela, Ahmedabad 380007 (Guj)
- Narsee Monjee Institute of Management Studies, V.L. Mehta Road, Vile Parle (West), Mumbai-400056. (Mah)
- National Institute of Advertising, Deen Dayal Upadhyay Marg, New Delhi 110002 (UT).
- National Institute of Design (NID), Paldi, Ahmedabad 380007 (Guj)
- Sir J.J. Institute of Applied Art, Dr. D.N. Road, Mumbai 400001
- University of Delhi, College of Art, Tilak Marg, New Delhi 110002

Advertising Sales Agents

Significant Points: Overall earnings are higher than average but can vary considerably because they are usually based on a salary plus performance-based commissions and bonuses. Pressure to meet monthly sales quotas can be stressful.

Nature of the Work: Advertising sales agents—often referred to as *account executives* or *advertising sales representatives*—sell or solicit advertising, including graphic art, advertising space in publications, custom-made signs, or television and radio advertising time.

More than half of all advertising sales agents work in the information sector, mostly for media firms, including television and radio broadcasters, print and Internet publishers and cable programme distributors. Other agents work for firms engaged in direct mail advertising or display and outdoor advertising, such as billboards and signs. Because most revenue for magazines, newspapers, directories and broadcasters is generated from advertising, advertising sales agents play an important role in their success.

Outside sales agents call on clients and prospects at their place of business. They may have an appointment, or they may practice "cold calling," arriving without an appointment. *Inside sales agents* work on their employer's premises and handle sales to customers who walk in or telephone the firm to inquire about advertising.

Some also may make telephone sales calls—calling prospects, attempting to sell the media firm's advertising space or time and arranging follow-up appointments between interested prospects and outside sales agents. Advertising sales agents should not be confused with *telemarketers,* whose duties are limited solely to soliciting orders for goods or services over the telephone and who work primarily in call centres that provide telemarketing services on contract.

Within the advertising and related services industry, media representative firms sell advertising space or time for media owners, including print and Internet publishers, radio and television stations and cable systems. Media representative firms maintain offices in major cities and employ their own teams of advertising sales agents.

These agents work exclusively with the executives at advertising agencies, called media buyers, who purchase advertising space for their clients. Media representative firms may represent any number of publications and radio or television stations, selling space to advertising agencies with clients who want to initiate a national advertising campaign or place advertisements outside their local market.

Sales agents employed in media representation normally do not cultivate new advertisers but maintain contacts with existing advertisers through the advertising agencies. A local television or radio station or publication would have a national sales manager to promote its best interests and coordinate the efforts of all the media representative firms on its behalf.

Local sales agents are employed by local publications or radio and television stations and are responsible for sales in a local territory. For these sales agents, obtaining new accounts is an important part of the job and they may spend much of their time travelling to and visiting prospective advertisers and current clients.

During a sales call, they discuss the client's advertising needs and suggest how their products and services can meet those needs. A critical part of building a relationship with a client is to find out as much as possible about the client and its products. Sales agents inquire about the client's current customers, prospective customers and the geographic area of the target market.

During the first meeting with a client, sales agents gather background information and explain how specific types of advertising will help promote a client's products or services most effectively. Next, the advertising sales agent prepares an advertising proposal to present to the client. This entails determining the advertising medium to be used, preparing sample advertisements and providing clients with estimates of the cost of the proposal. Consolidation in the media industries has brought the sale of different types of advertising under one roof. Sales are increasingly made of integrated packages that include advertisements to be placed in print, online and with a broadcast subsidiary.

After a contract has been established, advertising sales agents serve as the main contact between the client and the firm. They handle communication between the parties and assist the client in developing sample artwork or radio and television spots. They also arrange for commercial taping sessions and may accompany clients to the sessions.

Beyond selling, advertising sales agents have other duties as well. They analyze sales statistics, prepare reports and handle the scheduling of their appointments and work hours. They read about new and existing products and monitor the sales, prices and products of their competitors. In many firms, the advertising sales agent handles the drafting of contracts specifying the advertising work to be performed and its cost, as well as the billing and record-keeping for their customers' accounts—which may include customer service responsibilities such as answering questions or addressing any problems the client may have with the proposal. Sales agents also are responsible for developing sales tools, promotional plans and media kits, which they use to help make the sale.

Working Conditions: Selling can be stressful work because income and job security depend directly on the agent's ability to maintain and expand clientele. Companies generally set monthly sales quotas and place considerable pressure on advertising sales agents to meet those quotas. The added stress of rejection places more pressure on the agent.

Many advertising sales agents work more than 40 hours per week. Although the hours are long and often irregular, most have the freedom to determine their own schedule. The Internet and other electronic tools allow agents to do more work from home or while on the road, enabling them to send messages and documents to clients and coworkers, keep up with industry news and access databases that help them target potential customers. Advertising sales agents use e-mail to conduct much of the business with their clients. Use of e-mail has considerably shortened the time it takes to negotiate a sale and place the ad. Sales agents may accomplish more in less time, but many work more hours than in the past, spending additional time on follow-up and service calls.

Training, Other Qualifications and Advancement: Some employers prefer applicants with a college degree, particularly for sales positions that require meeting with clients. Courses in marketing, leadership, communication, business and advertising are helpful. For those who sell over the telephone or who have a proven record of successfully selling other products, a high school degree may be sufficient. After gaining entry into the occupation, successful sales experience becomes more important than education when looking for a position. In general, smaller companies are more willing to hire unproven individuals.

Personality traits are equally important as academic background. Because they represent their employers to the executives of client organizations, advertising sales agents must have excellent interpersonal and written communication skills. Employers look for applicants who possess a pleasant personality, honesty and a neat professional appearance. Self-motivation, organization, persistence, independence and the ability to multitask are required because advertising sales agents set their own schedules and perform their duties without much supervision.

Training takes place mainly on the job. In most cases, an experienced sales manager instructs a newly hired advertising sales agent who lacks sales experience. In this one-on-one environment, the supervisor typically coaches the new hire and observes as she makes sales calls and contacts clients. The supervisor then advises the new hire on ways to improve. To conduct more specialized training—for example, in selling to a particular market segment, such as real estate professionals or automotive dealers—the employer may bring in a consultant.

Advancement in the occupation means taking on bigger, more important clients. Agents with proven leadership ability and a strong sales record may advance to supervisory and managerial positions such as sales supervisor, sales manager, or vice president of sales. Frequent contact with managers of other departments and people in other firms provides sales agents with leads about job openings, enhancing advancement opportunities. In small firms, where the number of supervisory and management positions is limited, advancement may come slowly. Promotion may occur more quickly in large firms.

Employment: Advertising sales agents held over 154,000 jobs in 2004. Workers were concentrated in three industries: More than 3 in

10 jobs were in newspaper, periodical, book and directory publishers; 3 in 10 in advertising and related services; and 2 in 10 in radio and television broadcasting. A relatively small number of jobs were found in specialized design services, including industrial and graphic designers; printing and related support activities; computer systems design and related services; business support services; and cable and other programme distribution. Employment was spread around the country, but jobs in larger, well-known publications or radio and television stations were concentrated in big cities. Media representative firms also were concentrated in large cities with many advertising agencies.

Part-time employment of advertising sales agents was most common in advertising and related services and less common in publishing and radio and television broadcasting. Self-employment also was more common in advertising and related services. Overall, relatively few advertising sales agents were self-employed.

Job Outlook: Employment of advertising sales agents is expected to grow about as fast as the average for all occupations through the year 2014 because of growth in population and advertising revenue. Rising demand for advertising sales agents also will stem from fast growth in cable systems and from the expansion of firms into the growing Hispanic market.

The industries employing advertising sales agents experienced considerable consolidation in recent years and that trend is expected to continue over the next decade, although at a slower pace. This consolidation is not expected to affect employment of advertising sales agents significantly because prospective clients still will require sales agents to create and demonstrate advertising proposals.

Technology has made advertising sales agents more productive, allowing them to take on additional duties and improve the quality of the services they provide, without substantially lessening overall demand. Productivity gains have occurred mostly in the accounting, proposal creation and customer service responsibilities of sales agents, allowing them to provide improved services.

In addition to the job openings generated by employment growth, openings will occur each year because of the need to replace sales representatives who transfer to other occupations or leave the labour force. Each year, many advertising sales agents discover they are unable to earn enough money and leave the occupation. As a result, job opportunities should be good, especially for those with a college degree or a proven sales record. Advertising revenues are sensitive to economic downturns, which cause the industries and companies that advertise to reduce both the frequency of campaigns and the overall level of spending on advertising. Advertising sales agents must work hard to get the most out of every dollar spent on advertising under these conditions. Therefore, the number of job opportunities for advertising sales agents fluctuates with the business cycle.

Earnings: Most employers pay a combination of salaries, commissions and bonuses. Commissions are usually based on the amount of sales, whereas bonuses may depend on individual performance, on the performance of all sales workers in the group or district, or on the company's performance. For agents covering multiple areas or regions, commissions also may be based on the difficulty in making a sale in that particular area. Sales revenue is affected by the economic conditions and business expectations facing the industries that tend to advertise. Earnings from commissions are likely to be high when these industries are doing well, low when companies decide not to advertise as frequently.

Median annual earnings for all advertising sales agents were $40,300 including commissions, in May 2004. The middle 50 percent earned between $27,740 and $59,880 a year. The lowest 10 percent earned less than $20,210 and the highest 10 percent earned more than $89,720 a year. Median annual earnings for sales agents in May 2004 in the industries employing the largest numbers of them were as follows:

Advertising and related services	$44,900
Radio and television broadcasting	38,980
Newspaper, periodical, book and directory publishers	35,090

In addition to their earnings, advertising sales agents usually are reimbursed for expenses such as transportation costs, meals, hotels and entertaining customers. They often receive benefits such as health and life insurance, pension plans, vacation and sick leave, personal use of a company car and frequent flier mileage. Some companies offer incentives such as free vacation trips or gifts for outstanding sales workers.

Advertising and Public Relations Services

Significant Points: Competition for many jobs will be keen because the glamour of the industry traditionally attracts many more jobseekers than there are job openings.

California and New York together account for about 1 in 5 firms and more than 1 in 4 workers in the industry.

Layoffs are common when accounts are lost, major clients cut budgets, or agencies merge.

Nature of the Industry: Firms in the advertising and public relations services industry prepare advertisements for other companies and organizations and design campaigns to promote the interests and image of their clients. This industry also includes media representatives-firms that sell advertising space for publications, radio, television and the Internet; display advertisers-businesses engaged in creating and designing public display ads for use in shopping malls, on billboards, or in similar media; and direct mail advertisers. A firm that purchases advertising time (or space) from media outlets, thereafter reselling it to advertising agencies or individual companies directly, is considered a media buying agency. Divisions of companies that produce and place their own advertising are not considered part of this industry.

In 2004, there were about 47,000 advertising and public relations services establishments in the United States. About 4 out of 10 write copy and prepare artwork, graphics and other creative work and then place the resulting ads on television, radio, or the Internet or in periodicals, newspapers, or other advertising media. Within the industry, only these full-service establishments are known as advertising agencies. About 1 in 6 were public relations firms. Many of the largest agencies are international, with a substantial proportion of their revenue coming from abroad.

Most advertising firms specialize in a particular market niche. Some companies produce and solicit outdoor advertising, such as billboards and electric displays. Others place ads in buses, subways, taxis, airports and bus terminals. A small number of firms produce aerial advertising, while others distribute circulars, handbills and free samples.

Groups within agencies have been created to serve their clients' electronic advertising needs on the Internet. Online advertisements link users to a company's or product's Web site, where information such as new product announcements, contests and product catalogues appears and from which purchases may be made.

Some firms are not involved in the creation of ads at all; instead, they sell advertising time or space on radio and television stations or in publications. Because these firms do not produce advertising, their staffs are mostly sales workers. Companies often look to advertising as a way of boosting sales by increasing the public's exposure to a product or service. Most companies do not have the staff with the necessary skills or experience to create effective advertisements; furthermore, many advertising campaigns are temporary, so employers would have difficulty maintaining their own advertising staff.

Instead, companies commonly solicit bids from ad agencies to develop advertising for them. Next, ad agencies offering their services to the company often make presentations. After winning an account, various departments within an agency-such as creative, production, media and research-work together to meet the client's goal of increasing sales.

Widespread public relations services firms can influence how businesses, governments and institutions make decisions. Often working behind the scenes, these firms have a variety of functions. In general, firms in public relations services advise and implement public exposure strategies. For example, a public relations firm might issue a press release that is printed in newspapers across the country. Firms in public relations services offer one or more resources that clients cannot provide themselves.

Usually this resource is expertise in the form of knowledge, experience, special skills, or creativity; but sometimes the resource is time or personnel that the client cannot spare. Clients of public relations firms include all types of businesses, institutions, trades and public interest groups and even high-profile individuals. Clients are large and small for-profit firms in the private sector; State, local, or Federal Governments; hospitals, universities, unions and trade groups; and foreign governments or businesses.

Public relations firms help secure favourable public exposure for their clients, advise them in the case of a sudden public crisis and design strategies to help them attain a certain public image. Toward these ends, public relations firms analyze public or internal sentiment about clients; establish relationships with the media; write speeches and coach clients for interviews; issue press releases; and organize client-sponsored publicity events, such as contests, concerts, exhibits, symposia and sporting and charity events.

Lobbying firms, a special type of public relations firm, differ somewhat. Instead of attempting to secure favourable public opinion about their clients, they attempt to influence legislators in favour of their clients' special interests. Lobbyists often work for large businesses, industry trade organizations, unions, or public interest groups.

In an effort to attract and maintain clients, advertising and public relations services agencies are diversifying their services, offering advertising as well as public relations, sales, marketing and interactive media services. Advertising and public relations services firms have found that highly creative work is particularly suitable for their services, resulting in a better product and increasing their clients' profitability.

Working Conditions: Most employees in advertising and public relations services work in comfortable offices operating in a teamwork environment; however, long hours, including evenings and weekends, are common. There are fewer opportunities for part-time work than in many other industries; in 2004, 14 percent of advertising and public relations employees worked part time, compared with 16 percent of all workers.

Work in advertising and public relations is fast-paced and exciting, but it also can be stressful. Being creative on a tight schedule can be emotionally draining. Some workers, such as lobbyists, consultants and public relations writers, frequently must meet deadlines and consequently may work long hours at times. Workers whose services are billed hourly, such as advertising consultants and public relations specialists, are often under pressure to manage their time carefully. In addition, frequent meetings with clients and media representatives may involve substantial travel.

Most firms encourage employees to attend employer-paid time-management classes, which help reduce the stress sometimes associated with working under strict time constraints. Also, with today's hectic lifestyle, many firms in this industry offer or provide health facilities or clubs to help employees maintain good health. In 2004, workers in the industry averaged 33.8 hours per week, a little higher than the national average of 33.7.

2

A Systematic Approach to Strategic Planning

One of the largest companies in the world, with vast operations around the globe, has a very systematic strategic planning process. The organization is divided into many companies. Each year, all of the companies prepare a two-day presentation for corporate administrators to whom they report. They present highly detailed plans of the objectives the company will reach over the next few years, and the specific strategies that will be pursued in order to reach these goals. Hundreds of PowerPoint – style slides are used.

A rigid format is followed, so that the presentations of each company contain the same elements, and corporate executives know what to expect. In preparing for the presentations, company managers are very cautious. They are hesitant to bring up highly innovative ideas that could lead to dramatic changes, because the managers know that once they commit to their performance targets, the managers will be held accountable for reaching them. The managers are afraid to fail because the organization penalizes failure. In general, the organization does not reward unconventional thinking. Consequently, the company has been limping along for several years now, with many performance problems and low shareholder returns.

Intent-Focused

Strategic thinking is not a random process of trial and error. Instead, it involves *strategic intent, which* is a vision with regard to where an organization is or should be going. Strategic intent *implies a particular point of view about the long-term market or competitive position that a firm hopes* to build over the coming decade or so. Hence, it conveys a sense of direction. A strategic intent is differentiated; it implies a competitively unique point of view about the future. It holds out to employees the promise of exploring new competitive territory. Hence, it conveys a sense of discovery. Strategic intent has an emotional edge to it; it is a goal that employees perceive as inherently worthwhile. Hence, it implies a sense of destiny. Direction, discovery, and destiny. These are the attributes of strategic intent.

Comprehensive

Strategic thinking is based on a systems perspective that envisions the firm as a part of a complete end-to-end system of value creation. Furthermore, strategic thinking means that decision makers are aware of the interdependencies in the system. This type of thinking fits within the stakeholder view of the organization, which is one of the important perspectives on which our model of strategic management is based. Organizational managers each possess a mental model, which is a view of how the world works.

Mental models should include an understanding of both the internal and external organization. An industry-based model of the external environment has dominated for many years. However, a more promising model views the company not as a member of a single industry, but as a part of a larger business system that crosses a variety of industries. Companies co-evolve around innovations, and they work both in competition and cooperatively to satisfy the demands of a wide variety of stakeholders, including customers, suppliers, and broader society and its governments, as well as to create or absorb the next round of innovation. Organizations are a part of one or more value chains, to which they can contribute in many ways.

Managers who want to think strategically must also understand and appreciate the internal pieces that make up the whole of their companies.

The role of each person within the larger system must be identified, as well as the effect of that role on other people and groups with in the organization and on the outcomes of the organization. It is impossible to optimize an organizational system in, for example, satisfying customer needs, without understanding how individuals fit into the system. So the strategic thinker observes and understands the connections between and among the various levels of a business, as well as the linkages between the business and stakeholders in the external environment.

Diamond head and Trump: A Joint Venture

Deborah A. Vitale, the Chairman, CEO, and President of Diamond head, makes the case for the venture by stating: We believe a partnership with Trump Entertainment Resorts for this venture adds up to an ideal combination because of their experience, the value of the Trump brand, the location of our site on Interstate 10, and the vitality of the Gulf Coast market. We have the land, the location, and the desire to pursue a master plan for the entire tract that should not only enhance long-term shareholder value, but which should significantly enhance the surrounding economy. James B. Perry, President and CEO of Trump Entertainment Resorts, Inc., explains his firm's views on the proposed joint venture as follows:

As we renovate and re-brand our Atlantic City properties, we are also focused on our corporate development initiatives and expanding the Trump brand into new markets. We are excited about the prospect of bringing the Trump brand to the GulfCoast, and we hope to join private and public entities in redeveloping the region. We believe that this is a great opportunity to create value for our company, our shareholders and the citizens of Mississippi.

Opportunistic

Although strategic thinking is based on strategic intent, there has to be room for what might be called intelligent opportunism. *Intelligent opportunism* can be defined as the ability of managers at various levels of the organization to take advantage of unanticipated opportunities to further an intended strategy or even redirect a strategy. For example, Marriott saw an opportunity for growth in the lower-priced segment of the lodging industry when Courtyard was introduced. Of course, the company has a long history of bold entrepreneurship, beginning with a root beer stand started in 1927 by John and Alice Marriott. They added hot food, incorporated, and expanded their Hot Shoppes into a regional chain.

The next major movewas Marriott's first hotel, the Twin Bridges Marriott Motor Hotel, which opened in Arlington, Virginia, in 1957. With the increase in airline travel, Marriott built several hotels at airports during the 1970s. Each of these ventures was in response to an opportunity, and each was avital part of building the Marriott that exists today. Intelligent opportunism is consistent with the traditional strategic planning model. According to that model, strategies often come from taking advantage of opportunities that arise in the external environment.

Long-Term Oriented

Managers, especially in America, are often accused of making shortsighted decisions. Perhapsa renovation or expansion plan is cancelled because the payoff looks too far away, or employees are laid off when occupancies drop, only to be rehired within a few months. In contrast, strategic thinking is long-term oriented. Actions that a firm must make now should be linked to a vision of what the firm should become, based on the strategic intent of its top managers. This type of thinking is driving many hoteliers into international markets on a much larger scale.

Built on Past and Present

Although strategic thinking is long-term oriented, it does not ignore the present or the past. Infact, it might be referred to as "thinking in time" :Thinking in time (has) three components. One is recognition that the future has no place to come from but the past, hence the past has predictive value. Another element is recognition that what matters for the future in the present is departures from the past, alterations, changes, which prospectively or actually divert familiar flows from accustomed channels.... A third component is continuous comparison, an almost constant oscillation from the present to future to past and back, heedful of prospective change, concerned to expedite, limit, guide, counter, or accept it as the fruits of such comparison suggests.

Strategic thinkers need to consider the past. The past forms a historical context in which strategic intent is created. Learning from past mistakes helps the firm avoid making them again. Also, analysis of the past behaviours of important stakeholders, such as customers, competitors, unions, or suppliers, can help a firm anticipate how the stakeholders will react to new ideas and strategies. The present is also important to strategic thinking, because it places constraints on what the organization is able to accomplish. Strategic thinking is a creative process, but it is also a well-reasoned process. Although it may lead firms to consider unconventional ideas, the ideas that are actually pursued are selected based on rational analysis, including consideration of the organization's current resources, knowledge, skills, and abilities.

Hypothesis-Driven

Organizations should test their decisions to see if they are appropriate or likely to be successful. This process is similar to the scientific method, in which hypotheses are developed and tested.

Hypothesis *development* is a creative process built on brainstorming, whereas *hypothesis testing* is an analytical process.

A typical process begins as managers suggest ideas regarding what the firm might want to do. Those that are considered reasonable are then subjected to rigorous analysis of potential using a well-developed methodology. After analysis, managers determine which of the ideas are worthy of implementation. However, the company may decide not to make a full commitment to each of them at first. Instead, it may allocate enough resources to implement the ideas on a trial basis, so that the company will be able to tell whether the ideas are going to workout. The ideas that are successful are given additional resources. In this description, hypothesis testing occurred twice.

The first test was the rigorous analysis conducted by managers in the organization. The second test occurs as the company tries the ideas in the marketplace. If you combine all six of the elements of strategic thinking, what you have is a long-term thinker who builds a vision for the future on the foundation of the present and the past. It is someone who understands how the organization fits within its external environment, and who has a firm grasp of relationships with external stakeholders. Furthermore, it is someone who is willing to break out of traditional mind-sets and to seize opportunities, but who uses a rational approach to test ideas to prevent the organization from moving indefinitely in an inappropriate direction.

Motivating Managers and Employees to Think Strategically

Organizations can encourage strategic thinking in several ways. First, managers and employees can receive training that describes strategic thinking and how to do it. Second, an organization can encourage and reward employees who generate new ideas (hypotheses). For example, Disney allows some of its employees an opportunity each year to present new ideas to top managers.

With a similar philosophy, Virgin, well known for its unconventional airline, created a one-stop bridal-services company because one of its flight attendants was having a difficult time lining up those services for a friend's wedding. Virgin Bride, the name of the venture, is now Britain's largest bridal emporium. Third, a company can actually implement a strategic planning process that incorporates the elements of strategic thinking. Such a process would include a thorough evaluation of the external environment, with a special emphasis on relationships with stakeholders.

It would also include the generation of new ideas and facilitate their testing. Finally, to encourage strategic thinking, an organization has to be willing to take risks. It was risky for Kemmons Wilsonto develop the first Holiday Inn back in 1952, after returning from a family vacation disheartened at the lack of family and value-oriented lodging, but the strategy worked so well that Holiday Inn developed into a trusted name along the emerging interstate highway system.

Hotels and restaurants are among the most competitive businesses in the world. The hospitality industry primarily consists of businesses that provide accommodation, food and beverage, or some combination of these activities. Hospitality businesses provide services, which differ from tangible products because they are immediately consumed and require a people-intensive creation process. They differ from other service establishments by providing for those who are in the process of travelling away from home in contrast to local residence, although restaurant soften serve both travellers and local guests.

The offering of an experience is also becoming an important component of hospitality. In addition, a wide range of business structures exist inhospitality, such as direct ownership by chains, franchising, asset management, and consortia. Today, the hospitality industry has become more complex and sophisticated, with a movement away from the "mine host" (i.e., a view of hospitality in which the host personally and socially entertains visiting guests) and the cost-control frameworks of the past to a more strategic view of the business, in both investment and operations domains. "Travel and tourism" is a broad term used to capture a variety of interrelated businesses that provide services to travellers.

Tourism is the largest industry worldwide, the second largest services export industry, and the third largest retail sales industry in the United States. It is the first, second, or third largest employer in 30 of the 50 states. Besides the traditional hospitality businesses of hotels and restaurants, the tourism industry includes a broad range of businesses, such as airlines, cruise lines, car rental firms, entertainment firms, travel agents, tour operators, and recreational enterprises.

The focus of this textbook will be on those hospitality businesses primarily engaged in providing food and lodging to travelling guests. However, we will also include discussions of other travel-related businesses, such as casinos, airlines, cruise lines, time-shares, travel agents, tour operators, and governmental tourism institutions.

The Foodservice Industry — The Players

The foodservice industry consists of a wide variety of different businesses, including institutional providers and food contractors such as Aramark Corp., Sodexho Alliance, Autogrill SpA 's, HMSHost, and Compass Group. Institutional foodservice and military foodservice are small segments of the industry and consist of non-commercial institutions that operate their own foodservice.

Contractors operate for-profit services to commercial, industrial, university, school, airline, hospital, nursing home, recreation, and sports centres. Management is provided by the contractor of restaurant services, but the institution may provide the facilities and personnel for these operations. Contract companies are highly consolidated after aggressive merger and acquisition activities that gave them strong positions in the various on-site segments (e.g., school, corporate, and health care). Compass Group's Americas Division, for example, is the largest contract food service company, with $ 7.5 billion in revenues.

Its purchase of Bon Appetit Management Company, a$ 300 million provider of upscale foodservice for corporations and universities, is one example of its expanded coverage in various key segments. 65 Its parent company, Compass Group PLC, has worldwide revenues of $ 21 billion, with more than 400,000 associates working in more than 90 countries. Sodexho Alliance is the second-largest provider of foodservice worldwide, with operations in 79 countries employing 324,500 people. In the latest rankings, Aramark is the leading contract chain in U.S. system wide sales ($ 5.53 billion) and market share (28.8 percent share of aggregate sales of contract chains in top 100), followed by Canteen Services and Sodexho.

The restaurant industry is the largest private-sector employer in the United States, and consists of commercial dining and drinking establishments, such as restaurants, bars, cafeterias, ice cream parlours, and cafés. It dominates the foodservice industry. Within foodservice, the restaurant industry is by far the largest segment, with 935,000 restaurants in the United States, sales of around $ 537 billion in 2007, and an annual growth rate of around 8.4 percent.

Common convention is to split the restaurant industry into two main segments: quick-service and full-service. Quick-service, commonly called fast-food or fast-service, restaurants are defined as eat-in or take-out operations with limited menus, low prices, and fast service. This segment of the industry is further broken down into sandwiches (e.g., hamburgers and tacos), pizza, and chicken. Leaders in market share in the sandwich segment are McDonald's, BurgerKing, Wendy's, Subway, and Taco Bell, while the chicken segment is led by KFC (KentuckyFried Chicken), Chick-fil-A, and Popeye's Chicken and Biscuits. The pizza segment is led by two strong players: Pizza Hut with 43 percent of the market and Domino's Pizza with a 27 percent market share.

Full-service restaurants offer eat-in service, with more expansive menus, and prices that range from low to high. In providing annual comparisons, *Nation's Restaurant News* divides full-service restaurants into family, grill-buffet, and dinner house segments. Family chains include players like Denny's and IHOP (International House of Pancakes), and grill-buffet segment leaders include Golden Corral, Ryan's Family Steak House, and Ponderosa Steakhouse. Finally, the large dinner house segment is aggressively focusing on value-oriented menu items, advertising, and improved execution in operations, with several major players including Applebee's Neighbourhood Grill and Bar, Chili's Grill and Bar, Outback Steakhouse, Olive Garden, RedLobster, and T.G.I. Friday's. Other key players in this segment are the multi concept operators and franchisors like Dardenand Brinker. Large companies in the restaurant industry, such as Yum! Brands (which owns many of the aforementioned brands such as Pizza Hut and Taco Bell), are aggressively developing portfolios of restaurants, and international expansion continues to serve as a viable growth strategy for firms like Starbucks. Small operators and independent restaurants compete with the large chains in an industry known for its low barriers to entry and entrepreneurial opportunities.

The Lodging Industry — The Players

Lodging in the United States is a $ 113.7 billion industry, with more than 47,000 hotels and around 4.4 million guest rooms. 73 Like the foodservice industry, consolidation has been a theme for the last decade, with most of the largest companies being publicly owned. HyattHotels, owned by the Pritzker family, and Carlson Companies are exceptions to this rule, with Carlson being one of the largest privately held companies in the United States.

Segmentation

Providing a bed, bathroom, television, and phone are hotel basics, but additional amenities and services are common. *Segmentation* is a strategy that distinguishes properties on the basis of price, service, function, style, offerings, and type of guest served. Hotel chains have been utilizing segmentation, particularly since the 1980s, to enable growth, expand their customer base, and leverage corporate resources and expertise. A widely used approach to classifying segments of the lodging industry was devised by Smith Travel Research and Bear Stearns and includes five segments: luxury (upper upscale), upscale, midscale with food and beverage services, midscale without food and beverage services, and economy. Extended-stay hotels are also included in many classifications as either upper or lower tier, depending on the range of services they offer. Many of the largest hotel chains have developed brands in a variety of segments, from luxury to economy. Accor Hotels, for example, has the Sofitel brand in the upper upscale segment; Novotel, Mercure, and Suitehotel in the upscale and midscale segments; Ibis in the economy segment; and Etap, Motel 6, and Formula 1 in the budget segment.

Ownership Structures

A hotel may be owned by one company, franchised by another, and operated by a third, or anycombination of these situations. This complex web of business relationships often makes the question of business identity confusing for those who do not understand the structure of Carlson Companies began as the Gold Bond Stamp Company, providing consumer incentive programs for grocery stores, when founder CurtisL. Carlson started the business in 1938 with a loan of $ 55. When the trading stamp business reached its peak in the late 1960s, the company entered the hospitality industry, changing its name in the 1970s to reflect its transition into a marketing, travel, and hospitality leader.

Overall, the top players based on the number of rooms they hold around the world are, in that order: InterContinental Hotels Group, Wyndham Worldwide (formerly Cendant Hotel Group), Marriott International, Hilton Hotels Corporation, Choice Hotels International, Accor, Best Western International, Starwood Hotels & Resorts Worldwide, Carlson Hospitality Worldwide, and Global HyattCorporation. As this list suggests, 80 percent of the largest chains are headquartered in NorthAmerica, although this percentage drops to half when the list includes the top 50 corporations. Best Western International is the largest chain with independently owned and operated hotels, which explains why it has no managed or franchised hotels. Starwood also has 130 ownedhotels and 19 vacation ownership resorts in addition to its managed and franchised hotels. As firms in the industry have evolved and transitioned into more consolidated international operations, so too has the mind-set of managers moved to a more strategic way of thinking about the business.

Many of the assumed differences between hospitality firms and other businesses have disappeared, being replaced with a clear understanding of business practice. Although differences still exist between hospitality firms and firms of other types, in most ways hospitality firms are not that different. From one perspective, hotels and restaurants are a big assembly operation, much like a manufacturing operation. However, they are seldom studied in this manner.

Also, all hospitality firms can be studied in terms of their cash flows, just like other types of firms. They also all rely on markets for capital, human resources, customers, and supplies. They are subject to economic, sociocultural, technological, and political influences and trends. They have competitors. In summary, there are more similarities than differences between hospitality firms and firms of other types.

Consequently, the general strategic management process does not require substantial modifications to be applicable to hospitality firms. Similar to the manufacturing industry, the process begins with analysis of the firm and its environment, which forms the foundation for development of strategic direction, strategies, and implementation plans. The outcomes from this process are different for each hospitality firm, because results depend on the specifics of the situation. In addition, certain ideas require modification to understand their use and application in services. The most unique aspect of this book compared to general strategic management texts is the translation of these ideas into service contexts through the use of hospitality industry examples. These examples should help you as you learn the strategic management process. Also, they will help you become more aware of strategies and strategic issues in the industry. However, the most up-to-date theories and ideas of strategic management are also contained here. Non hospitality examples will occasionally be used when they better illustrate a point. One of the most important strategic issues facing the hospitality industry today is the ability to leverage human capital.

In particular, managers are concerned about human resource activities, such as attracting, retaining, and developing the workforce. Although human resources are an area of concern in every business, the hospitality business faces particularly great challenges because of relatively low wage rates and a large percentage of routine jobs. Managers are also very interested in effective use of capital, aligning the interests of stakeholders such as employees, customers, and owners, understanding their customers better, and applying information technology. Because of their importance to the industry, these issues will receive special attention in this book.

Strategic Management, a Tool of Leadership – Concepts and Paradoxes

The complete strategist's advice: if you want to make a sculpture of an elephant out of a block of granite, start cutting little parts away and then remove, fast, anything that does not look like an elephant the right change. Such data (i.e. well designed information) should structure signals, even weak signals, which impress the organisation with a sense of change in process. How to magnify and transform such signals into data is a managerial information task. Data can monitor change in the environment, or in the strategies applied in other institutions used as benchmarks.

But, more importantly, data should reflect the practice of the actors themselves, inside the organization or in its direct environment. It is clear today that a lot of significant information can be drawn from staff experience inside the organisation. It is difficult, however, for management to convince employees not only to expose their experience, but also to analyse it so that it can contribute to a database of useful information for the organisation. Information must be structured so that it is easily communicated, while providing useful data to the enquirer. Inside the organisation, it must be available to anyone who is concerned with specific elements of information: this means setting up open systems which are difficult to organise, but essential. Such a task represents a managerial challenge, especially when strong competition for positions exists inside the institution or, on the contrary, when the administration, interested in routines, prefers to retain information rather than to find time to disseminate it properly, thus risking the cultural fragmentation of the organisation.

Policies and Strategies

Policies deal with identity, with missions (what Max Weber calls *axiologic rationality*), with organisational climate. At this level of generality, they are usually expressed in broad terms, even symbolic ones. But such wording must have meaning for the people involved, as these policies define norms of behaviour and serve as fundamental references in case of serious conflicts between projects – or between people – within the institution. They play the role of a constitution in a State. Inside and outside the organisation, these norms represent institutional commitments and any interpretation which might lead to strongly divergent positions should be seriously debated, explained in writing and commented by the people in charge.

Too often, obscure or outmoded policies are just ignored, to avoid either the effort of updating or redefinition, or internal strife or potential conflicts with external regulators. It usually means that some of the more powerful and determined sub-groups in the organization are *de facto* imposing their own norms and objectives as if they were those of the whole institution. Alternatively, it leaves the way open for policies imposed from the outside by public authorities, the unions, resource providers or even by public opinion.

Doesn't this Ring a Bell in Universities?

Yet, the worst situation for an institution is a policy (statement of identity, expression of norms, etc.) which has no credibility; either because it has been expressed too vaguely, or because it is simply ignored or interpreted as fluctuating with circumstances. In such a case, most people, especially the managers, try to understand which is the real policy of the organisation and what this agenda really means for them.

It is often said that it is not possible, nor opportune, to explain all policies: some should be kept confidential, secret, in order to minimize potential opposition, while being implemented by a few people "in the know". But secrecy is difficult when implementation requires a wide distribution of information and an open exchange of experience.

Moreover, secrecy does not permit decentralized initiatives– it provides privilege to the happy few, leaving the other actors with a strong feeling of arbitrary behaviour, if not of mistrust. In fact, the formulation and implementation of strategies in the organisation are the test of the validity of institutional policies. When no strategic drive proves effective, there is an obvious need for change in policies.

Strategies describe types of changes and ways of transformation; they tell us what to do in order to implement policies (instrumental rationality, or efficiency). That is why they need to be expressed in operational terms: recalling objectives, they enunciate those activities selected to reach those objectives, the type of changes induced by such activities, the means which can be used – or kept untouched – to develop them, the allocation of individual sub-missions, resources and authority, the evaluation criteria for specific projects, the procedures to implement evaluation and those to take account of conclusions and recommendations. In other words, understanding the interaction between actors and strategies is at the core of any managerial process, and of the exercise of leadership.

Evaluation is thus the key to any policy and strategy, because it questions constantly the aims of the organisation, the institutional allocation of resources, the leadership and operational capacities, i.e., the norms, communication development, the criteria for quality, their implementation and their critical re-evaluation. At the level of the whole organisation, it is called institutional evaluation and deals with the basic orientation and norms of the institution. Functional evaluation of the departments, of specific activities or of the use of specific methods is a necessary complement to institutional evaluation but, too often, as it is easier to achieve and exploit, functional evaluation displaces or replaces institutional evaluation. Strategic management must make institutional evaluation possible and even desirable for the majority of actors, thus offering a frame of reference to functional evaluations that develop a critical approach to policies. Managing evaluation, as a collective process of change, in order to educate and motivate people for change, is thus at the core of strategic managerial capacity. This includes the ability to engage people in the evaluation process, as a critical understanding of what they do and why they do it. As a side benefit, this may help other members of the organisation to understand the managers' tasks and difficulties.

An internally-organised evaluation is essential to help institutional actors to question their goals and practices. An outsider's viewpoint is also useful – or even vital – to reconsider more objectively the organisation's aims and operations, its performance criteria or its public image. The outsiders could be external members of the administrative board, regular and influential in the governing process, as well as consultants or members of networks cooperating with the institution. The organisation's information system should be able to register this data even if it proves difficult to gather because of its informality, usually reflecting various actors' needs and motivation.

Moreover, the management of evaluation implies a proper follow-up of the recommendations made, i.e., getting people's support for change when they are shown the advantage of action adjustment. Wisdom consists here in showing that a non-change attitude, after the evaluation has pointed to areas of weakness, could lead to external adaptation pressures, and that immobility can only undermine present positions, making it all the more difficult to adjust later.

The Balance between Rationalisation, Innovation and Preservation

Often, managers are tempted to give priority to rationalisation, on the basis of efficiency criteria – usually a reduction of costs that leaves structures and roles as little affected as possible. Indeed, when change is the key, innovation cannot be developed without some rationalisation in order to provide transfer mobility in resource allocation as well as new models of action. Thus, rationalisation usually leads to reorganising organisational structures and to developing new functions while, however, keeping to the basics of the existing system. A classical way of developing innovation is to design experimental structures away from main stream activities in the organisation; areas of transformation are set up at the margin with their specific norms and evaluation criteria. This allows for focusing, in mainstream activities, on rationalisation and efficiency, thus allowing for some questioning of current practice. But, at some stage, innovation will need to be transferred from the periphery to the core resources for increased structural change. This should lead to a difficult act of balancing between rationalisation and innovation.

Too often, the drive for rationalisation and innovation, which professionally and even culturally proves rewarding for managers, underestimates the damage it can impose on situations that should be preserved in the longer term interest of the organisation. Ignoring the need for preservation can of ten endanger the institution or reduce its assets by wasting the professional and technical experience of staff, thus jeopardising quality, norms of cooperation, processes and communication or, more broadly, the organisational climate of the institution, i.e., its cultural norms. It is an illustration of badly managed change. Cultural organisations (universities in particular) – which are made up of traditions, individual motivations, weak leadership, fragmented and difficult communication procedures, as well as individual initiatives – are particularly at risk.

Rationalisation, innovation and preservation make up an interdependent system with it sown feedback loops. Designing and operating an appropriate balance within this system is at the core of strategic management, and therefore of leadership. It cannot be an *a priori* policy, but should flow from the implementation of change, while leaders remain aware of the danger of ignoring preservation.

3

Advertisement of Motivations

The Nature of a Break From Routine

Almost every respondent described the essence of a vacation as being a break from routine. These breaks could generally be classified into two categories, short-term and long-term. These appeared to resolve different types of disequilibrium. Short-term disequilibrium seemed to reflect a particular set of circumstances or events which were temporal disruptions to homeostasis. Typically, these were expressed as "pressures." In this situation, a break from routine was perceived to be a necessary and sufficient condition to restore homeostasis. Long-term states of disequilibrium could not usually be satisfied by a single pleasure vacation. Instead these states of disequilibrium were satisfied through an ongoing program of pleasure vacations. A break from routine was perceived as necessary to facilitate the resolution of long-term disequilibrium states, but the break alone was not sufficiently inclusive to resolve the state of tension. Long-term disequilibrium was perceived by respondents as being ever present but postponable. In contrast, short-term disequilibrium demanded immediate attention. In other words, the data suggested that a two tier system of disequilibrium was operating.

This is hypothesized to have meant continuation of doing the same kinds of things but in a different physical, or social context. The essence of "break from routine" was, in most cases, either locating in a different place, or changing the dominant social context from the world milieu, usually to that of the family group, or doing both of these things. The kinds of activities in which people engaged were generally not different, although they were sometimes more concentrated.

Respondents' life styles did not change. A break from routine often involved emphasizing particularly desired elements of the life style rather than changing the life style to incorporate different activities. The mundane elements in the routine were discarded, but the preferred discretionary elements of the normal life style were retained.

Motives Influencing Selection of Type of Pleasure Vacation and Destination

Once a desire to go on a pleasure vacation has been established, concern shifts from the impetus dimension of motivation to its directive dimension which serves to guide the tourist toward the selection of a particular type of vacation or destination in preference to all the alternatives of which the tourist is aware.

In most decisions more than one motive is operative. Priorities between alternative destinations are a function of the intensity of the particular combination of motives which are dominant in a hierarchy of motives at a particular moment of time. This hierarchy of motives construct helps to explain divergent reaction at different points in time by the same respondent to the same stimuli.

The data suggested that respondents' motives usefully could be conceptualized as being located along a cultural — socio-psychological disequilibrium continuum. Much of the tourist industry's modus operandi is based upon the assumption that tourists are attracted to a destination by the particular cultural opportunities or special attributes that it offers. However, the findings of this study suggested that for some respondents, the destination itself was relatively unimportant.

Respondents did not go to particular locations to seek cultural insights or artifacts; rather they went for socio-psychological reasons unrelated to any specific destination. The destination served merely as a medium through which these motives could be satisfied. The following sections of the analysis briefly discuss each of the motives empirically identified in this study, and categorize them as being located either toward the socio-psychological or the cultural end of the continuum.

Socio-Psychological Motives

Socio-psychological motives were rarely overtly identified by respondents in early discussion of their pleasure vacation experiences. These motives were difficult for respondents to articulate.

However, as the interview proceeded, it often became apparent that while initial concern and effort had been with selecting a vacation destination, the value, benefits, and satisfactions derived from the vacation were neither related to, nor derived from, a particular destination's attributes. Rather the satisfactions were related to social or psychological factors unique to the particular individual or group involved. In effect, these motives represented a hidden agenda. This suggests that one of the reasons that some people do not take pleasure vacations is unknown. The data suggested seven socio-psychological motives which served to direct pleasure vacation behaviour. These motives were: escape from a perceived mundane environment; exploration and evaluation of self; relaxation; prestige; regression; enhancement of kinship relationships; and facilitation of social interaction.

Escape from a Perceived Mundane Environment

A temporary change of environment was a frequently expressed respondent motive. Even the most prized living environments sometimes became mundane to those living there. For example, one respondent who lived on Cape Cod indicated that when crowds of people descend upon the Cape in the summer, many of the local residents go to Maine, New Hampshire, or Vermont to avoid the crowds. Escape was sought not only from the general residential locale but also from the specific home and job environments. There did not appear to be any single optimum type of environment that facilitated escape.

The critical ingredient was only that the pleasure vacation context should be physically and socially different from the environment in which one normally lives. For some respondents, the escape offered by a pleasure vacation was for a much longer time period than the actual trip. As Clawson and Knetsch (1966) have suggested, anticipation of the trip was an important ingredient of the total experience. One respondent commented that "You are sustained a little through the winter, first by anticipation of Christmas, then by anticipation of the trip in February or March. It is something to which I look forward in the long winter."

Exploration and Evaluation of Self

The data suggested that a pleasure vacation may be viewed by some people as an opportunity for re-evaluating and discovering more about themselves or for acting out self-images and in so doing refining or modifying them. For example, one respondent commented:

> *This trip put a lot of things in perspective for me. It helped me to get a clearer picture of myself because I put myself in different situations. I saw how I interacted with other people in other conditions. I had some constraints come up, some hardships, and I had to deal with that. It gave me a chance to see what is inside of me and how that would come out, without any outside pressures. You don't find this out when you go to the office from eight to five.*

Self-discovery emerged as a result of transposition into a new situation. The novelty of the physical and social context appeared to be an essential ingredient in the process. These insights into the person's self could not be achieved by staying at home or visiting friends and relatives. In the case of the latter there would be outside pressure serving to ameliorate hardship, and hence dilute the value of the experience, because of the accessibility of friendly other people. In the case of the former, there would be less likelihood of finding different situations or conditions.

Exposure to a different milieu sometimes caused a revision of existing perceptions of self-status and enhanced feelings of self-worth. A respondent who was a boat be of low status in that community, but on pleasure vacations, " I see people who are a lot worse off than I am, and I sort of appreciate what we do have." Other respondents stressed that exposure to a different milieu for a period of time served as a reference point re-evaluation of their own life style.

Self-discovery was not confined only to those respondents who went camping or sought inexpensive pleasure vacations. The wealthiest and most widely travelled respondent in the sample expressed similar sentiments. After a cruise vacation in which she found that she was not disposed to the socializing and organized activities which characterized the experience she commented, "I learned a lot about myself on that cruise."

Relaxation

The term relaxation was a constant respondent theme, but its use was often ambivalent. Generally, there was a reluctance on the part of respondents to relax physically. Respondents would say they felt relaxed and then admit that they came home physically exhausted. It was apparent that the term relaxation referred to a mental state rather than a physical relaxation. Given this interpretation it was possible to reconcile physical exhaustion or fatigue as being mentally refreshing and relaxing. Relaxation meant talking the time to pursue activities of interest. The activities selected were often a reflection of the increased time available at the vacation destination. In the rhythm of the normal routine, the mind was not directed toward these hobbies or interests. These interests were not selectively perceived because they were not pertinent to the prevailing train of thought or dominant motive.

Most respondents indicated that they were fatigued upon their return home from the exertions expended on the vacation and on associated travel. This fatigue factor together with the contribution the vacation has made to ameliorating tension states possibly accounted for the sentiment that respondents frequently expressed, "I am always delighted to go on a vacation, but I am just as delighted to return home again."

Regression

Some respondents suggested that a pleasure vacation provided an opportunity to do thingswhich were inconceivable within the context of their usual life styles. The things respondents' cited were often puerile, irrational, and more reminiscent of adolescent or child behaviour than mature adult behaviour. The opportunity to engage in this behaviour was facilitated by withdrawal from usual role obligations.

On vacation, respondents were freed of the mores that inhibit capacity for this type of enjoyment. One respondent stated, "My life style is free and more relaxed when I go away from home. I let my guard down more than I would at home." While puerility was the prevailing form of regressive behaviour, another form was identified by some respondents. This was the search for the life style of a previous era. This is sometimes referred to as the "nostalgia factor." In essence, the desire was to regress to a less complex, less changeable, less technologically advanced environment. For example, a respondent stated that she and her friends were:

> *Looking for the simple life. We are not looking for big cities, but are looking for peasants of the soil. A lot of us are very romantic. We want to go out and see the fields; to escape Americanism.*

Like the puerile regression state, this search for the life style of a previous era is a transitory, ephemeral tension state, and when homeostasis is restored, return to the routine of life is accepted. The actuality frequently is not congruent with the image, for as the same respondent commented, "It depends where they go, but a lot of people come back not always totally satisfied."

Enhancement of Kinship Relationships

Many respondents perceived the pleasure vacation as a time when family members were brought close together. Hence, the pleasure vacation served as a medium through which family relationships could be enhanced or enriched.

This enhancement is often facilitated by long drives in an automobile because family members are physically juxtaposed for long periods and forced to interact with each other. It is inevitable that a much greater exchange and understanding of each other is likely to occur than in the normal routine situation in which family members go in different directions interacting only spasmodically. The essence of this tension state was well expressed by a respondent who stated:

The important notion is being out of routine. It isn't that you are away from a place anymore than you are at a place. What is different is the act that you are together as a family. You are able to put aside the other kinds of responsibilities that each of you may have that would otherwise be impinging themselves upon that notion of focusing inwards and putting things together.

Facilitation of Social Interaction

It was evident that an important motive for some respondents going on a pleasure vacation was to meet new people in different locations. These trips were people oriented rather than place oriented. Like several of the other motives which were located towards the socio-psychological end of the disequilibrium continuum, respondents often became aware of this motive only after the trip was completed.

A variety of dimensions of this motive emerged from the data. For some respondents, an opportunity for transitory meetings with others from outside familiar reference groups to exchange views, was all that was sought.

Others were seeking more permanent relationships that would serve to extend their range of social contacts. Several observed that interaction with non-familiar people was more likely. In some cases, social contact was initiated by children, who were a common ingredient shared by some parties. The physical planning of accommodations was also perceived to be an ameliorating factor, for if the accommodations were closely juxtaposed they facilitated interaction.

Although several respondents expressed a desire to interact with local people in the destination area, they reported that this was frequently difficult to achieve. Most interaction was with other tourists in the area. There was little common identity with local people who were serving as waitresses, and much more with other tourists who were also waiting in line or visiting a particular attraction for the first time. Some respondents suggested that travelling with others may inhibit opportunities for interacting with local people at the destination. The availability of companions provided built-in entertainment and removed the urge to visit with others outside of the group; the natural tendency was to turn inward rather than outward.

The organized tour was a preferred type of vacation for some respondents because it served as a vehicle for facilitating social intercourse as well as being financially expedient. The prime ingredients inducing the camaraderie which respondents reported from tour experiences appeared to be the sharing of many dimensions of the experience and close physical juxtaposition with others. Some participated regularly in group tours which were arranged locally and were comprised of people who knew others in the group from the outset. In essence, these people were taking some of their home social environment with them to a different location. The existence of a nucleus of known people provided a good foundation upon which to establish new social relationships through introductions. In addition, the group often had a common interest which facilitated social interaction. For example, it may be comprised of lawyers, teachers, doctors, rose growers, or home builders.

Novelty

Novelty was defined by respondents in a variety of ways. Synonyms included curiosity, adventure, new and different. Novel meant new experience but it did not necessarily mean entirely new knowledge. Often respondents knew a lot about a place. The novelty resulted from actually seeing something rather than simply knowing of it vicariously.

A prefe*rence for going to a previously unvisited destination was a consistent factor. This* aspect had previously proved satisfactory, rather than to purchase a brand with which they have had no previous experience. Generally, this does not appear to apply to pleasure vacations. Cultural disequilibrium appears to be an on-going state which requires a supply of fresh cultural stimuli to restore homeostasis. In most cases, respondents anticipated that re-experiencing known cultural stimuli would not contribute as much as experiencing new stimuli to reducing the tension state. Hence, when the pleasure vacation product was purchased, a different destination brand was selected by respondents.

At the same time, there were some respondents who returned to a previously visited vacation destination. In some cases, the same destination was selected each year. While the data did not enable the reasons for this to be identified, it may be speculated that three factors account for this phenomenon.

First, habitual destination respondents may be motivated primarily by socio-psychological rather than cultural motives. Second, they may have restricted knowledge of the want satisfying attributes of other places. Returning to a proven destination reduces the risk that an unfamiliar alternative may not be as satisfying as those previously experienced. The third factor may be fear, or anxiety of the unknown, which is removed by revisiting a destination.

The urge for new and adventurous experiences was frequently compromised by the felt need to minimize rises of exposure to novelty which may be threatening. One respondent, who was a travel agent, pointed out that for some people, it was a fearful experience to go into an unknown situation in a country where the people did not speak your language. These people "would like to go away from home but they also have the desire to be taken care of. That is why you get tours and tour conductors, because it is a security blanket." People used organized tours to introduce themselves to travel, its problems and associated fears. Organized tours served to remove any anxiety or exposure to unfamiliar situations that may have been threatening.

An alternative strategy to the organized tour for reducing anxiety and fear was to experience the unknown by starting with the known and using that as a base. For example, a number of respondents indicated that they had visited the Mexican border towns, but had no intention of going further into Mexico.

The border towns were close to the perceived safety of the known United States and could thus be experienced relatively quickly with minimal anxiety. Similarly, some of the respondents who had visited Europe indicated that they started in the United Kingdom where they knew the language, or in a country that they had previously visited, so that there was some familiarity. From this relatively familiar base, sorties were made into new areas. When they felt comfortable there, the process was repeated and exploration extended to their new destinations.

Education

The positive influence of pleasure vacations on children's' education was exhorted by most respondents and in some cases was the primary consideration in the selection of a destination. Education was perceived as a means of developing a rounded individual. One respondent suggested, "As a generalization, those who have been on vacation, and have travelled, are usually more interesting to talk with than those who have not." It was perceived as almost a moral obligation to take the opportunity to visit a distinctive phenomenon, particularly if it was reasonably accessible. The sense of "ought" to see and experience a particular place frequently meant that circumstances, especially present location, had been the trigger which initiated selection of a destination. Cultural disequilibrium was not site or destination specific. It did not relate to one particular place, but it was generally applicable to all places. Hence, there was a feeling expressed by several respondents that, "I ought to go because I am here," particularly if it was anticipated that the present residential location was transitory. In this situation, it may have been perceived as the one opportunity in a lifetime to see particular cultural phenomena. If the opportunity was not grasped then educational benefits were lost.

Conclusions and Implications

Delineation of underlying motives offers useful insights into understanding the destination selection decision process. All else equal, preference is likely to be given to a destination which is perceived as most likely to service the dominant motive. Nine motives were identified. Seven of these were located towards the socio-psychological end of the disequilibrium continuum and two towards the cultural end. For ease of exposition, the motives were discussed as separate entities. However, they should not be considered as mutually exclusive, nor should any single tension state be selected as the determinant of behaviour. They operate in tandem or combination, for motives are multidimensional.

Thus, destination decisions were usually energized by several motives acting in tandem. The study suggested that any given destination can in principle attract customers whose motivations are neither homogeneous nor necessarily compatible. While the study gave no indication of the distribution of the two disequilibrium states in the population, it suggested that more attention usefully could be given by the tourist industry to socio-psychological disequilibrium in developing its product and promotion strategies than is presenting the case. The tourist industry's modus operandi is based upon the assumption that people go on vacation to do and see things. The data suggested that, for many respondents, this assumption is challengeable. They have been conditioned to thinking in terms of destination, but a number of motives emerged from the data which were not place specific. Consumers motivated by socio-psychological motives were not looking for uniqueness in the product. That is, some specific attribute it possessed which other destinations did not have. The pleasure vacation destination was not perceived by most respondents as a "speciality good."

There appear to be two directions which could usefully be pursued profitably by the tourist industry if it accepts the significance and role of socio-psychological tension states in pleasure vacation decisions suggested in this study. First, efforts are required to arouse people's awareness of their own real motives. The in-depth interviews caused many respondents to confront for the first time their real motives for going on a pleasure vacation. Several commented similarly to the respondent who stated, "This is interesting, I am learning all these things about myself." They expressed surprise at what they revealed, for the motives which ultimately emerged were often radically different from the reasons they were accustomed to giving for going on a vacation. The interviews proved to be an exercise in self-discovery. The role of the travel agent may be a factor. These details were discovered through interviews, then the counsellor would be in a much better position to recommend the most appropriate type of pleasure vacation and destination. The second direction lies in the development of the destination product and its promotion.

The motives may be used as a basis for market segmentation. They provide cues and insights around which destinations can develop and promote their product to target segments. Supplier efforts have generally focused on unique amenities and facilities of the destination. Socio-psychological tension states suggest that this may not be the most appropriate strategy. For example, the escape from a mundane environment, exploration of self, and regression motives, require only a destination which is physically and socially different from the residential environment. Literally thousands of destinations could meet these criteria and thus serve as direct substitutes. The detailed cultural attractions of a destination are not important in this context. The best promotion strategies for this market segment may be to stress the contribution the destination can make to reducing these disequilibrium states and to stress price advantages.

Those destinations seeking to cater to the relaxation motive may stress familiarity and the availability of facilities to enjoy preferred activities rather than a radically different environment or new activities. Destinations targeting at the prestige market segment may emphasize their unique qualities as a destination, rather than the activities or facilities available. This uniqueness must be fairly widely disseminated so that it is known to peer groups in order that they are able to confer upon members appropriate prestige for visiting it. At the same time it should not be promoted as a popular mass destination. The social interaction motive may be accommodated by physical juxtaposition of parties and organized programming, while enhancement of kinship relationships may be a useful theme for promoting family pleasure vacations.

Cultural disequilibrium referred to the desire to see new places or do things in a different environment. It is this motive to which most tourist supplier effort is presently directed. Two culturally oriented motives were identified. These were novelty and education.

Novelty implied that there was no desire to return to a previously visited destination no matter how successful the vacation. This lack of "brand loyalty" may be ameliorated by establishing a network of cross recommendations. That is, agreement between destinations to recommend satisfied consumers to a destination with similar characteristics in a different location. Chain and franchise organizations offer illustration of this at the individual motel or fast-food facility level. For example, if the vacationer enjoyed Dade County, Florida, they may be recommended to try the Rio Grande Valley region of Texas, or Orange County, California. This offers the credibility accrued by the proven destination that there is a good probability of the vacationer enjoying a similarly satisfying experience in a different cultural context.

To remove the fear inhibition present for some in contemplating a novel pleasure vacation, the organized tour may more prominently promote its anxiety reducing potential, rather than concentrating exclusively on price advantage which is its present tendency. Similarly destinations may stress the attributes with which vacationers were likely to feel familiar, that is their recognizable cultural ties, before pointing out cultural differences. Establishing the known before proceeding to the unknown.

Educational prowess may be useful in attracting vacationers for whom the education motive is dominant. Finally, many respondents changed residential location frequently. Location appeared to be an important ingredient in bringing the education motive state to the head of the hierarchy of motives.

This suggests that people are likely to be susceptible to promotions reminding them that the opportunity to visit a destination in reasonable proximity may not arise again. People went on pleasure vacation to satisfy a variety of different motives. As a result, the attributes which might attract them to a destination differed. The implications suggested in the above paragraphs are intended to be illustrative of how these data may be applied rather than exhaustive. Specific implications appropriate to a particular destination will according to its attributes, environmental niche and goals.

Theoretical Aspects of the Sustainable Tourism Strategies

In order to identify the importance and appropriateness of the sustainable tourism strategy in the growth and development of the industry, it has to identify the theoretical support. The major tourism theories are discussed here for identifying how the CSR concept is relevant in the tourism development and growth.

Tourism theories: Travel and tourism theories are mostly based on travel motivation. The basic factors that influence the travelling decisions are tourist need satisfaction, customer satisfaction and destination loyalty. Tourist motivation factors have higher influence on the tourist behaviour of travellers with regard to their destination choice, needs, goals and preferences.

In case of ecotourism, social psychological desire to break out from the habitual ordinary life is the primary push factor. The major pull factors which force travellers to take travel decisions are destination attributes such as natural attractions like wild life and immaculate environment.

As per the theory of Iso-Ahola interpersonal escape and interpersonal seeking motivate tourism and recreation among the individuals. In case of personal seeking and personal escape dimensions, tourism experiences have great role in motivation. Sporting events, beaches, amusement parks, and natural parks improves the motivational levels of tourism and recreational activities to a greater extent. Tourism motivation in holiday trips is the desire to travel for satisfying the internal needs and wants. Incentive tourism is a motivational tool among the employees as well as other organizational personnel.

Most of the weekend travel decisions are related to the intention to take rest and spend the weekend for relaxation. Travel behaviour among individuals can be described as a function of quantifiable aspects such as socio-demographic characteristics and physical characteristics of the region. Most of the travelling decisions are situational in nature.

Travel behaviour of individuals is influenced by individual personality, attitudes and perceptions. Attitude of travellers has influence on beliefs and behaviour in travel decision such as the frequency of use. Novelty seeking is the prime motivating factor that affects the travelling of most of the individuals. The positive and negative feed back from the travel affect their future decision to travel a particular destination.

The motivational factors have a key role in the tourist decision making behaviour. In the motivational factors, push and pull concept was introduced by Crompton and Chon in 1979.

Push factors affect the desire for travel whereas pull factors affect the actual destination choice. In the concept of Crompton 1979, there are nine motive factors influencing the leisure travellers. Seven of them are socio psychological factors and two are cultural motives.

Push factors are internal factors whereas pull factors are external The seven push factors include, making a change in the routine life environment, meeting self needs, relaxation, establishing social relationships, prestige and social interaction. Novelty and education are the pull factors. According to Iso-Ahola, 1980, there are mainly two motivational factors in tourist behaviour. The first feature is approach, focusing on recreational opportunities for intrinsic rewards, and the second feature is avoidance which is escape oriented. The increasing trend of shorter holiday breaks is a signal of escape dimension among the tourists behaviour.

The study by Teare (1994) on peoples' motives for selecting hotel leisure breaks in the UK states that there are six factors such as attending a pre arranged event, as a break from personal commitments, as well as employment pressures, to fulfil the desire of relaxation or visit a particular destination and to exploit the seasonal benefits of short breaks. The personal motivation factor may differ as per individual behaviour. When considering the theoretical concepts it revealed that protection of the natural environment is an essential factor for motivating the travellers to visit the destinations.

Through the keeping of novelty of the destination environment, its attraction can be sustained over a longer period of time. Thus the tourism theories better support the appropriateness of sustainable tourism strategy for the sustainable growth of the industry. Motivation for travel is a complex area of tourism research.

Sharpley (1994) identifies many factors which motivate people to travel. These include a personal need to escape from daily routines, to visit friends and relatives or to learn about other cultures. To understand an individual's motivation to travel, it is necessary to examine their desires, needs, experience and preferences and social, economic and demographic circumstances as well as prevailing social norms and customs.

Although there is a large amount of literature on what motivates people to undertake travel and tourism, the quantity of research into cultural tourist motivation is limited. In particular, there are few studies or surveys of international visitors' motivations and attitudes to Australia's cultural attractions, events and products, despite considerable interest in the Australian cultural tourism industry. Some people, like the English elite who undertook the Grand Tour in the sixteenth and seventeenth centuries, are motivated to travel because of culture.

Such visitors, therefore, can be termed 'specific' cultural or culturally motivated visitors. However, for most people, culture is not a sole motive for travel. Rather, participation in cultural activities is one potential component of a travel itinerary and may occur if opportunities arise. Visitors for whom this is the case can be called 'general' cultural visitors.

Studies of the Motivations of Cultural Visitors

According to some tourist motivation theories, motivations are developed as a result of 'pull' and 'push' factors. Pull factors relate to the characteristics or attractions of a travel destination. For cultural tourists visiting Australia, they include attractions such as the Sydney Opera House and Aboriginal sites.

Push factors relate to the needs and wants of individuals that lead them to 'buy' particular holidays. For cultural tourism and tourism as a whole, they include the desire for social interaction and relaxation, to experience something different and to learn about themselves and the places they visit for participating in cultural activities. Other researchers have identified more specific motivations.

Motivation Theory

"Crompton (1979) notes it is possible to describe the who, when, where, and how of tourism, together with the social and economic characteristics of tourist, but not to answer the question "why," the most interesting question of all tourist behaviour."

While motivation is only one of many variables in explaining tourist behaviour, it is nonetheless a very critical one, as it constitutes the driving force behind all behaviour. Motivation sets the stage for forming people's goals and is reflected in both travel choice and behaviour; as such it influences people's expectations, which in turn determine the perception of experiences. Motivation is therefore a factor in satisfaction formation.

Basic motivation theory suggests a dynamic process of internal psychological factors (needs, wants and goals), causing an uncomfortable level of tension within individuals' minds and bodies, resulting in actions aimed at releasing that tension and satisfying these needs. Motives, implying such an action, require the awareness of needs, as well as objectives, promising to satisfy these now conscious needs in order to create wants and move people to buy. Objectives or goals are presented in the form of products and services, it is therefore the role of marketing to create awareness of needs and suggest appropriate objectives, promising the satisfaction of these.

Several authors suggest that in the Western World free time and holidays are connected to the concept of self-actualisation or self-realisation. The latter defined by Grunow-Lutter (1983.) as *"a person's dynamic relationship between the real and the ideal self, constituting a process of decreasing the distance between these two cognitive systems, themselves subject to continuous change."* It is the individual's aim to achieve a state of stability, or homeostasis, which is disrupted when the person becomes aware of the gap between real and ideal self, or as Goosens calls it a need deficiency. The resulting need to self-actualise represents the motive, which under the constraints of the situation sets the stage for the process of motivation. But to what extent does tourism satisfy the intrinsic need for self-actualisation? Tinsley and Eldredge (1995) summarise 15 years of research into psychological needs, satisfied by leisure activities, and proposed leisure activities clusters such as novelty, sensual enjoyment, cognitive stimulation, self-expression, creativity, vicarious competition, relaxation, agency, belongingness and service. It is questioned however; whether these superficial needs are intrinsically motivated, suggesting that these motivations are merely culturally learned stereotypes or explanations for leisure behaviour. As Fodness (1994) states, a widely accepted integrated theory for needs and goals behind motivation is lacking. The question is of course why this is the case.

Research into motivation can be distinguished into two categories, the behaviourist and the cognivist approach. The discussion has therefore traditionally revolved around either push or pull factors influencing tourist behaviour. Push factors represent lasting dispositions, as they are internally generated drives. The individual, energised by such drives, will then search objects for the promise of drive reduction and develop a motive. The behaviourist view thus emphasises the emotional parameter of decision-making, while the cognivist approach focuses on situational parameters in which motives are expressed, consequently encompassing a certain knowledge which the tourist holds about goal attributes as well as a rational weighing up of situational constraints. This cognitive process results in motivations, which are more object specific than motives, as these only imply a class of objects and may result in a range of different behaviours, depending on the situation.

This unidimensional approach has been criticised however, as push and pull factors influence the consumer simultaneously, integrated by the concept of involvement, an unobservable state of motivation, arousal, or interest, which is evoked by stimulus or situations. This is the case, since pull factors such as marketing stimuli as well as the destination's and service's attributes respond to and reinforce push factors. Consequently research increasingly seeks to integrate emotions and cognition in the individual's decision-making process, indicating a more holistic approach.

As a result it became evident that people's intrinsic needs are influenced by external factors. Rojek (1990) asserts that in post-modern society the superstructure of advertising, television, fashion, lifestyle magazines and designer values increasingly take the role of forming knowledge and beliefs. People's needs are neutral, as motives however, they require an object towards which the need is directed, and when linked to actual situations, cultural and social impacts are also applied. Situations raise motives to the level of values, as such they are evaluations based on learned behaviour and perception.

If a drive is reduced satisfactorily the individual is likely to remember the behaviour and employ the same behaviour again, thus acquiring habits. Tourism experiences may therefore become learned behaviour and acquire the role of habit enforcers. Cognivists argue that knowledge and beliefs in future rewards, anticipatory in nature, are equally a product of formerly encountered situations, and external formation.

It may be concluded that motives merely represent learned behaviour, which are influenced by offered objects or tourism activities, while motivations represent knowledge and beliefs formed by society and culture or tourism marketers. The psychogenic need for self-actualisation, abstract in nature, is therefore operationalised in a learned and practical manner and expressed in values, which are learned strategies to either adapt one's environment to one's needs or adapt one's self to a given environment. Such values equally include effects of enculturation and socialisation. Furthermore the perceived gap between real and ideal self, may indicate both externally and internally controlled evaluations.

McCabe therefore asks what researchers can expect to know about individuals' drives, by asking them about their motivations and needs as these may not be available to individuals as part of their consciousness (2000a,). Iso-Ahola (1982) states that *"people do not walk around with numerous leisure needs in their minds and do not rationalise specific causes of participation if their involvement is intrinsically motivated"* (cited in Goosens 2000). Hence it may be assumed that needs are suggested by immediate social peers, and the wider context of particular social realities as well as the influence of the media. Yet as Weissinger and Bandalos (1995) stress, intrinsic leisure motivation, which is a global disposition and describes a tendency to seek intrinsic rewards, is characterised by self-determination, an awareness of internal needs and a strong desire to make free choices based on these needs.

While self-actualisation may be accepted as a need intrinsic to all individuals, society exercises a great deal of influence on the formation of the ideal self and thus perceived needs. However the notion of authentic or true self, determined by way of experience, offers a solution to the predicament. According to Waterman (1984), individualism symbolises four psychological qualities, the first one is a sense of individual identity, based on the knowledge of who one is and what one's goals and values are, as such it is related to the philosophical concept of true self, which indicates what an individual reckons personally expressive and what it is to be actualised. The second is Maslow's self-actualisation, which is the driving to be one's true self. The third quality is Rotter's (1966) internal locus of control, which reflects a willingness to accept personal responsibility for one's life, and finally principles (postconventional), moral reasoning, which involves consistency with general abstract principles.

Consequently, only if tourists become more autonomous and thus aware of intrinsic needs and motives are they able to self-actualise. As McIntosh and Goeldner (1990) explained, order is becoming less important in Western society and a desire for disorder in the tourism experience is becoming more important. Kim and Lee point out that *"opportunities for unplanned action and freedom from institutionalised regulations are distinctive of Western tourists"* (2000). This indicates that tourists exhibit a certain desire to liberate their identities. According to Krippendorf (1984), in order for tourists to cease being just users of holidays, they must come to know themselves, their motives and other cultures. It may therefore be assumed that self-actualisation is an intrinsic need, characteristic of any tourist, but must be understood in terms of true self as opposed to ideal self and as such is independent of societal pressures and involves the transcendence of habitual behaviours and mindstates. This proposition requires further elaboration and must be viewed in the context of modernity, which hinders this process but at the same time brought about its awareness.

The Escape Motivation

Recently, means-end theory has been applied to recreation and leisure settings by using the laddering method to investigate activities such as ski destination selection, spring break destination choice, nature park interpretation and marketing for urban tourism what a product is, what it does and what people get from it.

These form the three main elements of focus in means-end theory, starting with the physical, observable *attributes* (the "means"), *consequences* (benefits or costs) that follow from the attributes, which further lead to personal *values* (the "ends"). Means-end theory focuses on why and how product attributes are important. Attributes! Consequence (benefits or costs)! Value different) at either end based on personal values.

Individuals are attracted to a particular destination based on a variety of factors such as one's personal traits and leisure and travel motivation grounded within a broad conceptual push-pull scenario. Leisure and recreation are important motives for amenity migrants.

This model contends that motivation to reside specific to the Bow Valley include a desire to balance a mountain recreation lifestyle with work, to be with a friend or partner, to escape, to purchase a second home, to be in a place suits one's values, to be next to the (aesthetic lifestyle) mountains and to pursue a career in tourism or parks. Factor analysis results revealed two factor components labelled To Live and To Escape. The former included to pursue a career in tourism, hospitality or parks, to start a business, to balance work with a mountain recreation lifestyle and just to be with a friend or partner while the former included to own a second home and to escape.

Lived Experience of Negotiated Leisure. The leisure negotiation process is framed by the human-environment relationship and remains dynamic due to constant evaluations of the one's ability to negotiate aspects of a changing environment with one's personal resources. The lived experience component of the model includes the element of leisure and recreation behaviour.

Behaviour is important as it is postulated here that leisure/recreation behaviour imprints the destination through the expression of demand. For example, the persistent behaviour of mountain biking may result in the development of additional mountain trails, a built mountain bike park, or even the banning of mountain biking from certain or all trails. Likewise, the presence of upper middle class urban dwellers may bring about a perceived demand for up-scale restaurants and cafes. Or the presence of families with children may bring increased demand for traditional recreation facilities such as pools and ice arenas. Recreation behaviour is an expression of demand which is likely to impact supply thereby altering the environment.

Environment: The environment within a high recreation amenity destination can be characterized as having significant natural and cultural resources. It involves a strong social component of community and reference groups. The social element can also include detractions such as crowding, congestion and other forms of conflict such as with recent and long time residents. It also includes structural components such as the economy, housing, roads and health and educational infrastructure which all contribute to the negotiation. Physical, social and structural aspects of the environment are assumed to act both as a facilitator to one's leisure goals, and constraint or stressor at different times. It is also assumed that over time the nature and character of the Environment evolves (dotted line) as the physical and social aspects of the destination evolve.

Negotiation and Coping Strategies: From a leisure and recreation perspective negotiation with one's internal and external constraints is widely understood within the Leisure Constraints model which includes three basic levels of leisure constraint of intra-personal, interpersonal and structural. The Leisure Constraints model is perhaps best suited to understanding what aspect of the internal (personal traits and motivation) and external (physical, social and structural) environments are being negotiated and how. The Recreation Coping model is used to understand the way in which people respond to stressors within a recreation setting.

The Recreation Coping model posits that individuals will respond using one of more of four possible responses to stress within a recreation environment they include two cognitive based responses of rationalization and product shift and two behavioural based responses of displacement and direct action. It is postulated that an individual will begin leisure and recreation negotiations relying on typical leisure constraint negotiations for the selection and pursuit of activities and behaviours. With increased time at the site it is believed that an individual will rely more heavily on recreation coping strategies as various types of stressors persist and complimentary strategies are found. However, it is assumed that despite the shift in emphasis over time both leisure constraint and recreation coping negotiation strategies may be present at any one time.

Amenity Migrant Typology: Resulting from Motivation and the dynamic of the leisure centred human-environment negotiation is a typology of amenity migrants based on the findings of this investigation. The typology is primarily based on the qualitative data analysis and appears in Box A. The typology is a result of different types (what is being negotiated) and levels (intensity) of negotiation within the human environment. Various amenity migrant typologies appear in the literature. Factor analysis results revealed four distinct factor components based on importance of recreation amenities they include; back country, culture, recreation and entertainment.

Amenity Migrant Typology

1. Those who wish to pursue a mountain recreation lifestyle in the Bow Valley rely on it for their livelihood but can not negotiate the costs over the benefits and decide to leave;
2. Those who wish to pursue a mountain recreation lifestyle in the Bow Valley and rely on it for their livelihood but negotiate to overcome the costs for the benefit;

3. Those who live in the Bow Valley to pursue more urban recreation and hospitality & tourism careers within the area;
4. Those who wish to pursue a mountain recreation lifestyle but do not rely on the Bow Valley for their livelihood directly (commute or remote work situations); and
5. Those who wish to escape to the Bow Valley part-time (second home) and do not rely on the valley for their livelihood.

Place Attachment, Dependence, and Identity. The relationship the individual recreationist develops with the place over time can be understood using the concept of place attachment including underlying concepts of place dependence and identity.

Together, as place attachment, it is used to characterize the continuous manifestation of the human-environment negotiation as a relationship with the place. Place attachment, dependence and identity are assumed to be strong predictors of whether an individual will stay or leave a destination. Some will leave and others will remain. Even those who leave the site impact the evolution of the destination as was their behaviour an expression of demand for the tenure of their residency. Those who leave may be seeking other destinations more supportive of their identity, goals and personal resources. Those who remain impact the destination through their behaviour, and in other ways such as policy development, and through on-going, shared discourse that creates a collective understanding of place. Place attachment loops back (dotted line) to motivation as the individual's relationship with the place will be affected by the continuous negotiation process which is assumed to influence one's motivation to engage in future negotiations and in what manner. Place attachment loops back as an antecedent to the continuous negotiation process.

Affect on Destination and Recreation Supply. The final component of the models seeks to provide insight into how the leisure based human-environment relationship physically affects a high recreation amenity destination. It is postulated here that as population increases urban-type recreation supply increases and backcountry (outside of the townsite) generally remains stagnant or decreases. This general pattern has been previously observed. For example Glorioso & Moss (2006) discuss the rapid increase of urban amenities in the Santa Fe region during the 1980s to present in association with amenity migration. Moore, Williams & Gill (2006) report loss of recreation land adjacent to Whistler BC townsite as a result of residential and golf course development coupled with increased urbanization. As the destination evolves including the quantity and quality of urban and recreation supply this will result in an equally evolving image of the destination that will serve to attract different types of individuals. This is a simple displacement process similar the Plog's (2002) model, however based on tourists, whereby a destination evolves and as it does it attracts 'venturerers' at first then 'dependables' later on. Similarly, early, density-crowding-satisfaction models realized that within any one site varying conditions would attract different groups of people more or less comfortable with crowding conditions. The quantitative survey included a 27-item scale to assess whether residents perceived change in their recreation and structural environment in the form of increases or decreases in urban-type recreation, backcountry recreation, tourism activity, and structural elements such as jobs, housing and cost of living.

Factor analysis on the scale revealed seven factor components in accordance to where most change has been perceived (no particular direction of change) they were labelled as crowding, backcountry, urbane, town, outdoor recreation, and urban. A five-cluster solution revealed that overall some factor components were perceived to have increased and others decreased. More specifically, overall factor components 'crowding' (seven crowding related items) and 'urbane' (four items related to cafes, restaurants, and bars) were perceived to have increased while 'outdoor' (four items related to trails, ski areas, festivals), 'backcountry' (four items related to more remote outdoor activity), was perceived to have decreased while 'town' (five items related to structural aspects and public recreation) has remained about the same. The quantitative results generally support the final component of the model whereby in-town recreation supply increases while backcountry recreation increases. The results of cluster analysis on one of the four measures contained within the questionnaire. The sub-scale means for each of the clusters, the composite mean for each cluster, a cluster label and the results of the Scheffe test. The scale for Q8 was a six point scale with the final scale item of 'don't know' recoded as missing therefore it is based on a five point scale whereby 1 has increased greatly 3 is has not changed and 5 is has decreased greatly.

An ANOVA was conducted to determine if there were differences among the means of the clusters which yielded value of for each of the subscale items. A post hoc analysis of a Scheffe Test was conducted to determine which clusters are significantly different from which and in what direction. Numerous significant tests (p=.05) were reported with the direction of difference indicated by the arrow. Additionally Classification Results(a) test reported that 97.2% of the originally grouped cases were classified correctly.

Indicate that overall some factor components are perceived to be increasing and others are perceived to be decreasing for example if a cut off point of 2.5 within the scale is adopted whereby that which is less than 2.5 is perceived to be increasing and that which is over 2.5 is perceived to be decreasing than overall respondents report that 'crowding' and 'urbane' components are perceived to be increasing while 'town' has generally remained the same and 'outdoor', 'backcountry' and 'urban' (only one item) have all decreased. Also, that the five clusters are different however some basic patterns emerge. With respect to the 'crowding' subscale, cluster 1 (nothing is different) is different from the others. Cluster 2 (crowded out) generally differs from the others with respect to the 'urbane', 'outdoor', 'backcountry' and 'urban' subscales.

Overall, cluster 2 (crowded out, N=65) is different from others with respect to perception of change in the Bow Valley. In general, the exploratory findings support the assertion that change is occurring the direction of increased crowding and urban-type recreation amenities and opportunities with a perceived decrease in backcountry-type recreation amenities and opportunities

Relaxation

How Motivations, Constraints, and Demographic Factors Predict Seniors' Overseas Travel Propensity

As the trend in aging societies is growing all over the world, the travel and tourism market for senior citizens has attracted much attention recently from both practitioners and academics. The market shows great potential, not only because of its considerable population proportion, but also because of senior citizens' great contribution to a tourism economy. It is generally accepted that seniors in developed countries on average possess a relatively large share of discretionary income and time and are still in good health. These characteristics enable them to travel more, and many seniors have the time to travel and are willing to spend a significant amount of their savings on travel. In addition, the travel behaviour of seniors is characterized as travelling more frequently, going longer distances, staying away longer, spending more money, and relying more on travel agents.

Hence, senior travellers are important to the tourism industry and will grow in importance as their segment grows in size and wealth. Understanding seniors' travel decision behaviour is a crucial issue to travel marketers who compete for this important market.

The theory of tourism demand states that it is influenced by three major determinants: economic factors, socio-psychological factors, and exogenous factors. The economic factors include per capita income, cost of living, exchange rate, tourism prices, and transportation costs, among others. The social-psychological factors are associated with the decision-making of travellers such as demographic factors, travel motivations, constraints, images of destinations, and travel preferences, among others. The exogenous factors are associated with the business environment. The psychological determinants of demand in explaining some reasons why tourists travel and select particular destinations. Motivation is defined as the 'driving force behind all behaviour'. From the perspective of the traveller's decision-making process, travel motivations are seen as the energizers of demand that promote an individual to decide on a holiday. Travel behaviour can be predicted by underlying motivations.

Hence, those who are highly motivated might be those who are most likely to overcome constraints and participate in more leisure activities. The concept of travel motivations is based on the existence of "push" and "pull" factors. This has been extensively discussed and is a generally accepted concept. Push motivation refers to an individual's internal energy and an increase in the desire for people to travel, while pull motivation refers to a force external to an individual that influences where people travel, given the initial desire to travel.

Ryan (1991) finds that tourist travel motivations could be identified as wish fulfilment, shopping, escaping from a mundane environment, rest and relaxation, an opportunity for play, strengthening family bonds, prestige, social interaction, and educational opportunities. The most common motivations identified by related research regarding seniors' travel motivation are rest and relaxation, escaping from a mundane environment, social interaction, physical exercise, learning, nostalgia, visiting friends and relatives, and excitement. Shoemaker (1989) notes that among fourteen motivations, rest and relaxation as well as escaping from a mundane environment are the most salient two motivations, while knowing friends of a different gender and playing golf are the least important two motivations for senior travellers in Pennsylvania.

Interestingly, after ten years, Shoemaker (2000) finds that the main motivations of senior travellers shifted to visiting new places and experiencing new things. Regarding seniors' travel motivation, some main classifications can be identified in the literature such as rest/relaxation, social interaction, health, learning, seeking, escaping, attracting, cost, nostalgia and visiting historical sites.

Huang and Tsai (2003) reported that 'Get rest and relaxation' (35.6%) and 'Meet people and socialization' (20.1%) are found as the main travel motivation of Taiwanese seniors. In addition, considering both push and pull dimensions of Taiwanese senior travel motivations, Jang and Wu (2006) found the push motivations include 'ego-enhancement', 'self-esteem', 'knowledge seeking', 'relaxation', and 'socialization' while the pull motivations encompass 'cleanliness and safety', 'facility, event and cost', and 'natural and historical sites'.

Travel Constraints

Unlike motivations that serve as energizers, constraints towards travelling function as filters for tourism demand, preventing the decision makers from engaging in travel even though the motivation may exist.

Leisure constraints can provide a conceptual framework that may help understand why individuals do not participate in specific tourism activities. The hierarchical model proposed by Crawford and Godbey (1987) and Crawford et al. (1991), is the most accepted theoretical framework of leisure constraints.

Their studies categorize leisure constraints into three hierarchically organized levels: intrapersonal, interpersonal, and structural constraints. Furthermore, participation in leisure activities is seen as a process of overcoming the various constraints. The intrapersonal constraints are defined as individual psychological states and attributes, such as stress, anxiety, attitudes, and perceived self skill, that might inhibit one from participating in leisure activities. They exist when people fail to develop leisure preferences due to problems or misconceptions associated with personality needs, prior socialization, personal ability, and perceptions of reference group attitudes. The interpersonal barriers result from social interactions with friends, family, and others. The structural constraints include factors that block people's intentions from taking actions such as economic resources, availability of time, and accessibility. The most often cited constraints to travel in related research are a lack of time, financial considerations, physical and emotional costs, health status (objective and self-reported), perceived disability, age, security concerns, lack of information, family approval, and family responsibilities.

Regarding the dimensionality of leisure constraint measurement, Jackson (1993) identifies six dimensions of leisure constraints from eight studies: social isolation, accessibility, personal reasons, costs, time commitments, and facilities. The social isolation dimension can be deemed as an interpersonal dimension that is based on characteristics involving interaction between/among people. The accessibility dimension includes factors such as a lack of or limited access to transportation or 'getting there'.

The personal reasons dimension is an intrapersonal dimension that includes items pertaining directly to an individual's abilities or motivations. The cost dimension covers items related to the outlay of money. The time dimension represents a collection of items referred to as reasons that affect levels and intensity of participation among adults. Finally, the facility dimension relates specifically toleisure settings and individuals' perception. Although the theoretical hypothesis assumes a positive impact of travel motivation on travel propensity, it is acceptable to see a negative impact of *socialization* motivation on travel intention in this study.

The decision of whether to travel overseas or to travel domestically involves different decision-making considerations. The push power of travel motivation, such as socialization in general, can motivate seniors to travel in the domestic context due to familiar cultural and/or social customs, languages, etc. However, travelling overseas might be a barrier for seniors due to an unfamiliar or foreign environment. This is indirectly supported by about 70% of retirees choosing group package tours as their overseas travel mode in Taiwan.

The Psychology of Relaxation

The Gospel of Relaxation was the subject of a speech made by Mr. Herbert Spencer at a dinner given in his honour in New York City in 1882. Mr. Spencer called attention to the extreme form of "persistent activity' 3 which characterizes the American people. The energy of the savage, he said, was spasmodic. He could not apply himself persistently to work. He lived in the present and did not worry about the future. Civilized man more and more pursues a future goal and applies himself to work until it becomes a passion.

In America, said Mr. Spencer, this strenuous and high-pressure life has become extreme, and a counterchange a reaction must be imminent. We take our multitudinous responsibilities too seriously. There are too many lines in our faces, our gray hairs appear too early, our nervous breakdowns are too frequent. Damaged constitutions and a damaged posterity are among the results. Emerson, with his saying that the first requisite of a gentleman is to be a perfect animal, is a safer guide for us than Carlyle with his gospel of work.

More recently, Professor James, Annie Payson Call, and other writers 1 have eloquently preached this same gospel of relaxation. We are told that we are too breathless; that we live under too much stress and tension; that we are too intense and carry too much expression in our faces; that we must relax, let go, breathe deeply, and unburden ourselves of many useless contractions.

There seems to be a good deal of truth in this. Some of us manage to escape neu-rasthenia, but few of us are free from fatigue, chronic or acute. We hear with amazement now and again some one say, "I was never tired in my life." Surely under normal conditions we ought not to be so tired as we are, nor tired so often.

Impressed with the strenuous character of American life and the need of more rest and recreation, practical common sense, not waiting upon theory, has turned to discover means for relieving the excessive tension incident to our present habits of living. Some, as we have said, preach the gospel of relaxation, content to tell us that we are too intense. Others have established schools with practical and helpful rules and methods for relaxation and have brought comfort and relief to many. Again, a new and unique interest has suddenly arisen in play. Men and animals have always played; but now we have first become conscious of play and curious about it. We insist on play. If children do not play, we teach them to play. And we are anxious to know about the theory of play.

Finally, a score of movements, perhaps many score, have sprung into notice, whose purpose is to encourage or provide some form of relaxation. We recall the recreation movement; the physical-culture movement; the playground movement; the Boy Scouts; the Camp-Fire girls; the ever-increasing interest in athletics, not only in our colleges, but also in our high schools and grammar schools; the radical change in Young Men's Christian Associations from devotional to hygienic and athletic religion; the renaissance of the gymnasium and the Olympic games; the increased interest in outdoor life of all kinds; the renewed devotion to outdoor sports, like tennis, golf, baseball, and football; the rapid extension of the play motive into almost every branch of education; the new vacation schools and school excursions; finally the supervised playgrounds, supervised folk-dancing, supervised swimming, wading, tramping, gardening, singing, and storytelling. Even with very young children the Montessori system seeks to relieve the tension of the old task methods by making the child's activities natural and interesting as well as useful.

More than twenty-five hundred regularly supervised playgrounds and recreation centres are now maintained in about six hundred and fifty cities in this country. A brand new profession has appeared, that of play leader, employing nearly seven thousand professional workers.

The legislatures of some States have passed laws requiring every city of a certain size to vote on the proposition of maintaining playgrounds. New York City expended more than $15,000,000 on playgrounds previous to 1908.

The city paid $1,811,000 for one playground having about three acres. Chicago spent $11,000,000 on playgrounds and field houses in two years. Formerly the boy could play on the street, in the back alley, in the back yard. Now, the alley and back yard have disappeared, the street is crowded with automobiles, and the few remaining open spaces are given over to the lawn-mower and keep-off-the-grass signs, while more and more the school has encroached on the boy's precious period of growth, filling at least nine of the twelve months of the year and adding the evils of evening study and the dread of examinations.

For reasons which will be shown presently, boys must play. Take away the opportunity for legitimate play, and the play instinct, the instinct of rivalry, of adventure, of initiation, will manifest itself in antisocial ways. Hence the juvenile court and the reform school. "Better, playgrounds without schools," says one writer, "than schools without playgrounds." Up to the present time this is about as far as we have gone into the subject of relaxation. Its psychology has not really been studied at all. We have simply been impressed by the tense and strenuous character of our manner of life and have connected this with the increase of nervous disorders and nervous breakdowns and perhaps with the increase of insanity, and have felt the need, accordingly, of more recreation and play, and more harmony and poise in our way of living, and have taken, there fore, a few practical steps in this direction. But suddenly within the most recent days things have happened which have caused some of us to begin to think more deeply on the whole subject of work and play, and have suggested that it is not a local American problem at all, but a world problem of the present age, and that perhaps great social questions may be involved. The outbreak of recreation crazes in America was the first of these events, but it was the calamity of the European war which most distinctly called our attention to the need of a more careful study of the psychological conditions of our modern life.

Just as we thought the world to be getting very serious, and settling down to work and to problems of social and individual welfare and to political and moral reform, it has suddenly gone amusement-mad in America and reverted with unparalleled ferocity to primeval bloodshed in Europe. These amusement crazes have taken many forms, but the most virulent form was seen in the dancing mania, which has passed through various stages in North and South America and has been so widespread and so compelling that it has reminded us of the epidemics of the Middle Ages. At its height, according to the newspaper reports, a tribe of Indians in Nevada built a great dance-hall in the midst of their village, and imported a teacher of the tango.

Then came the moving-picture craze, which has seized the world like an obsession. No one can suppose that this colossal social phenomenon is to be explained by the mere fact of the discovery of the cinematograph, and that the people were merely waiting upon the invention in order to flock to the spectacles. The invention was an incident. The real significant fact was the psychological situation. Consider the following editorial from a recent number of the "Nation":

The historian will come to grief if he attempts to describe the cause of frivolity in the New York of 1915 A.D. as historians have depicted the frivolity of Rome under the early emperors, and to compare bread and the circus with lobster a la Newburgh and the cabaret. Going back to Rome, and assuming the grand manner, he will speak of a city that drew to itself the booty of the civilized world, of a population enervated by the largess of politicians doling out the plunder of three continents, of a citizenship lulled into civic indifference by gifts and amusements in other words, an imperial city gone rotten with prosperity.

If the parallel holds for New York, the historian would have to describe a city that went mad over cabarets because it had more money than it could spend wisely, because it had no serious interest in the problems of the civic and social life, because its serenity was undisturbed by wars or the fear of wars, because there was no unemployment problem, no city-budget problem, no workmen's compensation problem, no widows' pension problem, no Mexican problem, no German problem. Else how account for a city gone mad over the fox trot and the white lights? Life was much simpler in imperial Rome than it is in New York today, though even under the early Caesars the picture was not so uniform as the average historian has painted it.

At least we know today that the fact of 400,000 unemployed in New York City does not militate against the prosperity of the "movies," which are the circenses of the masses; and the fact of Wall Street's unemployed has not interfered with the prosperity of the cabarets. Quite the contrary. There is good reason for believing that not all the young men at the afternoon teas are professional idlers and parasites, but that a good many business men and brokers have taken to dancing in the afternoon because there was nothing to do downtown. Perhaps the grasshopper in La Fontaine's fable, who sang all summer, did so because business was rotten, and when the ant told him to go and dance in winter, he was only advising him to do the best possible thing under the circumstances.

To be sure it is no longer possible to dispose of such things as these by referring them to "frivolity" or to "luxury," but neither is it possible to say that they are due to idleness. For instance, a correspondent in a small mining-camp near the Mexican border writes that the Mexican labourers, who comprise six-sevenths of the population, are strictly amusement-mad, spending their last pennies at the "movies" or the merry-go-round or for intoxicants. May it not be that these amusement crazes are a form of reaction against a manner of life that is too serious and tense. May they not be indications of a lack of physiological adjustment. We are making great efforts in these days to secure better social adjustment through the study of social and economic conditions; but is it not possible that the trouble is not in the lack of social adjustment, but in the lack of physiological adjustment in the individual, so that what we have to strive for is not so much improved social conditions, as improved health and improved physical constitutions, to be gained by a different manner of life, a different kind of education, and a different proportion of work and play.

Then there is another cloud which has recently appeared on the social horizon leading us to think that the problem of work and play needs further study. We refer to the remarkable increase in the number of deaths from diseases of degeneration. A few years ago, rejoicing over the discoveries of Pasteur and his followers, we had great hope of increasing the span of human life by the conquest of the devastating parasitic diseases. These diseases have, indeed, to some extent been conquered. We have now less dread of typhoid, tuberculosis, pneumonia, and diseases of this class due to microscopic enemies, but the expected increase in racial stability has not come. Some, therefore, are beginning to ask whether the better way to lengthen human life is to remove the enemies which threaten it, or to increase our power of resistance to these enemies.

According to Mr. E. E. Rittenhouse, president of the Life Extension Institute, there is a marked decline in the power of American workers to withstand the strain of modern life. They wear out sooner than they did a few years ago. The chances of death after reaching the prime of life have increased because of the extraordinary increase in the death-rate from the breaking-down of the heart, arteries, kidneys, and of the nervous and digestive systems. Mr. Rittenhouse's conclusions as to the serious inroads of these diseases in modern life are based not on mortality records of the idle rich and such classes, but upon actual physical examination of a large number of male workers, including officials, clerks, and employees of banks and commercial houses, averaging about thirty years of age. The results show that these diseases of degeneration, so-called diseases of old age, are " reaching down into middle life and below, and increasing there, and apparently at all ages." These diseases, not being so quickly fatal as the parasitic diseases, produce decreased efficiency and increased misery, oftentimes through many working years.

The lesson which investigations such as this teach is that the problem of public health and longevity is not altogether a problem of hygiene in the narrower sense in which this word is commonly used. It is rather the deeper question of vitality, of biological adjustment, of racial stability; and it involves questions of heredity, of mental and physical balance, of manner of life, of physical education, of work and play.

Sociologists are becoming acutely conscious of the fact that our cultured classes are not self-perpetuating. The increasing number of childless marriages and small families in these classes indicates that a process of displacement is taking place in favour of peoples of hardier stock and simpler habits, depriving us at once of the advantages of physical heredity and making progress depend very largely upon social heredity alone. A given stock of people may cultivate its brains to the highest point of intellectual and moral efficiency, but, if it neglect the corresponding development of somatic vitality, if it neglect strength and vigour of muscles, heart, lungs, stomach, and reproductive system, it is doomed to extinction and cannot pass on to posterity the intellectual and moral power which it has itself inherited.

Finally, the increased desire for narcotics in the form of drugs, tobacco, and alcohol, prevalent in all civilized countries, is a further indication of some serious lack of balance between body and brain. There is a lack of adjustment somewhere, and the problem of the day is to find out where it is and how it may be remedied. It is not our purpose in this book to study this great problem, but rather a single phase of it, namely, the relation of work and play and the results both to the individual and to society of excessive work and insufficient relaxation. It is very probable that our modern strenuous life is bringing too heavy a strain upon the brain, particularly those parts of the brain immediately connected with the mental powers which condition that peculiar kind of progress which the world is now making. The tendency of the times is toward a very swift industrial, commercial, professional, and intellectual activity.

It is an age of great effort and endeavour, of stress and tension, of labour and strain, of scientific and inventive ability; an age of great efficiency and striving for efficiency; an age of variegation; a centrifugal age. It is not an age of peace, of calm, of poise, of relaxation, of repose, of measure, of harmony, of conservation. It is not a centripetal age. The spirit of the age is that of Francis Bacon. It is not the spirit of such greater minds as Buddha and Jesus and Sophocles and Plato and St. Francis.

What is likely to be the outcome of such tendencies as these? Our current sociology speaks almost exclusively of the proximate social results. What is perhaps more important is to speak of the immediate physiological and psychological results, because they throw light upon certain ultimate and still more important social consequences.

The immediate social results of an age of such great activity and great expenditure are clearly pointed out, for instance, by Professor Giddings in his "Democracy and Empire." These are, in brief, (i) an increase of wealth, culture, and refinement, followed by a marked increase of population; (2) a movement of the people toward the large cities; and (3) a displacement of the higher types of people by the lower, followed by an increase of crime, vagabondage, suicide, and feeble-mindedness.

These social results we may leave to the sociologist. But what is the effect of such an age of great activity and great expenditure upon the individual? This we believe to be just now the important question, and it is to the answer to this question that we hope the studies in this book may be a contribution.

The result, in a word, is a rapid and extreme fatigue of the higher brain and an unusual and imperative demand for rest and relaxation. Nature has provided various means for rest and relaxation, in sleep, play, sport, laughter, etc. But what will happen when the claims made upon the working brain are in excess of the powers of repair provided by these natural means of relaxation, or when these means themselves are neglected ? There will be increasing irritability and probably reactions more or less violent and spasmodic, and if there are any artificial means of relieving the strain and temporarily restoring the balance, there will be recourse to such aids.

The craving for narcotic drugs, tobacco, and alcohol, will be an example of the latter, and the recurrence of recreation crazes will be an illustration of the former. Finally, it is altogether possible that society as a whole may suffer from such excessive mental activity and such excessive tension, and that great social upheavals may follow, such, for instance, as war. Thus we may understand why the psychologist in treating the laws of relaxation may bring together in one volume subjects apparently so unlike as play, sport, laughter, profanity, alcohol, and war.

The principle involved in all the forms of relaxation here studied is relief from tension or release from some form of restraint. Although this tension and restraint on the part of the individual are necessary conditions of all social evolution, they have been greatly intensified by the manner of life which characterizes the nineteenth and twentieth centuries. The repression of primitive impulses to the end of growing social needs is the fundamental law of human progress. Such continual repression necessitates constant effort, constant strain, and constant exercise of voluntary attention. It involves those higher brain centres whose development has conditioned human progress, and brings upon them a severe and constant strain, making rest and relaxation imperative.

When this everlasting urge of progress is excessive, as it has been in recent times, we may say that there is in a way a constant subconscious rebellion against it and a constant disposition to escape from it, and the method of escape is always the temporary reversion to simpler and more primitive forms of behaviour, a return to nature, so to speak. Sudden momentary and unexpected release from this tension, with instinctive reinstatement of primitive forms of expression, is laughter. Daily or periodic systematic return to primitive forms of activity is sport or play. War is a violent social reversion to elemental and natural in-tertribal relations. Profanity is a resort to primitive forms of vocal expression to relieve a situation which threatens one's wellbeing. Alcohol is an artificial means of relieving mental tension by the narcotizing of the higher brain centres.

Thus the reader may understand why we have associated in a single volume these seemingly diverse kinds of human behaviour they are all forms of relaxation. That which is common to all these phenomena is the relief from the tension of our modern strenuous life by means of a return to nature, or a return to early and elemental forms of behaviour which offer rest or release from the burdens of life. All therefore appear as forms of relaxation, some helpful and normal, others abnormal and brutalizing.

If we should succeed in tracing all of these modes of human behaviour to their psychological sources, we may contribute something to the clearing-up of certain difficult social problems of the day. We may, for instance, be enabled to see very clearly that evil and destructive forms of relaxation cannot be banished except by substituting normal and healthful forms.

The growing worldwide craving for alcohol, tobacco, and other narcotic drugs and the fatal and inevitable recurrence of war, with its fearful toll of human life and its still more fearful toll of hard-earned human savings, perplexing though they are as social problems, nevertheless might become much clearer in the light thrown upon them by the study of the laws of mental relaxation.

In the present stage of human culture, war seems like a species of insanity. It is no longer taken for granted. It no longer fits in as a part of the natural order of events. It seems anomalous and grotesque. It has lost its glory and seems now barbaric. We have been so long accustomed to have our disputes settled by courts of law, whose decisions are based upon principles of justice, that an appeal to mere brute force in the settlement of international disputes appears to us more and more absurd.

Recently the reversionary character of war has been startlingly revealed to us by the reversionary logic and the reversionary morals which accompany it. And yet wars one after another, each more terrible than the last, are flaunted in the face of nineteenth and twentieth century civilization, are flaunted directly in the face of worldwide movements for international conciliation. In like manner the use of alcohol, from the standpoint of modern science, appears as a kind of insanity. Scientific study has now shown that alcohol has none of the good effects upon the body or mind which formerly it was supposed to have, and that it is not even a stimulant. Yet the consumption of alcohol steadily increases.

Under these circumstances we should welcome any light, however small, which psychology can throw upon these subjects. The desire for alcohol and the instinct for war are phenomena which lie in the field of psychology, and reformers will make little headway against these evils unless they take into account the psychological motives.

We may, if we choose, redouble again our efforts against alcohol, but it would be the part of reason to find out, if we can, the causes of this growing desire in order that they may, if possible, be removed. So we may, if we choose, redouble our efforts toward universal peace, but a more rational method would seem to be to find out the deep-lying causes of war and see whether anything can be done to remove them.

In the chapters which follow, an attempt is made to treat these subjects psychologically and in particular to consider them from the standpoint of phylogenetic experience. We must call to mind not only the animal and savage past from which man has emerged, but also the forces or tendencies which are manifest in his development. It is not sufficient to explain war by recalling that man is a fighting animal, that he has literally fought his way up to manhood. It is far more important to understand that his constant advance has been attended by conditions of tension and stress which have made his periodic and temporary reversion to primitive habits an actual condition of renewed progress. It is still more important to learn how the supreme intelligence with which evolution has finally crowned mankind may be used to devise some means by which these periodic reversions to savagery may be made unnecessary.

Lately we have seemed to forget that human progress is rhythmical, that mankind advances by a series of relapses and recoveries, and that after each recovery there is new ground gained, sometimes very much new ground.

It may be that we have here the explanation of war, and it may be that there are conditions present in the social life of our times which intensify these rhythmical reversionary tendencies, so that no manner of humanitarian effort can withstand the periodic demand for war, just as no manner of prohibitive legislation and no manner of science sermons can stem the desire for alcohol. Especially in the last century has "progress," as it is called, been very rapid, progress in science, in industry, in invention, in everything, and the tension and rapidity of our lives have become correspondingly great. After great tension there must be great relaxation. There is a limit to the strain which the social mind can stand. It is imperative that we study the laws of mental tension and mental relaxation. The psychology of play may throw much light on the psychology of war.

No engineer or architect undertakes to build a bridge or skyscraper without an accurate knowledge of the strength of material. Modern life is a kind of social skyscraper. The minds of the individuals who constitute society are the material. This material is put under too much tension. A collapse necessarily follows. In our social life these collapses appear as reactions or reversions, sometimes cataclysmic, as in the case of the war in Europe, sometimes sporadic, as in the dancing crazes and the amusement crazes in America.

In the following pages an attempt has been made to study the strength of this human material, to study the causes of the social strains and the forms and directions taken by the social reactions. If these studies teach us nothing more, they will at least show that the folly of explaining war by referring it to mere political rivalries is no less than that of referring amusement crazes to "frivolity" and the desire for alcohol to "depravity."

Educational Opportunity

Educational Tourism

During the past decades, the educational tourism have evolved and developed number of ways such as the student exchanges or the urge of the young people to travel to another country in order to study and learn as well as analyse the language and culture of other people; special holidays on the other hand, is the urge to travel to learn something new (1999). There is no doubt that educational industry has already become one of the most popular types of special interest tourism. According to and (1997), the world market for international education travel was estimated to increase from 4.8 million trips up to more or less 8 million trips in 1996, showing that it had increase 66% of its total trips.

Tourism industry has been one of the most important industries in the world during the past few decades that have helped many countries and nations to improve their economies by increasing sales, employment and the foreign currency earnings (1991). Tourism has been part of the normal daily life of many people in the world (2006).

That is why most of the countries and places in the world are doing their best in focusing on their tourism industry because of the fact that the said industry has obtained the leading position of becoming the most important source of income and foreign investments (2006). (2006) believes that the growth of the tourism industry will continue to expand in the near future and will maintain its growth to become the most important industry in the world.

Special Interest Tourism

Special interest tourism is a controversial and a hot label that often used incorrectly or interchangeably to define a form of tourism that refers to the mass tourism (2000). According to the World Tourism Industry or WTO, special interest tourism can be defined as the specialized tourism that involved individual or group tours by those people who wishes to develop their given interests or visit sites and places that has a relation or connection with their specific interest or subject (2003). According to, people are travelling because of their particular interest for a particular subject that are available or can be seen in a given country or place (2003).

On the other hand those people who are into the special interest tourism are called special interest tourist. They are motivated by their desire and urge to pursue their particular interest, hobby or activity than can be a sport like, scuba diving, golf or mountain climbing or bird watching; another thing that can motivated them is their love for heritage interest like folk music, educational pursuit and periodical architecture. They are choosing their destination based on the can offer them a better and unique way of enjoying their hobbies and interest (2000 century).

Shopping

One-day Shopping Tourism as a Situation Specific Experience

Motives for a Shopping Trip : The motivational basis for purchasing and shopping has been studied by consumer behaviour researchers for decades. The seminal attempt to classify buyers according to their orientation was made by Stone (1954). He identified four different shopper types: the economic consumer, the personalizing consumer, the ethical consumer and the apathetic consumer. Later, several studies have been conducted in order to increase understanding on shopping orientation. According to Tauber (1972) shopping behaviour is motivated by a variety psychosocial need beyond those relating to the products being acquired. In this way, Tauber identified both personal and social motives to be influential in shopping behaviour. Personal satisfaction gained from shopping according to Tauber are: 1) the opportunity to enact a culturally prescribed role; 2) diversion from daily routines; 3) provision of self-gratification; 4) learning about new trends, fashions and innovations; 5) obtaining physical exercise; and 6) receiving sensory stimulation from the retail environment.

The satisfaction of a social nature arises from 1) social interaction outside the home; 2) communication with others having similar interests; 3) affiliating with reference group; 4) obtaining increases in social status; 5) achieving success in bargaining and negotiation. Later, Bellenger and Korgaonkar (1980) introduced their twofold shopper typology: economic shoppers, who dislike shopping or are neutral toward it and recreational shoppers, who enjoy shopping as a leisure-time activity.

Westbrook & Black (1985) introduced a motivation-based shopper typology based on Tauber's work. According to Westbrook & Black, there are seven major dimensions of shopping motivation: 1) anticipated utility; 2) role enactment; 3) negotiation; 4) choice optimization; 5) affiliation; 6) power and authority; and 7) stimulation.

These dimensions may vary across individuals and shopping situations due to personality, learning, products being shopped and the types of retail institutions. Dawson, Bloch & Ridgway (1990) used Westbrooks & Blacks results as starting point in their research of how shopping motives and emotional states influence retail outcomes.

They divided motives to product-oriented motives and experiential motives. Product-oriented motives include 1) find variety of new products; 2) find unique crafts or foods; 3) see new things; 4) find good prices; and 5) keep up with new crafts or foods when experiential motives are 1) watch other people; 2) enjoy the crowds; 3) see and hear entertainment; 4) meet new people; 5) experience interesting sights, sounds and smells; 6) get out of the house. Babin, Darden & Griffin (1994) use same kind of duality in their research of shopping value.

Babin et al. argue, that shopping includes both 1) utilitarian outcome resulting from some type of conscious pursuit of an intended consequence and 2) an outcome related more to spontaneous hedonic responses.

As the entertainment aspect of retailing came more recognized, also the hedonic shopping motivations came more apparent. Arnold & Reynolds (2003) focused only on hedonic shopping motivations and developed a scale, which consists of 1) adventure; 2) gratification; 3) role; 4) value; 5) social; and 6) idea shopping motivations.

One remarkable feature in the studies on shopping motivation is that both utilitarian and hedonistic motivations are apparent and important in explaining different aspect of purchasing behaviour. According to Arnold & Reynolds (2003) the importance of the recreational and hedonistic aspects is emphasized in modern markets. Shopping goes beyond mere purchasing and product acquisition in that it emphasizes recreation and gratification. The growth of the size of shopping malls and the change of their style into more entertaining has led to increase in consumers' interest.

It appears as, for example, long shopping trips and increase in time spent in shopping malls. Ikea is one of those shopping centres, which tempt customers from long distance to receive stimulation, buy products and spend leisure time. Travellers spend hours in a car, bus or train just to spend one day in Ikea. The aim of this paper is to understand the main motives of this kind of a shopping trip. The objective is to describe and analyse the motivation orientation of the people going on a one-day trip to Ikea by bus. This study represents a new approach of shopping orientation study in that it concerns the whole trip, not only the store.

Motivational Orientation for One-day Shopping Trip to Ikea

This one day shopping tourism trip to Ikea cannot be specified solely as tourism or shopping. For some consumers, the trip might be just travelling and for others it is mainly shopping. Shopping is experiential and satisfying in nature and not only instrumental in getting the products and services needed. In this way it can be seen to be something in between everyday and holiday. It contains tourism-like features when both movement and changing places are included. On the other hand, shopping is an important activity in tourism, shopping and dining have said to be the most popular activities among tourists. In its broadest sense, shopping is seen as a significant element of tourism. Sometimes shopping may be the foremost motivation for travelling. When the prime reason for the trip is to shop, tourist shopping has been defined as 'shopping tourism', while 'tourism shopping' is used when shopping is just one of many other activities undertaken during the trip.

The similarities between shopping and tourism are evident especially in outshopping, i.e. when the shopping trip is extended beyond the boundaries of one's local retailing area. What is evident is that consumers do not go to a shopping trip just for purchasing or goods. It can be presumed that on a shopping trip motives to travel and motives to purchase are both present. In this research the interest lies in the tension between the recreational motives and the purchasing oriented motives on a one-day bus trip to Ikea. On these shopping trips, travellers spend hours in a bus, shop hours in Ikea and spend hours on the way back home. The first challenge here is to analyse the ability of the motivational orientations to categorize differently motivated travellers.

In order to analyse the motivational orientation of Ikea travellers a Likert-scale consisting of 25 items based on previous research on shopping and travelling motives was developed. Altogether 104 persons were interviewed on bus on their way to Ikea. The motivational data was factor analysed in order to reveal the orientation dimensions. Thinking about the aim of this study, two factor model appeared to be the most clear to interpret. Only the most heavily (>.50) loaded statements.

The two factors explain 38 per cent of the total variance.

Items describing recreational reasons for participating a shopping trip, push from everyday life and pull of the experiential aspects of a shopping trip were loaded on the first factor. In order to capture both the pull and push motivations the factor is termed as "variety from everyday". Items loaded on the second factor conventionally included elements of purchasing behaviour, namely information gathering and product buying. This factor is named as "purchasing". The two factors resemble well the motivational orientations of recreational and task-orientation found by Kaltcheva & Weitz (2006).

In order to reveal different shopping traveller groups a cluster analysis was conducted by using the factors as variables. The five cluster solution presented, offers a grouping that can be justified with good reasons argued for.

The two factors of purchasing and variety from everyday life turned out to be able to discriminate between the clusters of consumers. However, because of the relative small sample size we are not able to make any far reaching interpretations of the clusters. The results suggest, however, that the recreational factor of variety from everyday life seems to be somewhat better discriminator than the task-related purchasing factor. Most of the travellers attended on the Ikea trip in order to buy something. Especially consumers in group A went to Ikea in order to purchase something. On the other hand group B consumers were not inspired by purchasing. They were presumably there just to escort or to elapse time. The C and D shoppers emphasized the recreational and experiential aspects of the shopping trip with the difference that for the C consumers purchasing was more important. On the other hand, the E consumers regarded the shopping trip more as an everyday activity that has to be attended to in order to get something needed.

Clusters are relatively close to origin. It can be assumed, that travellers' motives on this kind on shopping trip to Ikea are not strongly related to variety from everyday life or to purchasing, but various things combine in the motivation structures of the travellers. Falk and Campbell (1997) argue that while shopping, hedonistic and utilitarian motivations become so closely intertwined it is not reasonable to separate them. Consumers often justify their shopping with some rational reason, which might also increase the amount of utilitarian motives. Shopping trip is a sum of several elements, which is why it should be considered as different, partially overlapping processes.

Shopping Trip as an Experience

Since the hedonistic motives to shopping became apparent, the consumer has been seen as an individual emotionally involved in a shopping process, in which the multisensory, imaginary and emotive aspects are sought and appreciated. Shopping is not only buying, but also a socioeconomic means to socialize, enjoy oneself and the company of another person. In this way, shopping can be seen as an experience with an important emotional meaning, founded on the interaction with the products and services consumed. According to Schmitt (1999), an experience is a sum of different elements: sense, feel, think, act and relate.

In order to gain deeper understanding of a shopping trip as an experiential phenomenon, 104 Ikea travellers were interviewed on the way back home from Ikea. The travellers were asked to describe their trip and the best and worst things of it. These descriptions were analysed with content analysis using the elements of experience by Schmitt (1999) as a loose conceptual grid. All of these elements were present in Ikea traveller's descriptions. In addition, to own and to be privileged came up in the descriptions.

Owning has an important role on a shopping trip: buying things and the joy of possessing get travellers into a good mood. Thinking on a shopping trip is both creative and thoughtful. A shopping trip is imagination, gaining new insights and pondering of things. A shopping trip to Ikea is full of stimulation for senses: people try different tastes, see attention awaking new things, smell the scents of new goods, touch coverings of soft pillows and smooth leather couches and listen to the sounds of the department store. Sitting in a bus is a large part of physical action on a shopping trip to Ikea. However, the trip also includes a lot of other kind of action: eating, talking and laughing. To relate is an important element in a shopping trip. Good company might make the trip worth going and friends are needed for backup while making purchasing decisions.

Feelings on a shopping trip can be everything from wonderful and lovely to awful and horrible.

Travellers' descriptions of their trip express a large spectrum of experiences. Every consumption experience is unique and includes thinking, action, relating, feeling and sensing in varying degree. We can assume that this consumption experience itself is somehow valuable, although the desired products are not always found, the prices are too high or the time runs out too fast. Also Westwood (2006) argues that for shopping tourists, already sense of being somewhere different was a defining feature of their experience. Ikea travellers have an experience that makes them somehow privileged compared to those, who have not visited Ikea.

Wonderful Shopping or Endless Torture?

It is amazing, how many different elements are attached to one shopping trip to Ikea. Pleasantness or unpleasantness of the trip is a consequence of many different elements. Sometimes one element affects a lot and sometimes small things create large entities. The pleasantness of the trip might derive from good company, meeting an old friend or spending time with family. Good plans, new ideas, reasonable purchases and money saving make the trip nice. People can relax and enjoy buying and travelling on the Ikea trip. Seeing new products and the large store is exciting and shopping in good company cheers up. The store's selection is nice to watch; scents from cafeteria arouse hunger and food tastes amazingly good after wandering. For some of the travellers, motivational orientations defines the pleasantness or unpleasantness. One of the travellers, who was strongly oriented for variety from everyday life found, that the best thing about the trip was "*The trip itself (possibility to get away from home once in a while)*", when the worst thing was, that Ikea was only "*An ordinary store*". One of the purchasing-oriented travellers described the best thing about the trip "*I got all the things I needed*".

But for many of the travellers on Ikea-trip, situational factors seem to define the pleas ant and unpleasant elements of the experience. One traveller, who was not purchasing oriented at all, thinks that the best thing about the trip was "*many good purchases*", when the worst thing was that "*all of the plans did not come true, I could not find suitable things*".

Sometimes one good or bad occurrence is the one that is remembered about the trip. For some travellers, the fact that restaurant closed earlier than they assumed, was definitely the worst thing about the trip, despite of their motivational orientation. In one trip, there were some problems with the seats on the bus on the way back and everybody could not sit next to their friend. This was worst thing about the trip to many travellers, although they were purchasing-oriented.

This might be due to the experiential and intensive nature of the one-day shopping trip. This trip is not solely purchasing or leisure, it combines rationality and emotionality. This trip includes many different aspects, and the comprehensive experience is a combination of all of these.

According to Buttle (1992) shopping trips are basically made in terms of logical force, but motives for shopping are also linked to particular shopping context. Our findings support Buttles conclusions: most of the Ikea travellers are purchasing oriented, and attend the trip to buy desired products. Tourism, on the other hand, is considered to be hedonic activity, which determines the shopping context. On the shopping trip to Ikea, travel context brings in the hedonic motives for the trip.

Travellers' motivational orientation differs in the way they wish to gain also immaterial consequences on the trip. Most of the travellers are oriented to buy something, but they are not all interested in the recreational aspects of the trip. According to Westwood (2006) leisure-like aspects are more important than purchasing while shopping. This might be true with shopping-oriented travellers, but our results indicate that there are also purely purchasing oriented travellers on a trip to Ikea. The fact, that some consumers try to justify their shopping with rational reasons, might affect to this.

Because of the small differences in Ikea-travellers' motivational orientation, we suggest that a shopping trip should be seen as different processes, which might also be overlapping. We examined these processes as experiential aspects of a shopping trip. Ikea travellers' experience includes the elements suggested by Schmitt (1999) and in addition the elements named to own and to be privileged arouse from travellers descriptions.

These elements can be assumed to occur from the special characteristics of the shopping trip. Pleasantness and unpleasantness on this kind of intensive one-day shopping trip seems to arise from situational factors. For some travellers, motivational orientation defines the best and worst things about the trip. But it is not unusual, that same elements affect the pleasantness or unpleasantness, despite the motivational orientation of the travellers.

This might be due to the experiential nature of the trip. One-day shopping trip to Ikea is not purely a shopping trip; it is an intensive experience, which includes many different elements.

Offering experiences is a great opportunity for retailers to succeed. Experiential retailing aims to offer customers satisfactory total consumption experiences by chancing the store atmospherics.

Types of Tourist

Tourism is a travel for predominantly recreational or leisure purposes. Tourism also refers to the provision of services in support of this act. Tourism is defined as the study of man (the tourist) away from his usual habitat, of the touristic apparatus and networks responding to his various needs, and of the ordinary (where the tourist is coming from) and nonordinary (where the tourist goes to) worlds and their dialectic relationships. Such conceptualisations extend the frame beyond the earlier trade-oriented notions or definitions mostly devised to collect data and calculate tourist arrivals, departures, or expenditures. Significantly, it is this holistic view which accommodates a systemic study of tourism: all its parts, its interconnected structures and functions, as well as ways it is influenced by and is influencing other forms and forces relating to it.

Tourism Behaviour

The concept of behaviour in tourism considers customers and their behaviour specifically as it relates to tourist activities. Some distinctive behaviour topics include cross-cultural interaction, authenticity, tourist-guide interaction and post travel attitudes. This subsumes both the observable behaviour of tourists and their mental and psychological processes involving decision-making, motivations and cognition. The study of tourist satisfaction provides a link to business and management research. Knowledge of the behaviour of tourists in space and time is valuable to assist planners and managers of attractions and environments. Tourist behaviour and experience is assessed by survey studies as well as observational and field research.

Decision Process

Many models have been proposed to simulate the decision-making process for tourism-related products. However, this is a very complicated procedure, and it increases in complexity as more people become involved. The concepts of image, utility maximisation, knowledge acquisition and others are all involved. In addition, various socioeconomic characteristics affect decision making in different ways. Tourism has become one of the world's most powerful components of economic development. Many countries have established tourism development as a high priority concern.

However, increases in discretionary time and money, as well as the variety of vacation choices, have given the potential traveller more flexibility of choice. As a result, the factors influencing travel decisions are becoming more complex. If a travel or tourism organisation wants to influence a travel decision, it needs to understand who is making the decision and how that decision is made.

The 'decision process' has been described as a simple association between a stimulus and a response. It has also been described as a very complex interaction among many behaviour determinants (, 1966). An effective travel decision-making model must incorporate important factors affecting the decision (such as sociodemographic, sociological and psychographic characteristics) and provide an understanding of the relationships between these variables. Travel decisions may also be affected by factors such as travel characteristics, destination attributes and past travel patterns. One of the key steps in tourism planning and marketing is to develop travel behaviour choice models by analyzing these travel factors.

Consumer Behaviour

Consumer behaviour can be viewed as the study of how, why and how often individuals make decisions to spend their available resources (such as money, time or energy) on consumption-related items (and, 1990). Many factors affect the consumer decision process. Factors can come from marketing (including such things as perceived product quality, price and distinctiveness), social sources (which includes family and reference groups), individual differences (such as sociodemographics, lifestyle and personality types), or psychological processes (like motivation, or destination perceptions). Sociodemographics, travel characteristics and psychographic variables have all been recognized as important factors influencing travel decisions. One of the strategic approaches in tourism planning and decision-making is to develop travel choice models by analyzing these travel factors. Models can be defined as 'systems of hypotheses relating one or more dependent variables to several independent variables' (1989).

In studying travel and tourism, dependent variables could be the choice of a tourist destination, hotel or accommodation, the likelihood of taking a future trip, the length of stay or the total number of visits. On the other hand, independent variables could include factors such as sociodemographics, psychographics, travel characteristics, destination attributes or economic variables.

Tourism Motivations: Factors affecting the Decision Making Process: According to the sociologist Max Weber, motivation lies at the core of human behaviour. Consequently, the study of motivation is central to any social scientific undertaking since it provides understanding, explanation and prediction. It goes beyond the how questions of description to the why questions of interpretation and causality. As one domain of interpersonal activity, tourism is no exception to this general observation. Indeed, 'why do people travel?' is probably the most fundamental issue in tourism research today (2000). (1994), points out that there are several concrete social influences conditioning the decision to travel. He identifies the family, reference groups, social class, the surrounding culture and the work place as the most important of these. The latter is particularly significant since it is conductive to compensatory and spill over effects in various types of travel.

1. Social interaction is commonly identified as a tourism motivation. Early research on the latter incorporated the underlying hypothesis that an individual has a need for love and affection and the desire to communicate with others. Further explorations revealed enhancement of kinship and friendship relationships and the facilitation of varied and increased social interaction as motives which directed vacation choice and behaviour.

2. Cultural motivators are strong push factors for the development of tourism. Cultural motivators lead the tourist into learning about and experiencing the culture of societies other than their own.

Senior Tourism

An exponential increase in the number of senior citizens throughout the world has made this group an attractive niche market for tourism with its own particular needs. Tourism marketers in countries like Australia, Canada and the United States are beginning to sharpen their focus on older people. Seniors roughly constitutes up to a third of the adult population in each of these countries. Many of these seniors have the desire and means to travel for pleasure, discovery and learning. The main purpose of travel is Holiday. Seniors stay more in lower cost accommodation. They tend to stay more with friends, relatives or their own property.

Trip Characteristics

1. Senior Tourists travel longer.
2. Senior Tourists travel to more destinations.
3. Senior Tourists have less ties to employment.

Senior Tourists are people of later age (after 55) who travel for leisure and whose earning and family obligations decrees and finally disappear. A-first-distinction can be made in young-old (aged 55-64), old (aged 65-74) and very old (aged 75 and over).

Economic Aspects

The WTO forecasts that earnings from international tourism will grow an average of 6-7% annually – double the growth rate for the world economy as a whole. In the coming decades tourism activity will become one of the main economic sectors of the world. Senior Tourists are attractive as consumers because:

1. They have the financial means.
2. They have time.
3. They have a better education than in the past.
4. They belong to a generation, which has travelled.
5. They are relatively healthy and know that activities like tourism and recreation contribute to a healthy lifestyle.

Senior Tourists differ in age (chronological-biological), health, economic status, tourism experience and cultural background.

People do not change their travel behaviour because they turn 60 or retire. Travel experience and patterns will have an important influence on travel behaviour.

Youth Tourism

Youth Tourism has taken many forms over time, most of which seem to have been a simple expression of youthful energy and curiosity about the world beyond their bounded society. Their travels were usually a form of alternatives to prevailing tourism. Historically, these involved travels to medieval universities and such institutions as the "Grand Tour", with its year abroad for young scholars and their tutors.

Youth travel itself is not a new phenomenon. For centuries, young people have been travelling around the world with their families, in groups, or on their own. The World Tourism Organization (WTO) defines the 'young' tourism market as travellers 16-25 years old, who take a trip of at least one night's stay. The Canadian youth market is defined as young people 30 years of age and under, who are travelling outside the family unit, not for business, and not primarily to visit friends or relatives, and whose travel includes at least one overnight stay.

Youth Travel Market

Different groups within the youth travel market have unique characteristics and motivations for travel, and require different products to suit their needs. The youth travel market is divided into two broad categories: independent you travel and youth travel group.

Youth Group Travel

This group is consisting of six or more unrelated young people travelling together. Youth travel group is divided into two groups: student travel or school-based youth group travel and non-school based youth group travel. Youth travel is specifically sanctioned by the sponsoring school, board or school district. School based youth group travel may be driven by curriculum-related activities an/or semi-curricular or extracurricular activities like music performances and sports competition.

Travel and activities are generally undertaken as a group, accompanied by teachers, school personnel and/or adult chaperones. Non-school-based youth group travel is often referred as youth travel grope. This travel is organized by a group such as a sports team, church group, cultural/musical performance troupe or Scouts/Guides.

Travel is often undertaken as a group, but may also occur in smaller groups, led by parents or other adult chaperones. Youth group travellers are price sensitive, in the sense that they are more strongly influenced by price related issues that the average business or convention traveller.

Independent Youth Travel

Sometimes referred to as 'free independent youth travellers', or foreign independent youth travellers', independent youth travellers travel alone, or in small informal groups. Today's independent youth travellers tend to be well educated, well informed, and Internet savvy. Students between the ages of 18 and 26 mostly comprise this group, although some are young professionals who are either unemployed or taking time off between school and settling down.

Most independent youth travellers head for destinations farther from home stay longer and spend less daily but more in total than the average adult tourist spends. They appear to be price sensitive for travel, housing and food, but less for entertainment, shopping and attractions. Domestic independent youth travellers tend to plan shorter trips, to one or two specific destinations. Foreign independent travellers tend to have longer stays, and are experience-driven.

Independent Youth Traveller Characteristics

1. Between 15 and 30 years old.
2. Well-educated – most often students or previous students.
3. Travel independently, or with 1-2 friends.
4. Risk-friendly, experience oriented.
5. Responsive to destination/experience based marketing initiatives.
6. Detailed pre-trip planning.
7. Lower incomes, but willing to save/combine travel with work in order to finance travel.
8. Lower daily spending, but longer stays resulting in higher overall spending per trip.

Organised Mass Tourists

The organized mass tourist was the least adventurous and was confined to his environmental bubble, while the drifter was most adventurous and felt at ease with strangeness. The organized mass tourist preferred guided tours, air-conditioned bus with fixed itinerary because of the need of maximum familiarity and minimum novelty.

The degree to which strangeness and familiarity prevailed in the tourist role determined the nature of the tourists' experience as well as the effect on the host society. Cohen (1979) further distinguished five modes of tourist experience by analyzing the different meanings which interest in and appreciation of the culture, social life. The typology further confirmed the different behaviour of travellers in relation to their motivation

Individual Mass Tourist

The individual mass tourist was similar to the organized mass one but he allowed more flexibility in his time and itinerary and so his tour was not well preplanned. He would make the major arrangements through a travel agent, as familiarity was dominant in his total trip experience, but he still accepted somehow the experience of novelty.

The explorer tried to leave the environmental bubble by associating himself with the local people visited and the language they spoke. However, the explorer was still cautious to avoid too rough a visiting experience, and therefore he normally needed comfortable accommodation and reliable transportation.

The Explorer

The explorer tourists are thole one, who travel to or into (unfamiliar or unknown regions), esp for organized scientific purposes. Archeologists, Environmental schientist etc. are the examples of this group.

Exploration is the act of searching or travelling a terrain for the purpose of discovery, e.g. of unknown people, including space (space exploration), for oil, gas, coal, ores, caves, water, (Mineral exploration, botanical exploration, or prospecting), or information.

Although exploration has existed as long as human beings, its peak is seen as being during the Age of Discovery for Europe's contact with the rest of the world, and Major explorations after the Age of Discovery for scientific exploration in the modern era.

The Drifter

A Drifter is an itinerant person. Such people may be called drifters, tramps, rogues, or hobos. A vagabond is characterised by almost continuous travelling, lacking a fixed home, temporary abode, or permanent residence. Vagabonds are not bums, as bums are not known for travelling, preferring to stay in one location.

Historically, "vagabond" was a British legal term similar to vagrant, deriving from the Latin for 'purposeless wandering'. Following the Peasants' Revolt, British constables were authorised under a 1383 statute to collar vagabonds and force them to show their means of support; if they could not, they were jailed. Under a 1495 statute, vagabonds could be sentenced to the stocks for three days and nights; in 1530, whipping was added. The assumption was that vagabonds were unlicensed beggars.

By the 19th century the vagabond was associated more closely with Bohemianism. The critic Arthur Compton-Rickett compiled a review of the type, in which he defined it as men "with a vagrant strain in the blood, a natural inquisitiveness about the world beyond their doors." Examples included Henry David Thoreau, Michael John Arthur Bujold, Walt Whitman, Leo Tolstoy, William Hazlitt, and Thomas de Quincey. A notable 20th century vagabond was the Hungarian mathematician Paul Erdos.

Allocentric vs. Psychocentric

Allocentric tourist – enjoys varied activities and gets a thrill from the unexpected

Psychocentric tourist – nonadventurous and self-inhibited

Allocentric tourists are constantly searching for the new destination, as package tours start spreading into past midcentric and even allocentric destinations. Examples of this include the Caribbean becoming increasingly more midcentric (people between the extremes) as travel becomes less expensive.

- In 1974, Stanley Plog developed a theory which allowed the US population to be classified into a series of interrelated psychographic types. These types range from two extremes:
- The 'psychocentric' type is derived from & apos; psyche & apos; or ' self-centred & apos; where an individual centres thoughts or concerns on the small problem areas of life. These individuals tend to be conservative in their travel patterns, preferring 'safe' destinations and often taking many return trips. For this latter reason, market research in the tour-operating sector labels this group as ' repeaters & apos;.
- The 'allocentric' type derives from the root 'allo' meaning 'varied in form'. These individuals are adventurous and motivated to travel/discover new destinations. They rarely return to the

same place twice, hence their market research label ' wanderers & apos.

The Expectation-Evaluation Paradigm

Tourists and vacationers go through a complex decision-making process in determining their level of post-purchase satisfaction. Most tourist satisfaction models follow a positivists approach, in which tourists are viewed as rational beings who evaluate their level of satisfaction or dissatisfaction through a disconfirmation paradigm.

That is, tourists purchase a trip with certain expectations (i.e., destination, amenities, and activities), and subsequently evaluate satisfaction based on whether than absolute truth, and that such research produces findings "with a focus on meaning and understanding the situation or phenomenon under examination".

He recommends building multiple methods approaches that involve the researcher with those being researched and focus on in-depth study of a small sample.

Stewart and Floyd (2004) capture the rationale for including post-positivistic philosophies within recreation and leisure studies with their observations: "The anxiety amongst leisure researchers is a reflection of a broader crisis within the social sciences about any account that claims to have directly or completely captured someone's lived experiences and social reality". They cite an increasing interest in post-positivistic philosophy as a means for addressing this inability to fully represent people's lived experiences.

Employing a post-positivistic philosophy, this study focuses on understanding and interpreting the process and factors of satisfaction evaluation, rather than on prediction and control. Utilizing mixed qualitative methods, this study examines the complexity involved in tourists' satisfaction with their travel experiences, moving beyond the rational decision-making principles found in positivistic approaches such as Moutinho's, towards an interpretivistic approach.

"Travellers want more than merely observing things and listening to lecture, they want to get actively involved". Tourists may have expectations about the level of active involvement they will experience during a trip that would lead to a disconfirmation paradigm, however active involvement seems to be a more complex variable in the evaluation of satisfaction than what can be captured and measured using Moutinho's model.

For this reason, it has been chosen as a variable to be further explored. Geva & Goldman (1999) define group dynamics as "...the relations and interactions among group members, the cohesion and morale of the tour group, manner in which free time was spent...". Bettenhausen (1991) suggests that belonging to a group had a great impact on an individual's sense of self, in shaping behaviour and attitudes, in creating a shared culture, and in creating the "rites, rituals, and social roles that provide continuity and order". Arsenault and Gale (2004) report findings from their study of Travel Suppliers and Tour Operators, which indicate a relationship between small group interaction, bonding, friendship formation, and satisfaction via the dimension of positive memory creation

The Tourist Experience

Tourism is a quest for experiences that are in contrast to, and sometimes an extension or intensification of, daily experience. In this sense, tourism is a pioneering example of the emerging "experience economy". The quality of experiences constitutes the key to the success of tourism development. However, despite the importance of the "tourist experience," this is still an ambiguous term. Although various constituents of the tourist experience, such as motivations (curiosity, novelty, change, authenticity meaning, identity, self), satisfactions, feelings, and emotions, have been well researched in psychology, anthropology, sociology, and other disciplines, the literature on the tourist experience as a *gestalt* phenomenon has still been understudied. This is not to deny that there exists a small literature on the tourist experience per se. But many questions still remain unanswered. For example, how is the formulation of the tourist experience related to itineraries?

Itinerary is a frequently used term in the tourism industry, especially in tonnst brochures, but it is rarely seen as an academic term. The reason for this situation could be simple. The itinerary is seen as too self-obvious, too simple, and too trivial to deserve serious academic treatment. At best, it is treated as a component of tourism linking to tour operation. Such a common-sense view of the itinerary should be challenged! however. Rather than being trivial, itineraries act as important media through which the tourism industry interacts with the tourist in the production and consumption of the tourist experience. Itineraries shape the formulation and organization of the tourist experience and become an arena in which the tourist experience is socially produced. As *temporal-spatial carriers* of tourist experience, itineraries are significant in the ways that tourism is consumed and in the ways that tourists' experiences are shaped.

Surely, the tourist experience cannot completely be equated with, or reduced to, itineraries, but it is equally true that the tourist experience is shaped by itineraries. There are at least two reasons that the itinerary deserves study in its own right. First, a number of paradoxes involved in tourism have their roots in itineraries. These paradoxes involve dualisms including authenticity and inauthenticity, autonomy and passivity, freedom and determinations, agency and structure. For example, while tourism is regarded as a quest for authenticity, what is experienced often ends up as "staged authenticity" of the front zone, partly because of the temporary and transient nature of itineraries that constrain tourists from penetrating the back zone of toured reality. While tourism is hailed as freedom, it often ends up as the loss of freedom, partly because of the rigidity of itineraries. While tourism is thought to restore the autonomy and agency that have decreased in daily routines, it creates its own constraints over autonomy and agency because of the constraining, pre-determining, and disciplining nature of itineraries. As Minea and Oakes put it in this volume's introduction, tourism is a performance through which various binaries, such as subject and object, are constantly re-enacted. Relatedly, itineraries are performances in which the paradoxes of modernity are enacted and embodied. The itinerary is thus one of the best dimensions of tourism from which the paradoxes and ambivalence of modernity can be revealed.

Second, as spatial-temporal carriers of tourism commodities, itineraries constitute the media that bridge experiences and goods, services and products, hospitality and attractions, movement and rest, time and space, the quantitative side and the qualitative side of tourism, the ordinary supportive consumption and extraordinary peak consumption, tourist consumers and tourism suppliers. Thus, the itinerary is one of the best domains of tourism from which the mechanisms of social, economical, and cultural production of tourism can be better understood.

This chapter deals with the issue of how the production and consumption of itineraries bring about and reinforce a series of paradoxes in tourism, and how the formation of itineraries are related to wider social, economical, and cultural processes. Just as tourism reveals the ambivalence of modernity and globalization, the same is true of the itinerary. The itinerary provides an alternative perspective from which the paradoxes of tourism can, perhaps more clearly, be revealed.

The following pages consist of three parts. The first concentrates on the issue of how itineraries constitute the *commodity form* of the tourist experience and how the commoditization of itineraries leads to a number of paradoxes. The second examines how itineraries become a way of circulation of tourism products and the associated paradoxes. The third focuses on the role that itineraries play in shaping the consumption of tourism, and the consequential "consuming paradoxes". Finally, in the conclusion, the paradoxes of tourism are discussed in relation to the rationalization of the tourist experience within the context of postmodernity.

Itineraries as the Commodity form of Tourism

In contemporary societies, the tourist experience is sold as a commodity, which is a result of the commoditization of travel and associated pleasant experiences under the condition of modernity. However, what is the commodity *form* of tourism? This is still an unanswered question. For a commodity to come into being, it must have a form.

For example, for a commodity to become the object of desire, it must be designed in order to take a particular appearance of colours, shape, size, and so on. This type of appearance can be called the *material form* of a commodity. However, in addition to the material form of commodities, there also arise *dematerialized forms* of commodities. In postindustrial economies, the commoditization of information and services leads to the *dematerialization* of commodity forms. The increasingly dominant part that the economy of services plays in postindustria] economies makes the nonmaterial form of commodities increasingly significant. As an integral element of the service industry, tourism also assumes a nonmaterial form, which is exemplified by itineraries.

The itinerary is a system of links between the temporal and spatial arrangements of tourist activities on the tourist journey. From the perspective of the tourism industry, an itinerary is a salable product that links, bridges, and puts together the various components that are necessary to the consumption of tourism. These components include accommodation, transportation, restaurants, attractions, entertainment, and tourist sites. Obviously, for tour operators and travel agencies, itineraries are the commodity form of mass tourism products.

But they are the nonmaterial form, despite the fact that tourism contains such material elements as food, means of transport, and hotels. The itinerary is nonmaterial because it is "virtual", existing in both tourists' and suppliers' imaginations; illustrated in tourist brochures, guidebooks, or TV programs; and only instantiated or materialized in the stage of consumption. Although itineraries are the non-material form, this does not mean that itineraries have nothing in common with the material form. The material commodity form consists of the arrangements of material elements. By contrast, the nonmaterial commodity form is constituted by the temporal and spatial arrangement of procedure, process, and activities. Thus, itineraries, as the nonmaterial commodity form of tourism, are temporal-spatial connections.

They constitute the temporal-spatially organizing processes in which discrete tourist "raw materials" are integrated and sold as a packaged commodity. At the same time, they themselves become the boundaries organized and constrained by the larger economic, social, political, and cultural contexts. Why does tourism take the commodity form of itineraries? The answer should be found from the process of the commoditization of travel experiences.

First, the commoditization of travel experiences is confronted with the problem of *intangible* experiences. In order to turn intangible experiences into "tangible" products in managerial terms, a certain organizing form must be imposed upon the journey.

Thus, itineraries are a way in which travel experiences are objectified, operationalized, and temporally and spatially "materialized." In a literal sense, we cannot sell experiences or pleasures per se, but we can sell the itineraries that are the "containers," carriers, or confines of experiences and pleasures. In short, itineraries are the "tangible" temporal-spatial carrier of intangible travel experiences, which can be produced, circulated (in the form of tourist brochures), and sold in the tourist market. Second, the essence of the commoditization of travel experiences is to make profit through creating an exchange value of tourism commodity. In so doing, travel experiences, as a qualitative subjective state, must be turned into precisely quantifiable and priceable products. Itineraries thus become the quantifiable, profitable, and saleable products of travel experiences.

Third, the commoditization of travel experiences reduces risk and uncertainty arising out of journeys. In order to transform the "raw materials" of risky and uncertain travel into tourism commodities, itineraries become a necessary form through which risks, chances, and uncertainties linking to journeys are eliminated or diminished. For examples, flight seats, hotel rooms, and restaurant tables are secured; safety and hygiene are ensured; access to attractions is guaranteed with tickets booked in advance. With itineraries, the risk-related and uncertain journeys are turned into clearly arranged, certain, standardized, and predictable commodities of tourist experiences.

Itineraries thus embody the rationalism in capitalist commoditization, and hence act as a rational way in which the tourism industry controls and manages mobile experiences. Itineraries are particularly attractive to *mass tourists* who want to create order out of chaos, risks, and uncertainties on their journeys to unfamiliar environments, even though they might also want to defy that order at the same time. Itineraries are thus an indispensable commodity form of modern tourism and act as an integral dimension of the commoditization of the tourist experience. However, while tourism is successfully commoditized with the help of itineraries, it also faces a paradox derived from itineraries. Part of the essence of the tourist experience is to get out of daily routines, order, schedules, and constraints. As mentioned above, in order to turn the tourist experience into a commodity, it is necessary to make tourism assume a commodity form, namely, itineraries. The latter, however, imposes an emergent routine, order, schedule, and constraint upon the tourist experience.

Thus, tourism, the very act of escape from daily constraints, ends up as an alternative constraint. In relation to the *elimination of chance, risk, and uncertainty* and the increase of security and certainty, tourism is wheeled to the position of diminishing the real charms and appeals of travel, namely, a suitable extent of risk-taking, challenge, improvisation, independence, flexibility, freedom, creativity, and authenticity. Thus, while tourism is put on with the commodity form of itineraries, it paves a way to the demise of the authenticity of travel. As a response to such a strong commoditization of tourism, an increasing number of tourists tend to abandon overscheduled and itinerized mass tourism and adopt more individualist, independent, and flexible forms of travel.

These individual tourists take responsibility for then-own itineraries and leave enough room for adapting and changing primary schedules. The increasingly popular "backpacking" form of travel is such an example. This process can be called the *decommoditization* of itineraries. What Edensor (1998,105-14) describes about tourist behaviours at the Taj is a typical example of differentiation of decommoditized itinerary from commoditized itinerary.

For package tourists, visits to the Taj are highly regulated, predetermined, restrained, and disciplined in time and space. As a result of commoditization of itineraries, package tourists are usually allowed to stay for a quite limited time and to walk around within a limited range when they visit the Taj. By contrast, backpackers have much wider room for improvisation and for changing their itineraries as much as they wish.

For ex ample, they usually spend much more time and cover a wider spatial range at the Taj. Decommoditization of itineraries is thus a tourist action that seeks to transcend the rigidity, constraints, and disciplines of the itinerary of package tourism and that seeks more individual freedom, autonomy, and creativity. However, after getting rid of the itineraries of package tourism, independent travellers find themselves involved in an alternative form of commoditization.

For example, independent travellers often have to buy guidebooks in order to plan an itinerary. Here, guidebooks, such as Lonely Planet and Rough Guides, are themselves a specific way of commoditization of itineraries, or more precisely, the commoditization of the *knowledge* of potential itineraries. In guidebooks, itineraries become the content, rather than the commodity form, of guidebooks. The consumption of this content accompanies independent travellers' journeys. The itineraries described in guidebooks are thus the *hidden* itineraries of the tourism system that shape and organize independent travellers' concrete itineraries.

These *hidden itineraries,* such as the network of schedules, traffic lines and prices, and booking systems of transportation and hospitality, constitute alternative constraints on travel. While the itineraries of package tours are the first level of touristic constraints, the itineraries of the tourism system as a whole are the second level of touristic constraints. Thus, while independent travellers can get rid of the first level of itineraries (overt itineraries) that are sold by travel agencies as packaged tours, they cannot get rid of the second level of itineraries (covert itineraries), itineraries that are hidden in the tourism system and are described by guidebooks and other travel materials.

Itineraries as the Way of Circulation of Tourism Products

Itineraries are not only scheduled journeys, but also mark a spatialization of those journeys. To put it another way, itineraries are about "what" will happen "when" and "where." While the issue of the scheduled journeys has been touched on above, we now turn to the issue of the spatialization of tourism, namely, the issue of "where" tourist activities will take place.

Itineraries are not only the commodity form of tourism, but also the form of access to tourist attractions. Itineraries are the way to circulate tourism products in tourist markets. In the market of goods, it is commodities that are circulated and delivered to consumers for consumption. In the market of temporal spatial experiences of tourism, however, it is tourist consumers that are "circulated" and "delivered." They are taken to tourism products, that are not deliverable in a literal sense. Thus, when tourists travel to destinations, are in a sense "delivered" to tourists. Itineraries can thus be regarded as a way of the circulation of tourism products, despite the fact that itineraries are themselves an integral part of those products.

As a result, once tourist sites are visited by tourists, the "experiences" of these sites are in reality "delivered" and "circulated" to the tourist simultaneously. Therefore, the directions of tourist flows or itineraries are of significance to tourist destinations.

Itineraries are thus not only the way in which people move, but also the way in which landscapes, cultures, and heritage are "circulated". The integration of places into the networks of tourist itineraries turns the places into "experiential commodities" circulated among tourists. Thus, it is no small wonder that tourist destinations compete for access to the network of tourists' itineraries. The simultaneity and synchronization of *circulation* and *consumption* of the tourism products makes the directions and coverage of tourists' itineraries vital to the success of tourism development.

Paradoxes may occur when tourist destinations vie for inclusion into the network of tourists' itineraries. In reality, to compete for this inclusion is to develop a favourable image that is in congruence with targeted potential tourists' tastes and demands.

In this sense, to promote the circulation of a product of "tourist destination" is an issue of developing and establishing a desired image about the destination. In general, a favourable tourist image of a destination tends to allow tourists to include this destination into his or her itineraries, whereas a negative image, on the other hand, tends to deter potential tourists from visiting the destination. However, a favourable image of a destination may involve a paradox.

For example, in sightseeing tourism, the inclusion of a destination into his or her itineraries this time simultaneously implies the exclusion of this place next time, for sightseers always want to seek variety and novelty. Therefore, while a favourable image increases a destination's attractiveness, it may at the same time pave a way to the demise of that attractiveness. That is why a destination has its own life cycle. In postmodernity, with the help of mass media and the Internet, images increasingly become cultural fashions, whereas cultural fashions are always transient and temporary. Moreover, with the bombardment of images, images seem to become an autonomous world, a world that is "virtual reality." Thus, while image-making on the part of a destination is originally aimed at directing potential tourists' journeys and competing for the inclusion of the destination into their itineraries, it may often end up as distracting those tourists because they may get lost in the bombardment of tourist images. In this situation, word of mouth regains its significance in a world with too much information and too many images.

Itineraries as Menus for Tourism Consumption

Tourism is essentially an activity of consumption. What is consumed in tourism consists of two types of "materials." The first is the "material" serving of such daily consumption needs as eating, drinking, and sleeping. This does not mean that the material of this kind needs to be same with that of everyday life. Rather, a certain variety is necessary. Moreover, the consumption of this material takes place in a nondaily context, that is, the context of a journey, mobility, and an itinerary. New meanings of the consumption of the daily material can be derived from such a nondaily context. The second is the "material" of attractions at destinations and the journey itself. This type of material is beyond the reach of daily consumption. The consumption of the first type can be called "consumption *on* the journey," and the consumption of the second type can be called "consumption o/the journey." The consumption *on* the journey is the primary tourism consumption, and the consumption o/the journey is the secondary tourism consumption. The former is the extension of daily consumption to the journey; it is the base and support of the secondary consumption. By contrast, the latter is a transcendence of daily consumption; it is an extraordinary consumption. Both kinds of consumptions constitute *mobile* consumerism, or mass consumption *on the move.*

In both the primary and the secondary consumption, itineraries function as the temporal-spatial carriers of the two. In the primary tourism consumption, itineraries act as the nondaily *context* where daily functions of consumption are performed. In the secondary tourism consumption, itineraries become not only an *object* for consumption (journeys, services, and experiences), but also a *means* of "consumption *elsewhere*" consumption that takes place in other places and that transcends daily consumption. The secondary tourism consumption can thus be called *"peak consumption"*.

The rise and the spread of mobile or touristic consumerism relates to the rise of tourist citizenship in contemporary societies. Tourist citizenship means a specific type of consumer citizenship, a democratized right to consume extraordinary experiences that transcend one's daily reach and that are accessible only through travel. In relation to this, itineraries act as the *carrier* of extraordinary experiences. However, problems arise with the question of "what is the extraordinary experience?" The extraordinary is always relative. What is extraordinary for children could not be so for adults. What is extraordinary for the first-time travellers could not be so for experienced travellers. For island residents, the sea is not the source of extraordinary experience. However, the sea is so for inhabitants from desert areas. Therefore, the extraordinary is relative to different potential tourists with different experiential backgrounds and characteristics. Relatedly, in tourism marketing, tourism is segmented into different typologies and packaged as various types of products in order to serve the varying needs of potential tourists with different tastes.

As a result, the functions of itineraries as illustrated in tourist brochures are similar to the functions of menus in restaurants. Just as menus help customers in selecting courses of foods that best fit their tastes and preferences, so itineraries presented in tourist brochures serve clients in choosing types of tourist experiences that best satisfy them. In short, itineraries function as menus for tourism consumption.

According to Levi-Strauss (1983), for foods to be edible, they must be cooked. In this sense, cooking is a cultural practice. The same is true of potential tourist resources. For these resources to be consume-able by potential tourist consumers, they must also be culturally "cooked." Itineraries are thus one of the cultural ways of "cooking" these resources. Just as menus represent certain cuisines by means of which foods are cooked, itineraries embody touristic "cuisines" by means of which potential tourist resources are "cooked" and "packaged." As itineraries are often displayed and illustrated in tourist brochures, it is more precise to regard itineraries *as presented in tourist brochures* that are the "menus" of tourist experiences.

Just like a certain type of cuisine produces some consistency in foods, itineraries also embody a certain theme or consistency in tourist experiences. A "touristic cuisine" that produces this consistency is "thematized." As a result of thematization, each itinerary is often centred around certain common themes, such as the itineraries of "Beautiful China," "Classic China," "China Adventure," and "the Silk Road." All these itineraries select some of the components from the "raw materials" of China and combine them as a thematic itinerary. Itineraries are thus the cultural combination of tourist experiences, in which the criteria for inclusion and exclusion of the components of tourist resources are culturally, as well as economically, determined. In short, it is culture that determines what type of packaged tourist experiences suit what kind of potential tourists. Via such criteria of selection, discrete tourist spots are integrated as a whole and objectified as an itinerary. Itineraries thus reflect people's views, evaluations, and imagery of the world.

They are the categorization of peoples, cultures, places, and heritage in the world. In this sense, itineraries form *institutional circuits* in which contemporary people are "circulated" to examine and renegotiate the meanings of their relationships with the world. Itineraries are not only culturally structured as thematic experiences, but also dramatized as progressive stories. Itineraries are *scripts* in which the tourist journeys—like courses for a meal—can be organized as the beginning, the middle, the climax, and the end. Accordingly, tourists are performers who make their own stories with the itinerary unfolding across time and space. Just as dramatization creates meaning, the intensified dramatization of human experiences in itineraries indeed helps foster and reproduce meanings in human Use. Therefore, the consumption of itineraries is in reality a way of *consumption of meanings,* that are created beyond the confines of daily life and that make human life more colourful and meaningful.

However, with the mass production and consumption of itineraries or tourism, there arises a paradox of objectification of meanings, a paradox inherent in what Simmel (1990) calls "the objectification of culture" in western modernity. Itineraries are the temporal-spatial carriers of tourist experiences and their associated meanings. Under the condition of the commoditization of tourism, itineraries are often supplied in massive, homogenized, and standardized ways. The new marketing strategy of the segmentation of tourism does not forsake these standardizations but merely divides them into several domains. As a result, the meanings related to itineraries are objectified, standardized, and thematized.

In pre-modern ages, every single journey was linked to unique, subjective, and personal meanings. Under the condition of modernity, by contrast, such subjective and personal meanings of travel are increasingly diminished. Instead, tourism is packaged as various types of itineraries with thematic, categorized, homogenized, and objectified meanings In tourism advertisements, there are a number of "musts."

Once these "musts" are seen, this means "you have been there." If you go to Paris, you "must" find the scene of a romantic couple kissing each other. If you go to London, you "must" enjoy beers in a typical English pub. If you go to Beijing, you "must" see the torrent of bicycles on streets, Tiananmen Square, the Forbidden City, and the Great Wall at Badaling. All these "musts" signify the typical, objectified, standardized, and commonly acceptable meanings derived from the journeys to these places. Itineraries are thus organized in terms of socially, culturally, and objectively sanctioned and defined "worthiness" of visits. This site is included in our itineraries, just because everybody says it must be seen. That activity is also an item of our itinerary, just because everybody thinks such a kind of activity is a "must" in such a place. To miss such a "must" is not only a pity, but also a loss of value we pay for the journey Thus, in a hidden way, itineraries lead to a cultural and social conformism to objectified and stereotyped meanings that are already circulated within society, mass media, and the tourism industry.

However, for individual tourists, the problem could be, "why 'must' we see this site or participate in that activity at such a place?" "Could we look at the place from our own perspectives and find something meaningful with our own eyes?" Yes, you could. However, even independent travellers are in pursuit of the experiences that are informed by guidebooks, brochures, maps, and holiday programs on TV that are seen at home.

Thus, it becomes obvious that tourism is a kind of cultural practice in which each tourist participates to reproduce the code of meanings regarding the status quo, what is "sacred," and what is "heritage." The meanings derived from itineraries are thus unavoidably objectified and stereotyped. Accordingly, the consumption of these meanings serves to reproduce consumerist values of a society. Thus, tourists begin with a search for personal meanings but end up with the disappearance of *personal* meanings. Tourists want to keep a distance from reality but end up with a stronger conformity to the objectified semiotic order that a society needs. Such a paradox is one of exemplifications of what Miles (1998,5) calls the "consuming paradox." In this, the consumers' pursuit of freedom through economic means ends up maintaining "a dominant order that potentially constrains personal liberty". He describes the consuming paradox as the idea that, on the one hand, consumerism appears to offer us individuals all sorts of opportunities and experiences, on the other hand, as consumers we appear to be directed down certain predetermined routes of consumption which ensure that consumerism is ultimately as constraining as it is enabling. (Miles 1998,147) Itineraries embody the same consuming paradox.

As the form of circulation and consumption of tourism products, itineraries are the bearer of touristic consumerism. On the one hand, itineraries offer tourists "menus" for free choices and ease and order on the journey. On the other hand, itineraries direct tourists to the "predetermined routes of consumption" (Miles 1998,147), which may trigger complaints about the very ease and order linking the itineraries because of their constraints on freedom and spontaneity. Itineraries initially offer tourists menus for free choice, but they finally deprive tourists of freedom of choice on the journey. Itineraries are thus constraining as well as enabling. While tourism becomes a reaction to the ambivalence of modernity (Wang 2000), it itself brings about its own ambivalence.

The quest for the tourist experience is essentially a reaction to the Logos-modernity which is about the realm of institutions characterized by reason and rationality (Wang 1996, 2000). However, in so doing, the tourist experience is itself rationally organized. The tourist experience appears to be an escape from the overwhelmingly rationalizing institutions, but finally ends up as the rationalization of that experience, with the tourism industry being its rational agent. Itineraries, then, become a way in which the tourist experience is rationally organized. In this sense, the paradoxes of tourism derived from itineraries represent the paradoxes of the Logos-modernity that is characterized by overarching rationalization in contemporary societies.

In effect, the rationalization of experiences often turns the tourist experience into its opposite, namely, the non-flexible and rigid schedules and itineraries.

The Tourist as Outsider or Guest

Everyone who has ever travelled to another country knows that feeling. The feeling of being the outsider, the one who doesn't blend it, that everyone knows is totally outta place. And most of us know that when some tourist shows up in your home town, you feel the exact same way about them. Some try their best to blend in, others don't care that you laugh at them.

The Tourist Resort Zone

The Descriptive Approach

Tourist destinations are in a state of continuous change. This development is more intense in the case of island destinations due to their geographic limitations

Transport is a fundamental component of tourism, providing the vital link between the tourist generating areas and destinations. Hence there are very close links between the transport and tourism industries where a two-way relationship exists. On the one hand good accessibility, which is determined by the transport services provided, is essential for the development of any tourist destination. Conversely for the transport industry, there can be substantial benefits from tourism because of the additional demand which this type of travel can produce.

Aviation is an increasingly important mode of transport for tourism markets. Whilst geography has meant that, in modern times, air travel has always been the dominant mode for long distance travel and much international tourism, moves towards deregulation, and in particular the emergence of the low cost carrier sector, have also increased aviation's significance for short and medium haul tourism trips. Thus, developments in aviation are having very major implications for many leisure and business tourism markets. However, the characteristics and needs of leisure travellers are generally so very different from business travellers that this necessitates a separate consideration of these markets if a detailed understanding of the relationship with aviation is to be gained.

In spite of the obvious closeness between the aviation and the leisure tourism industries, there are very few specialist texts on this subject. Most tourism focused books consider aviation as just one component of the tourism industry which needs to be discussed, whereas aviation specialist texts rarely concentrate on just leisure travel. In addition there is very little literature that gives a detailed appreciation of the complexities and potential conflicts associated with the development of coherent and effective aviation and tourism policies. Therefore it is the aim of this book to fill this important gap which exists with a comprehensive, in-depth study of the relationship between aviation and leisure travel.

4

Image Promotions

Introduction

The unprecedented growth in the tourism industry during the last fifty years has created major challenges in tourism marketing. As more and more areas of the world are developed for tourism, the destination choices available to consumers continue to expand. Furthermore, today's consumers, facilitated by increased leisure time, rising levels of disposable income and more efficient transportation networks, have the means to choose from among this much larger variety of destinations. As a result, tourism marketers are now faced with influencing consumer decision making in an increasingly complex and competitive global marketplace.

One of the most significant marketing challenges arising from this situation is the need for an effective destination positioning strategy. In order to be successfully promoted in the targeted markets, a destination must be favourably differentiated from its competition, or positively positioned, in the minds of the consumers. A key component of this positioning process is the creation and management of a distinctive and appealing perception, or image, of the destination.

Tourism has been long accepted as an economic activity of attracting tourists and catering to their needs, which has rapidly grown into the world's largest industry and surpassing other important sectors such as automobiles, steel, agriculture and so forth. As demand for tourism increased, more and more areas developed for tourism and the choices of destination available to tourists continue to expand. As a result, destinations compete, and this phenomenon would lead to a fierce competition between tourism destinations. In this case, to be successfully promoted in targeted market, a destination must be favourably differentiated from its competition and has strong image to be positioned in the mind of the tourists. Thus, destination image play an important role in making the tourism destination viable for long-term tourism business Tourists today have to be enticed since the tourism destination is an intensely competitive and many destinations competing with one and another to attract the same potential tourists.

Therefore, a better understanding of destination image is vital in order to develop appropriate marketing strategies that based on tourists' perception and behaviour so that more competitive destinations' products are delivered to current and potential tourists. The research of destination image can be traced back to the early of 1970s. In this era, images signify a pretesting of the destination which, can be referred as transpose representation of the destination into potential tourist's mind. Natural environment or beautiful beaches are the images held that likely to detract or contribute to the important role in tourism development and this become the concerns of Hunt study. His influential work has been expanding and later, several studies also highlighted the aspect of image and travel behaviour such as Mayo (1973), Gunn (1972), which since then and after 30 years, destination image become the most researched topics in the field of tourism.

Factors that Influencing the Destination Image Formation

The understanding of image formation is a one way to develop a competitive image or good impression of tourist destinations to the market. A positive image of tourist destination is considered as pulling factors among the flood of total impression that attract visitors to the destination. However, there are several types of factors that vital in the destination image formation which is pushing the tourists to the destination. Previous section has explained the importance of variety and types of information sources in image formation. Thus, this section attempts to highlight personal factors which refer to individual's personal characteristics, as well as psychological characteristics which influence destination image formation. On top of that, the differences in tourists' cultural values and past travel experiences are also important factor to be included.

Past Travel Experience

Previous studies have shown a significant effect on what tourist has perceived and acted based on previous experiences. According to

Perdue (1985), past travel experience explain the reason why repeat visitors only visit several or specific destination. It is because of specific intention or certain level of knowledge that pulled them to the destination again. On the other hand, first time visitors travelled to more destination and visited more attractions than repeat visitors (Oppermann, 1997).

This was supported by Fakeye and Crompton (1999) study that shows repeat visitors rated attraction-based images significantly higher than first-timer or even the potential tourists. Potential tourists have limited knowledge about the attributes of a particular destination and they have no previous experience, while previous visits affect familiarity with the destination.

For instance, Millman and Pizam (1995) found that individuals with past experience at a destination had a more positive image of the destination, and is more likely to revisit compared with individuals who were aware of, but had never experienced in the destination. They also found that individuals with no awareness of a destination were similar in their intention to visit compared with individuals with some level of destination awareness. This has enlightened that past experience reduces the risk of unfamiliarity of the environment and unsatisfactory experience which in turn result in accepting or rejecting a destination in a choice set.

Destination awareness is about knowledge or how much the tourist knows about the destination product. This term of awareness was used in purchasing and consumption behaviour which reveals whether the consumer has experienced or familiar with the product, and followed by repeat purchase.

In this case, for repeat visitation to be occurred there must lead to a first trial or first visit. Nevertheless, the awareness may not always lead to purchasing behaviour. In other words, information collected by tourists is not necessarily influence their travel behaviour perhaps there are many situational factors that may affect tourists travel behaviour. If satisfaction occurs as the result from the first visit, repeat visitation will follow.

Personal background characteristic, psychological factors and cultural values Every individual is different in nature. Personal characteristic, psychological factors and cultural values do affect the formation of image. The amount of external stimuli which is being exposed to the tourist determines the level of beliefs toward the attributes of the destination. Nevertheless, the internal factors such as sociodemographic characteristics perhaps lead to the various developments of mental picture about the destination, which produces their own version of images prior to individual's needs, motivation, knowledge, preferences and other personal characteristics.

A tourist destination can be described as a combination of services, resources and experiences. The destination image is basically measured through the cognitive-affective dimension which tells what images should be promoted based on what tourist has perceived or preferred. On the other hand, the amount of external stimuli which is being exposed to the tourist as well as, the motivational aspects that took place will initiate the action based on the image preferred.

The development of mental images will be later modified during the actual contact of the destination. As a result, the outcome of the experience affects the overall perception of the destination. This influences the post-decision for the future selection of holiday or visitation whether revisited or rejected.

The proposed theoretical framework identified the process as discussed in the literature. The question remains on how this process being examined as a complete cycle of image preference. This involve before the tourist making visit, during and after visitation as well as, the next process in intention to revisit. Therefore, this paper proposed a theoretical framework that need for further inquiries based on the given phenomenon.

Measures of Physical Attractiveness

Definition

To define a Tourist Attraction is not simple. Here are two definitions:

1. A physical or cultural feature of a particular place that individual travellers or tourists perceive as capable of meeting one or more of their specific leisure-related needs. Such features may be ambient in nature (e.g. climate, culture, vegetation or scenery), or they may be specific to a location, such as a theatre performance, a museum or a waterfall.
2. Positive or favourable attributes of an area for a given activity or set of activities as desired by a given customer or market, including climate, scenery, activities, culture.
   (a) Man made attractions are physical structures (Sydney Harbour Bridge) or events (Olympics).

(b) Natural attractions are physical phenomena deemed unusual and /or beautiful (Bungle Bungles).

(c) Secondary attractions have tourist appeal, but are not the primary reason for visiting a location.

(d) A negative attraction is an attribute of an area that tends to make some customer or market choose not to visit as for example pollution or crime.

Types of Attractions

There are basically two types of attractions:

- Built Attractions.
- Natural Attractions.

In attempting to embrace the core values of these definitions, Tourism Western Australia has developed the following set of essential and desirable recognition criteria for assessing a Tourist Attraction. The use of these criteria will ensure that uniform standards provide a fair and equitable assessment of all Tourist Attractions. A Tourist Attraction will need to meet all of the essential recognition criteria before a recommendation is made to Main Roads Western Australia or a local government for the erection of appropriate road signs.

Built Attractions – Recognition Criteria

Essential Criteria

Most importantly:

- Tourism must clearly be an important part of the business In addition, the attraction must:
  * Provide a substantive tourist experience in addition to, or part of, the commercial establishment's normal activities.
  * Have all relevant State and Local Government licenses and approvals to operate as a commercial tourist attraction including health, planning, parking and disabled access facilities.
  * Be a member of a recognised local tourism organisation.
  * Be open on weekends and three other days of the week including public holidays.
- Clearly display opening times (if not open 7 days):
  * At the entrance to the property or establishment.
  * In brochures and all promotional mediums (advertisements, web sites, etc.).

- Be open at least between 10am and 4pm.
- Produce a leaflet or brochure describing the attraction.
- Be distinctly signed at the property line so that the attraction can be easily identified.
- Be clean and well presented at all times.
- Have clean and conveniently located toilet facilities.

Desirable Criteria

It would be desirable for the attraction to also:

- be open every day.
- be Quality Assured by Tourism Council Western Australia.
- provide a parking area for coaches and caravans.
- keep a record of visitor numbers (e.g. by way of a visitors book).

Other Considerations

Arts & crafts outlets, nurseries, garden centres and the like are generally not considered to be tourist attractions unless the premises are significantly large and they provide some kind of value added experience such as having a well known or established artist in residence, or they conduct interpretative tours of their premises.

Wineries must provide wine tastings and cellar door sales. Wineries, which are only 'open by appointment', are not considered to be a tourist attraction for road signage purposes. Historic sites, buildings, etc. must be classified by the Heritage Council of WA.

Natural Attractions-recognition Criteria

Natural attractions comprise geographic or other natural features of tourist interest:

- National Parks and Reserves.
- Waterfalls, lakes, dams and other water catchment areas.
- Beaches.
- Caves, rock formations.
- Scenic lookouts, viewing areas, vistas and areas of impressive natural beauty.

Essential Criteria

The natural attraction must:

- be managed by a recognised agency or body.

- be recognised by Tourism Western Australia as a significant feature of tourist interest.
- be accessible to the public at least 9 months of the year.
- clearly display when the attraction is closed (if not open year round).
    - at the turn-off to the attraction.
    - in brochures and all promotional mediums (advertisements, websites, etc.).
- have adequate designated parking areas at the site.
- be distinctly signed at the entrance point so that the natural attraction can be easily identified.
- have clean and well presented visitor facilities.
- have access roads, walking tracks and viewing platforms maintained in a safe and satisfactory condition all year-round by the management body responsible.

Desirable Criteria

It would be desirable for the natural attraction to also:

- have clean and conveniently located toilet facilities.
- provide a parking area for coaches.
- be interpreted.

The Economic Impacts of Tourism

Businesses and public organizations are increasingly interested in the economic impacts of tourism at additional, state, and local levels. One regularly hears claims that tourism supports X jobs in an area or that a festival or special event generated Y million dollars in sales or income in a community. "Multiplier effects" are often cited to capture secondary effects of tourism spending and show the wide range of sectors in a community that may benefit from tourism.

Tourism's economic benefits are touted by the industry for a variety of reasons. Claims of tourism's economic significance give the industry greater respect among the business community, public officials, and the public in general. This often translates into decisions or public policies that are favourable to tourism. Community support is important for tourism, as it is an activity that affects the entire community. Tourism businesses depend extensively on each other as well as on other businesses, government and residents of the local community.

Economic benefits and costs of tourism reach virtually everyone in the region in one way or another. Economic impact analyses provide tangible estimates of these economic interdependency and a better understanding of the role and importance of tourism in a region's economy.

Tourism activity also involves economic costs, including the direct costs incurred by tourism businesses, government costs for infrastructure to better serve tourists, as well as congestion and related costs borne by individuals in the community.

Community decisions over tourism often involve debates between industry proponents touting tourism's economic impacts (benefits) and detractors emphasizing tourism's costs. Sound decisions rest on a balanced and objective assessment of both benefits and costs and an understanding of who benefits from tourism and who pays for it.

Tourism's economic impacts are therefore an important consideration in state, regional and community planning and economic development. Economic impacts are also important factors in marketing and management decisions. Communities therefore need to understand the relative importance of tourism to their region, including tourism's contribution to economic activity in the area.

A variety of methods, ranging from pure guesswork to complex mathematical models, are used to estimate tourism's economic impacts. Studies vary extensively in quality and accuracy, as well as which aspects of tourism are included. Technical reports often are filled with economic terms and methods that non-economists do not understand. On the other hand, media coverage of these studies tend to oversimplify and frequently misinterpret the results, leaving decision makers and the general public with a sometimes distorted and incomplete understanding of tourism's economic effects.

How can the average person understand these studies sufficiently to separate good studies from bad ones and make informed choices? The purpose of this bulletin is to present a systematic introduction to economic impact concepts and methods.

The presentation is written for tourism industry analysts and public officials, who would like to better understand, evaluate, or possibly conduct an economic impact assessment. The bulletin is organized around ten basic questions that either are asked or should be asked about the economic impacts of tourism.

What is an Economic Impact Analysis?

A variety of economic analyses are carried out to support tourism decisions. As these different kinds of economic analysis are frequently confused, let's begin by positioning economic impact studies within the broader set of economic problems and techniques relevant to tourism. These same techniques may be applied to any policy or action, but we will define them here in the context of tourism. Each type of analysis is identified by the basic question(s) it answers and the types of methods and models that are appropriate.

Types of Economic Analysis

Economic impact analysis : What is the contribution of tourism activity to the economy of the region? An economic impact analysis traces the flows of spending associated with tourism activity in a region to identify changes in sales, tax revenues, income, and jobs due to tourism activity.

The principal methods here are visitor spending surveys, analysis of secondary data from government economic statistics, economic base models, input-output models and multipliers. (Frechtling 1994a) Fiscal impact analysis – Will government revenues from tourism activity from taxes, direct fees, and other sources cover the added costs for infrastructure and government services? Fiscal impact analysis identifies changes in demands for government utilities and services resulting from some action and estimates the revenues and costs to local government to provide these services.

Financial analysis : Can we make a profit from this activity? A financial analysis determines whether a business will generate sufficient revenues to cover its costs and make a reasonable profit. It generally includes a short-term analysis of the availability and costs of start-up capital as well as a longer-range analysis of debt service, operating costs and revenues. A financial analysis for a private business is analogous to a fiscal impact analysis for a local government unit.

Demand analysis : How will the number or types of tourists to the area change due to changes in prices, promotion, competition, quality and quantity of facilities, or other demand shifters? A demand analysis estimates or predicts the number and/or types of visitors to an area via a use estimation, forecasting or demand model. The number of visitors or sales is generally predicted based on judgement (Delphi method), historic trends (time series methods), or using a model that captures how visits or spending varies with key demand determinants (structural models) such as population size, distance to markets, income levels, and measures of quality & competition.

Benefit Cost analysis (B/C) : Which alternative policy will generate the highest net benefit to society over time? A B/C analysis estimates the relative economic efficiency of alternative policies by comparing benefits and costs over time. B/C analysis identifies the most efficient policies from the perspective of societal welfare, generally including both monetary and nonmonetary values. B/C analysis makes use of a wide range of methods for estimating values of non-market goods and services, such as the travel cost method and contingent valuation method.

Feasibility study : Can/should this project or policy be undertaken? A feasibility study determines the feasibility of undertaking a given action to include political, physical, social, and economic feasibility. The economic aspects of a feasibility study typically involve a financial analysis to determine financial feasibility and a market demand analysis to determine market feasibility. A feasibility study is the private sector analogue of benefit cost analysis. The feasibility study focuses largely on the benefits and costs to the individual business or organization, while B/C analysis looks at benefits and costs to society more generally.

Environmental Impact assessment: What are the impacts of an action on the surrounding environment? An environmental assessment determines the impacts of a proposed action on the environment, generally including changes in social, cultural, economic, biological, physical, and ecological systems. Economic impact assessment methods are often used along with corresponding measures and models for assessing social, cultural and environmental impacts. Methods range from simple checklists to elaborate simulation models. Benefit cost analysis and economic impact analysis are frequently confused as both discuss economic "benefits". There are two clear distinctions between the two techniques. B/C analysis addresses the benefits from economic efficiency while economic impact analysis focuses on the regional distribution of economic activity. The income received from tourism by a destination region is largely offset by corresponding losses in the origin regions, yielding only modest contributions to net social welfare and efficiency. B/C analysis includes both market and non-market values (consumer surplus), while economic impact analysis is restricted to actual flows of money from market transactions. While each type of economic analysis is somewhat distinct, a given problem often calls for several different kinds of economic analysis. An economic impact study will frequently involve a demand analysis to project levels of tourism activity. In other cases demand is treated as exogenous and the analysis simply estimates impacts if a given number of visitors are attracted to the area. A comprehensive impact assessment will also examine fiscal impacts, as well as social and environmental impacts. Be aware that an economic impact analysis, by itself, provides a rather narrow and often one-sided perspective on the impacts of tourism. Studies of the economic impacts of tourism tend to emphasize the positive benefits of tourism.

On the other hand environmental, social, cultural and fiscal impact studies tend to focus more on negative impacts of tourism. This is in spite of the fact that there are negative economic impacts of tourism (e.g., seasonality and lower wage jobs) and in many cases positive environmental and social impacts (e.g., protection of natural & cultural resources in the area and education of both tourists and local residents). An economic impact assessment (EIA) traces changes in economic activity resulting from some action.

An EIA will identify which economic sectors benefit from tourism and estimate resulting changes in income and employment in the region. Economic impact assessment procedures do not assess economic efficiency and also do not generally produce estimates of the fiscal costs of an action. For many problems economic impact analysis will be part of a broader analysis. Environmental, social, and fiscal impacts are often equally important concerns in a balanced assessment of impacts.

What Economic Impacts does Tourism have?

Tourism has a variety of economic impacts. Tourists contribute to sales, profits, jobs, tax revenues, and income in an area. The most direct effects occur within the primary tourism sectors —lodging, restaurants, transportation, amusements, and retail trade. Through secondary effects, tourism affects most sectors of the economy. An economic impact analysis of tourism activity normally focuses on changes in sales, income, and employment in a region resulting from tourism activity.

A simple tourism impact scenario illustrates. Let's say a region attracts an additional 100 tourists, each spending $100 per day. That's $10,000 in new spending per day in the area. If sustained over a 100 day season, the region would accumulate a million dollars in new sales.

The million dollars in spending would be distributed to lodging, restaurant, amusement and retail trade sectors in proportion to how the visitor spends the $100. Perhaps 30% of the million dollars would leak out of the region immediately to cover the costs of goods purchased by tourists that are not made in the local area (only the retail margins for such items should normally be included as direct sales effects). The remaining $700,000 in direct sales might yield $350,000 in income within tourism industries and support 20 direct tourism jobs. Tourism industries are labour and income intensive, translating a high proportion of sales into income and corresponding jobs.

The tourism industry, in turn, buys goods and services from other businesses in the area, and pays out most of the $350,000 in income as wages and salaries to its employees. This creates secondary economic effects in the region. The study might use a sales multiplier of 2.0 to indicate that each dollar of direct sales generates another dollar in secondary sales in this region.

Through multiplier effects, the $700,000 in direct sales produces $1.4 million in total sales. These secondary sales create additional income and employment, resulting in a total impact on the region of $1.4 million in sales, $650,000 in income and 35 jobs.

While hypothetical, the numbers used here are fairly typical of what one might find in a tourism economic impact study. A more complete study might identify which sectors receive the direct and secondary effects and possibly identify differences in spending and impacts of distinct subgroups of tourists (market segments). One can also estimate the tax effects of this spending by applying local tax rates to the appropriate changes in sales or income. Instead of focusing on visitor spending, one could also estimate impacts of construction or government activity associated with tourism. There are several other categories of economic impacts that are not typically covered in economic impact assessments, at least not directly. For example:

- *Changes in prices* — tourism can sometimes inflate the cost of housing and retail prices in the area, frequently on a seasonal basis.
- *Changes in the quality and quantity of goods and services* – tourism may lead to a wider array of goods and services available in an area (of either higher or lower quality than without tourism).

- *Changes in property and other taxes* – taxes to cover the cost of local services may be higher or lower in the presence of tourism activity. In some cases, taxes collected directly or indirectly from tourists may yield reduced local taxes for schools, roads, etc. In other cases, locals may be taxed more heavily to cover the added infrastructure and service costs. The impacts of tourism on local government costs and revenues are addressed more fully in a fiscal impact analysis.
- *Economic dimensions of "social" and "environmental" impacts-* There are also economic consequences of most social and environmental impacts that are not usually addressed in an economic impact analysis. These can be positive or negative. For example, traffic congestion will increase costs of moving around for both households and businesses. Improved amenities that attract tourists may also encourage retires or other kinds of businesses to locate in the area.

Direct, Indirect and Induced Effects

A standard economic impact analysis traces flows of money from tourism spending, first to businesses and government agencies where tourists spend their money and then to:

- *Other businesses* — supplying goods and services to tourist businesses,
- *Households* – earning income by working in tourism or supporting industries, and
- *Government* — through various taxes and charges on tourists, businesses and households Formally, regional economists distinguish direct, indirect, and induced economic effects.

Indirect and induced effects are sometimes collectively called secondary effects. The total economic impact of tourism is the sum of direct, indirect, and induced effects within a region. Any of these impacts may be measured as gross output or sales, income, employment, or value added.

Direct effects are production changes associated with the immediate effects of changes in tourism expenditures. For example, an increase in the number of tourists staying overnight in hotels would directly yield increased sales in the hotel sector. The additional hotel sales and associated changes in hotel payments for wages and salaries, taxes, and supplies and services are direct effects of the tourist spending.

Indirect effects are the production changes resulting from various rounds of re-spending of the hotel industry's receipts in other backward-linked industries (i.e., industries supplying products and services to hotels).

Changes in sales, jobs, and income in the linen supply industry, for example, represent indirect effects of changes in hotel sales. Businesses supplying products and services to the linen supply industry represent another round of indirect effects, eventually linking hotels to varying degrees to many other economic sectors in the region.

Induced effects are the changes in economic activity resulting from household spending of income earned directly or indirectly as a result of tourism spending. For example, hotel and linen supply employees, supported directly or indirectly by tourism, spend their income in the local region for housing, food, transportation, and the usual array of household product and service needs.

The sales, income, and jobs that result from household spending of added wage, salary, or proprietor's income are induced effects. By means of indirect and induced effects, changes in tourist spending can impact virtually every sector of the economy in one way or another.

The magnitude of secondary effects depends on the propensity of businesses and households in the region to purchase goods and services from local suppliers. Induced effects are particularly noticed when a large employer in a region closes a plant. Not only are supporting industries (indirect effects) hurt, but the entire local economy suffers due to the reduction in household income within the region. Retail stores close and leakages of money from the region increase as consumers go outside the region for more and more goods and services. Similar effects in the opposite direction are observed when there is a significant increase in jobs and household income.

Final demand is the term used by economists for sales to the final consumers of goods and services. In almost all cases, the final consumers of tourism goods and services are households. Government spending is also considered as final demand. The same methods for estimating impacts of visitor spending can be applied to estimate the economic impacts of government spending, for example, to operate and maintain a park or visitor centre.

Regional Economic Models

An input-output model (I-O model) is a mathematical model that describes the flows of money between sectors within a region's economy.

Flows are predicted by knowing what each industry must buy from every other industry to produce a dollar's worth of output.

Using each industry's production function, I-O models also determine the proportions of sales that go to wage and salary income, proprietor's income, and taxes. Multipliers can be estimated from input-output models based on the estimated re-circulation of spending within the region. Exports and imports are determined based upon estimates of the propensity of households and firms within the region to purchase goods and services from local sources (often called RPC's or regional purchase coefficients). The more a region is self-sufficient and purchases goods and services from within the region, the higher the multipliers for the region.

Input-output models make a number of assumptions. The basic ones are that:

- All firms in a given industry employ the same production technology (usually assumed to be the national average for that industry), and produce identical products.
- There are no economies or diseconomies of scale in production or factor substitution. I-O models are essentially linear–double the level of tourism activity/production and you double all of the inputs, the number of jobs, etc.
- The model doesn't explicitly keep track of time, but analysts generally report the impact estimates as if they represent activity within a single year.
- One must assume that the various model parameters are accurate and represent the current year. I-O models are firmly grounded in the national system of accounts, which relies on a standard industrial classification system (SIC codes) and various federal government economic censuses, in which individual firms report sales, wage and salary payments and employment. I-O models will generally be at least a few years out-of-date, although this isn't usually a major problem unless the region's economy has changed significantly. An I-O model represents the region's economy at a particular point in time. Tourist spending estimates are generally price adjusted to the year of the model.
- Multiplier computations for induced effects generally assume that jobs created by additional spending are new jobs, involving new households in the area. Induced effects are computed assuming linear changes in household spending with changes

in income. Estimates of induced effects may be inflated due to the violation of these assumptions. Induced effects tend to account for the vast majority of the secondary effects of tourism, and therefore should be used with caution.

What are Multipliers and Multiplier Effects of Tourism?

Multipliers capture the secondary economic effects (indirect and induced) of tourism activity. Multipliers have been frequently misused and misinterpreted in tourism studies and are a considerable source of confusion among non-economists. Multipliers represent the economic interdependency between sectors within a particular region's economy.

They vary considerably from region to region and sector to sector. There are many different kinds of multipliers reflecting which secondary effects are included and which measure of economic activity is used (sales, income, or employment).

For example,

* The Type I sales multiplier = direct sales + indirect sales direct sales.
* The Type II or III sales multiplier 1 = direct sales + indirect sales + induced sales direct sales.

Multiplying a Type I sales multiplier times the direct sales gives direct plus indirect sales. Multiplying a Type II or III sales multiplier times the direct sales gives total sales impacts including direct, indirect and induced effects. The multipliers defined above are called ratio type multipliers as they measure the ratio of a total impact measure to the corresponding direct impact. Comparable income and employment ratio type multipliers may be defined by replacing sales with measures of income or employment in the above equations. Ratio multipliers should be used with caution.

A common error is to multiply a sales multiplier times tourist spending to get total sales effects. This will generate an inflated estimate of tourism impacts. The problem is that tourism spending or sales is not exactly the same as the "direct effects", appearing in the multiplier formula.

Tourist purchases of goods (vs. services) are the primary source of the problem. To properly apply tourist purchases of goods to an input-output model (or corresponding multipliers), various margins (retail, wholesale and transportation) must be deducted from the "purchaser price" of the good to separate out the "producer price". In an I-O model, retail margins accrue to the retail trade sector, wholesale margins to wholesale trade, transportation margins to transportation sectors and the producer prices of goods are assigned to the sector that produces the good.

In most cases the factory that produces the good bought by a tourist lies outside of the local region, creating an immediate "leakage" in the first round of spending and therefore no local impact from production of the good.

Before applying a multiplier to tourist spending, one must first deduct the producer prices of all imported goods that tourists buy (i.e. only include the local retail margins and possibly wholesale and transportation margins if these firms lie within the region). Generally, only 60 to 70% of tourist spending appears as final demand in a local region. While all tourist purchases of services will accrue to the local region as final demand, only the margins on goods purchased at retail stores should be counted as local final demand. The ratio of local final demand to tourist spending is called the capture rate.

Capture Rate = Local Final Demand / Tourism Spending in Local Area

The distinction between Type II and Type III multipliers involves a technical difference in how the induced effects are computed. Type II approaches include households as a sector of the economy and invert the technical coefficient matrix including the household sector, while Type III approaches treat households as exogenous.

Capture rates, like multipliers, will vary with the size and nature of the region as well as the kind of tourist spending included. One must therefore be cautious in taking a multiplier or capture rate cited in one study and using it in another.

Another way of calculating a multiplier (generally the preferred approach among economists) is as a ratio of income or employment to sales. This kind of multiplier is sometimes called a Keynesian multiplier or response coefficient.

Type III Income multiplier = Total direct, indirect, and induced income direct sales.

Type III Employment multiplier = Total direct, indirect, and induced employment direct sales.

This income (employment) multiplier produces total income (employment) impacts when multiplied by the direct sales. One must still be careful in distinguishing between tourism spending/sales and direct sales effects. Some studies may embed the capture rate in the multiplier, expressing the ratio in terms of tourism spending rather than direct sales.

How are Tourism's Economic Impacts Measured?

The economic impacts of tourism are typically estimated by some variation of the following simple formula:

Economic Impact of Tourism = Number of Tourists.

* Average Spending per Visitor

* Multiplier.

The formula suggests three distinct steps and corresponding measurements or models: Estimate the change in the number and types of tourists to the region due to the proposed policy or action.

Estimates or projections of tourist activity generally come from a demand model or some system for measuring levels of tourism activity in an area. Economic impact estimates will rest heavily on good estimates of the numbers and types of visitors. These must come from carefully designed measurements of tourist activity, a good demand model, or good judgement. This step is usually the weakest link in most tourism impact studies, as few regions have accurate counts of tourists, let alone good models for predicting changes in tourism activity or separating local visitors from visitors from outside the region.

Estimate average levels of spending (often within specific market segments) of tourists in the local area.

Spending averages come from sample surveys or are sometimes borrowed or adapted from other studies. Spending estimates must be based on a representative sample of the population of tourists taking into account variations across seasons, types of tourists, and locations within the study area. As spending can vary widely across different kinds of tourists, we recommend estimating average spending for a set of key tourist segments based on samples of at least 50-100 visitors within each tourism segment.

Segments should be defined to capture differences in spending between local residents vs. tourists, day users vs. overnight visitors, type of accommodation (motel, campground, seasonal home, with friends and relatives), and type of transportation (car, RV, air, rail, etc.).

In broadly based tourism impact studies, it is useful to identify unique spending patterns of important activity segments such as downhill skiers, boaters, convention & business travellers. Multiplying the number of tourists by the average spending per visitor (be careful the units are consistent) gives an estimate of total tourist spending in the area.

Estimates of tourist spending will generally be more accurate if distinct spending profiles and use estimates are made for key tourism segments. The use and spending estimates are the two most important parts of an economic impact assessment. When combined, they capture the amount of money brought into the region by tourists. Multipliers are needed only if one is interested in the secondary effects of tourism spending. Apply the change in spending to a regional economic model or set of multipliers to determine secondary effects. Secondary effects of tourism are estimated using multipliers or a model of the region's economy. Multipliers generally come from an economic base or input-output model of the region's economy. In many cases multipliers are borrowed (often improperly) or adjusted from published multipliers or other studies. One should not take a multiplier estimated for one region and apply it in a region with a quite different economic structure.

Generally, multipliers are higher for larger regions with more diversified economies and lower for smaller regions with more limited economic development. A common error is to apply a statewide multiplier (since these are more widely published) to a local region. This will yield inflated estimates of local multiplier effects. Multipliers can also be used to convert estimates of spending or sales to income and employment. Simple ratios can be used to capture how much income or jobs are generated per dollar of sales. These ratios will vary from region to region and across individual economic sectors due to the relative importance of labour inputs in each industry and different wage and salary rates in different regions of the country. Be aware that job estimates are generally not full time equivalents, making them difficult to compare across industries with different proportions of seasonal and part time jobs. Income or value added are generally the preferred measures of the contribution of tourism to a region's economy.

What are the Typical Approaches for an Economic Impact Assessment?

At the simple, "quick and dirty" end of the spectrum are highly aggregate approaches that rely mostly on judgement to determine tourism activity, spending and multipliers. Such estimates can be completed in a couple hours at little cost and rest largely on the expertise and judgement of the analyst. At the other extreme are studies that gather primary data from visitor spending studies and apply the spending estimates to formal regional economic models for the area in question. In between are a wide range of options that employ varying degrees of judgement, secondary data, primary data, and formal models. Different levels of detail and corresponding expense (time and money) and accuracy are possible for each of the three steps — estimating tourist volume, spending, and multiplier effects. Four typical approaches illustrate the levels of detail that are possible and the associated methods.

1. Subjective estimates that rely mostly on expert opinion.
2. Secondary data in aggregate form, adapting existing estimates to suit the problem.
3. Secondary data in disaggregate form, permitting finer adjustment of data to fit the situation.
4. Primary data and/or formal models, usually involving visitor surveys and regional economic models.

The National Park Service's "Money Generation Model " is a simple fill-in-form for generating economic impacts. While an extremely simple approach, it captures the essential elements, of an economic impact analysis. The number of visits, average spending per visitor and an aggregate sales multiplier are entered on a simple work sheet to generate estimates of the direct and total sales effects of visitor spending. Sales effects are converted to income and jobs using simple ratios of income to sales and jobs to sales.

Tax effects of visitor spending can also be estimated by applying local tax rates In an engineering approach, one estimates the costs of producing a "trip" by itemizing typical costs for each input-e.g., a typical overnight visitor party of 4 staying two nights will incur $50 per night for motel room, $20 per person per day for meals, $10 for half tank of gas, and $50 for souvenirs = total of $320 per party per trip to sales estimates. With sound judgement in choosing the parameters, the MGM model can yield reasonable ballpark estimates of economic impacts at minimal cost.

This approach, however, provides little detail on spending categories or which sectors of the economy benefit from either direct or secondary effects. The aggregate nature of the approach also makes it difficult to adjust recommended spending rates or multipliers to different applications (USDI, National Park Service 1990.).

5

Advertisement Process

The travel market is often divided into four segments: personal business travel, government or corporate business travel, visiting friends and relatives, and pleasure vacation travel. This study focuses on the pleasure vacation travel segment.

The objectives of the research were to identify motives which directed respondents' selection of destination, and to develop a conceptual framework that would integrate such motives. It was anticipated that the motives might provide a basis for subdividing or segmenting those travelling for pleasure.

The concept of a stable equilibrium state is either stated or implied in most theories of motivation. Disequilibrium or tension in the motivational system occurs when some need arises. Disturbance of equilibrium drives the organism to elicit a course of action which is expected to satisfy the need and to restore equilibrium. The action ceases when equilibrium is restored as the result of the need being met. Hence, satisfactory resolution of the tension state is the criterion against which alternative actions are compared, contrasted,: and evaluated.

In the study reported here, the concern was to identify states of tension or causes of disequilibrium which provoked respondents' decisions to select particular vacation destinations. It is recognized that motivation is only one of many variables which may contribute to explaining tourist behaviour.

To expect motivation to account for a large portion of the variance in tourist behaviour is probably asking too much since there may be many other interrelated influences operating. Nevertheless, motivation is considered a critical variable because it is the impelling and compelling force behind it all.

Just what motivates people What does Florence have over sitting in front of the television? Why the Fjords of Norway over Icing on a beach in the sun? Why Bali-or Acapulco? u — or wherever? Even more interestingly, why do some people choose not to take holidays at all? Are they just poor, or do they have ideological objections?

It has been suggested that it is possible to describe the who, when, where and how of tourism, together with the economic and social characteristics of tourists, but not to answer the question "why". Lundberg (1976) in the most recent edition of his basic text devotes a chapter to "Why Tourists Travel," but prefaces it with the comment:

Because research and established theory are lacking, the comments included here are necessarily impressionistic and made principally to stimulate investigation...the observations that follow make no claim to validity other than a validity based on observation and reflection. Most discussions of tourist motivation have tended to revolve around the concepts of "pull" and "push." The push factors for a vacation are socio-psychological motives. The pull factors are motives aroused by the destination rather than emerging exclusively from within the traveller himself. In this study, this latter category of motives is termed "cultural". These motives reflected the influence of the destination in arousing them. Traditionally, push motives have been thought useful for explaining the desire to go on a vacation while pull motives have been thought useful for explaining the choice of destination.

For example, Dann (1977) states: While a specific resort may hold a number of attractions for the potential tourist, his actual decision to visit such a destination is consequent on his prior need for travel. An examination of "push" factors is thus logically, and often temporally antecedent to that of "pull" factors. Prominent among the "pull" studies is the world reported by Williams and Zelinski (1970). They studied international tourism flows and partially explained these flows by the term "heliotropic." Gray (1970) suggested a synonymous term "sunlust" which may be a more descriptive term referring to the same phenomenon. Sunlust characterizes vacations which are motivated by the desire to experience different or better amenities for a specific purpose than are available in the environment in which one normally lives. It is prominent with particular activities such as sports, and literally occurs with the search for the sun. Williams and Zelinski (1970) effectively define this phenomenon when they state:

Specifically in those cases where Country B offers singly or in combination contrasting or desirable climatic characteristics, scenic attractions, cultural and historical features, sports, shopping facilities, night life, and so on, either missing or in short supply in Country A, one might expect a significantly high flow from A to B. Gray (1970) suggested that an alternate appeal to sunlust, that destinations may satisfy, is wanderlust. He defined wanderlust as: That basic trait in human nature that causes some individuals to want to experience different existing cultures and places, or the relics of past cultures in places famous for their historical associations, ruins and monuments.

Tourism researchers and writers have displayed a preference towards "cultural" motives in seeking to explain why tourists travel. Similarly, the tourist industry generally has focused on cultural factors in seeking to attract tourists. As a result, a review of the published literature reporting why people select one destination rather than another reveals that relatively little empirical research has been undertaken into socio-psychological motives. It is these motives which emerged as being of prime importance in the study reported here.

The most comprehensive empirical studies reported in the literature which are concerned with socio-psychological motives of tourists are those undertaken by Hill (1965), Plog (1976), and Dann (1977). The studies by Hill and Plog, like the study reported here, both used unstructured interviews to collect their data, focusing upon interpretation of individual responses in search of qualitative insights and understanding. Hill's (1965) study, which was commissioned by the Irish Tourist Board, identified some underlying motives for going on a vacation. These were used by the Irish Tourist Board as primary themes upon which to base its advertising and promotional efforts. Plog (1976) empirically derived typical vacationer profiles, which included motives, of each stage of the life cycle.

Dann (1977) confirmed his hypotheses that the answer to the question "What makes Tourists Travel" lies primarily in the socio-psychological concepts of "anomie" and "ego enhancement." In addition, both of these motives had a strong fantasy component. Underlying the anomie hypothesis is the need that man has for love and affection and the desire to communicate with his fellow man. Dann suggested that there is a desire to transcend the feeling of isolation obtained in everyday life, and that this need for social interaction can only be fulfilled by the individual getting away from it all on vacation. Similarly, Dann argued that man requires to be recognized, and that travel provides opportunity for ego-enhancement or self recognition.

Hill (1965) concluded:

> *A holiday is undertaken in response to a sense of internal damage or depletion and represents a period of replenishment and restoration. When he goes on holiday, the holiday maker is hoping to taller in and store "internal goods" with which he will return enriched,* regenerated and recharged to his own environment.

This appears to support the assumption of most writers in the field of tourism who generally express the primary motive for taking a pleasure vacation in terms of personal enrichment of one kind or another. However, personal enrichment may not be the exclusive prerogative of the pleasure vacation.

Howard and Sheth (1968) distinguish between specific and non-specific motivation. If motivation is specific, it is uniquely satisfied by the pleasure vacation experience. If it is non-specific it can also be satisfied by alternative opportunities available from other sources. For example, Hill reported that for those respondents who could easily give up the opportunity to go on a pleasure vacation, the same tension reliever or internal refreshment was sought in some other kind of activity:

> *It was noticeable that when alternatives to the holiday were mentioned, there existed a fundamental notion of repair and renovation to internal objects. However, for the majority of Hill's respondents, a pleasure vacation was regarded as a more or less essential period of refreshment. It was regarded as virtually priceless. If it has to be forfeited because of pragmatic constraints, this forfeiture was regarded as only temporary.*

The study explored the contention that socio-psychological motives may be useful not only in explaining the initial arousal, energizing, or "push" to take a vacation, but may also have directive potential to direct the tourist toward a particular destination. This differs from the traditional conceptual framework described earlier, in which the primary utility of socio-psychological motives lies in explaining the initial decision to go on a vacation, and the consequent decision, choice of destination, is conceived to be primarily a function of the cultural pulling power of the destination. Motives were a primary focus and typically recurred at a number of points throughout the interviews. The interviews were tape recorded, subsequently transcribed, classified and their content analysed to isolate all data which pertained to motives. The content analysis yielded patterns of responses which provided the basis for the conceptual framework formulated in this paper.

The respondents consisted of a sample of adults who were conveniently available. They resided either in College Station, Texas or in the Greater Boston area of Massachusetts. Nineteen respondents were female and twenty were male. Thirty were married, four were single, and the spouses of five were deceased. Only five respondents did not have children. The age and occupational profile of the sample. The occupational data suggests that the sample primarily was comprised of middle-class respondents.

It is important to note that the study reported here was essentially a qualitative study. Its objectives were limited to identifying, and obtaining insights into, tourists' motivations. Because of the research design, data collection technique, and the limited sample size, this study was not concerned with identifying the distributions of these motives in a population. An investigation into the distribution of these motives, which builds upon the basic work reported here, is currently being undertaken by the author as a subsequent project.

Analysis

A conceptualization of the role and relationships of respondents' underlying states of disequilibrium which emerged from patterns in the data. It identifies four main components.

First, a state of disequilibrium. Second, a break from routine, which was conceptualized as an initial overt manifestation of disequilibrium. Third, three behavioural alternatives: stay at home, go on a pleasure vacation, or travel for other purposes such as visiting friends and relatives or going on a business trip, each of which may provide a break from routine. Fourth, the particular motives which help determine the nature and destination of the pleasure vacation if that alternative is selected. These are aligned along a continuum as being primarily either socio-psychological or cultural.

The Nature of a Break From Routine

Almost every respondent described the essence of a vacation as being a break from routine. These breaks could generally be classified into two categories, short-term and long-term. These appeared to resolve different types of disequilibrium. Short-term disequilibrium seemed to reflect a particular set of circumstances or events which were temporal disruptions to homeostasis. Typically, these were expressed as "pressures." In this situation, a break from routine was perceived to be a necessary and sufficient condition to restore homeostasis. Long-term states of disequilibrium could not usually be satisfied by a single pleasure vacation. Instead these states of disequilibrium were satisfied through an ongoing program of pleasure vacations. A break from routine was perceived as necessary to facilitate the resolution of long-term disequilibrium states, but the break alone was not sufficiently inclusive to resolve the state of tension. Long-term disequilibrium was perceived by respondents as being ever present but postponable. In contrast, short-term disequilibrium demanded immediate attention. In other words, the data suggested that a two tier system of disequilibrium was operating.

This is hypothesized to have meant continuation of doing the same kinds of things but in a different physical, or social context. The essence of "break from routine" was, in most cases, either locating in a different place, or changing the dominant social context from the world milieu, usually to that of the family group, or doing both of these things. The kinds of activities in which people engaged were generally not different, although they were sometimes more concentrated. Respondents' life styles did not change. A break from routine often involved emphasizing particularly desired elements of the life style rather than changing the life style to incorporate different activities. The mundane elements in the routine were discarded, but the preferred discretionary elements of the normal life style were retained.

Motives Influencing Selection of Type of PleasureVacation and Destination

Once a desire to go on a pleasure vacation has been established, concern shifts from the impetus dimension of motivation to its directive dimension which serves to guide the tourist toward the selection of a particular type of vacation or destination in preference to all the alternatives of which the tourist is aware. In most decisions more than one motive is operative. Priorities between alternative destinations are a function of the intensity of the particular combination of motives which are dominant in a hierarchy of motives at a particular moment of time. This hierarchy of motives construct helps to explain divergent reaction at different points in time by the same respondent to the same stimuli. The data suggested that respondents' motives usefully could be conceptualized as being located along a cultural — socio-psychological disequilibrium continuum. Much of the tourist industry's modus operandi is based upon the assumption that tourists are attracted to a destination by the particular cultural opportunities or special attributes that it offers. However, the findings of this study suggested that for some respondents, the destination itself was relatively unimportant.

Respondents did not go to particular locations to seek cultural insights or artifacts; rather they went for socio-psychological reasons unrelated to any specific destination. The destination served merely as a medium through which these motives could be satisfied. The following sections of the analysis briefly discuss each of the motives empirically identified in this study, and categorize them as being located either toward the socio-psychological or the cultural end of the continuum.

Socio-Psychological Motives

Socio-psychological motives were rarely overtly identified by respondents in early discussion of their pleasure vacation experiences. These motives were difficult for respondents to articulate.

However, as the interview proceeded, it often became apparent that while initial concern and effort had been with selecting a vacation destination, the value, benefits, and satisfactions derived from the vacation were neither related to, nor derived from, a particular destination's attributes. Rather the satisfactions were related to social or psychological factors unique to the particular individual or group involved. In effect, these motives represented a hidden agenda. This suggests that one of the reasons that some people do not take pleasure vacations is unknown. The data suggested seven socio-psychological motives which served to direct pleasure vacation behaviour. These motives were: escape from a perceived mundane environment; exploration and evaluation of self; relaxation; prestige; regression; enhancement of kinship relationships; and facilitation of social interaction.

Escape from a Perceived Mundane Environment

A temporary change of environment was a frequently expressed respondent motive. Even the most prized living environments sometimes became mundane to those living there. For example, one respondent who lived on Cape Cod indicated that when crowds of people descend upon the Cape in the summer, many of the local residents go to Maine, New Hampshire, or Vermont to avoid the crowds. Escape was sought not only from the general residential locale but also from the specific home and job environments. There did not appear to be any single optimum type of environment that facilitated escape.

The critical ingredient was only that the pleasure vacation context should be physically and socially different from the environment in which one normally lives. For some respondents, the escape offered by a pleasure vacation was for a much longer time period than the actual trip. As Clawson and Knetsch (1966) have suggested, anticipation of the trip was an important ingredient of the total experience. One respondent commented that "You are sustained a little through the winter, first by anticipation of Christmas, then by anticipation of the trip in February or March. It is something to which I look forward in the long winter."

Exploration and Evaluation of Self

The data suggested that a pleasure vacation may be viewed by some people as an opportunity for re-evaluating and discovering more about themselves or for acting out self-images and in so doing refining or modifying them. For example, one respondent commented:

> *This trip put a lot of things in perspective for me. It helped me to get a clearer picture of myself because I put myself in different situations. I saw how I interacted with other people in other conditions. I had some constraints come up, some hardships, and I had to deal with that. It gave me a chance to see what is inside of me and how that would come out, without any outside pressures. You don't find this out when you go to the office from eight to five.*

Self-discovery emerged as a result of transposition into a new situation. The novelty of the physical and social context appeared to be an essential ingredient in the process. These insights into the person's self could not be achieved by staying at home or visiting friends and relatives. In the case of the latter there would be outside pressure serving to ameliorate hardship, and hence dilute the value of the experience, because of the accessibility of friendly other people. In the case of the former, there would be less likelihood of finding different situations or conditions. Exposure to a different milieu sometimes caused a revision of existing perceptions of self-status and enhanced feelings of self-worth. A respondent who was a boat be of low status in that community, but on pleasure vacations, " I see people who are a lot worse off than I am, and I sort of appreciate what we do have." Other respondents stressed that exposure to a different milieu for a period of time served as a reference point re-evaluation of their own life style.

Self-discovery was not confined only to those respondents who went camping or sought inexpensive pleasure vacations. The wealthiest and most widely travelled respondent in the sample expressed similar sentiments. After a cruise vacation in which she found that she was not disposed to the socializing and organized activities which characterized the experience she commented, "I learned a lot about myself on that cruise."

Relaxation

The term relaxation was a constant respondent theme, but its use was often ambivalent. Generally, there was a reluctance on the part of respondents to relax physically. Respondents would say they felt relaxed and then admit that they came home physically exhausted. It was apparent that the term relaxation referred to a mental state rather than a physical relaxation. Given this interpretation it was possible to reconcile physical exhaustion or fatigue as being mentally refreshing and relaxing.

Relaxation meant talking the time to pursue activities of interest. The activities selected were often a reflection of the increased time available at the vacation destination. In the rhythm of the normal routine, the mind was not directed toward these hobbies or interests. These interests were not selectively perceived because they were not pertinent to the prevailing train of thought or dominant motive.

Most respondents indicated that they were fatigued upon their return home from the exertions expended on the vacation and on associated travel. This fatigue factor together with the contribution the vacation has made to ameliorating tension states possibly accounted for the sentiment that respondents frequently expressed, "I am always delighted to go on a vacation, but I am just as delighted to return home again."

Prestige

Although some respondents suggested prestige was a primary motivating factor in other people's trips, few of them accepted that there was any prestige motive involved in their own pleasure vacation decisions. It may be that as travel has become more frequent, it is perceived to be less prestigious. Travel may have become part of the indigenous life style rather than symbolic of a higher life style. Prestige potential disappears with frequency of exposure.

Regression

Some respondents suggested that a pleasure vacation provided an opportunity to do thingswhich were inconceivable within the context of their usual life styles. The things respondents' cited were often puerile, irrational, and more reminiscent of adolescent or child behaviour than mature adult behaviour.

The opportunity to engage in this behaviour was facilitated by withdrawal from usual role obligations. On vacation, respondents were freed of the mores that inhibit capacity for this type of enjoyment.

One respondent stated, "My life style is free and more relaxed when I go away from home. I let my guard down more than I would at home." While puerility was the prevailing form of regressive behaviour, another form was identified by some respondents. This was the search for the life style of a previous era.

This is sometimes referred to as the "nostalgia factor." In essence, the desire was to regress to a less complex, less changeable, less technologically advanced environment. For example, a respondent stated that she and her friends were:

> *Looking for the simple life. We are not looking for big cities, but are looking for peasants of the soil. A lot of us are very romantic. We want to go out and see the fields; to escape Americanism.*

Like the puerile regression state, this search for the life style of a previous era is a transitory, ephemeral tension state, and when homeostasis is restored, return to the routine of life is accepted. The actuality frequently is not congruent with the image, for as the same respondent commented, "It depends where they go, but a lot of people come back not always totally satisfied."

Enhancement of Kinship Relationships

Many respondents perceived the pleasure vacation as a time when family members were brought close together. Hence, the pleasure vacation served as a medium through which family relationships could be enhanced or enriched.

This enhancement is often facilitated by long drives in an automobile because family members are physically juxtaposed for long periods and forced to interact with each other. It is inevitable that a much greater exchange and understanding of each other is likely to occur than in the normal routine situation in which family members go in different directions interacting only spasmodically.

The essence of this tension state was well expressed by a respondent who stated:

The important notion is being out of routine. It isn't that you are away from a place anymore than you are at a place. What is different is the act that you are together as a family. You are able to put aside the other kinds of responsibilities that each of you may have that would otherwise be impinging themselves upon that notion of focusing inwards and putting things together.

Facilitation of Social Interaction

It was evident that an important motive for some respondents going on a pleasure vacation was to meet new people in different locations. These trips were people oriented rather than place oriented. Like several of the other motives which were located towards the socio-psychological end of the disequilibrium continuum, respondents often became aware of this motive only after the trip was completed.

A variety of dimensions of this motive emerged from the data. For some respondents, an opportunity for transitory meetings with others from outside familiar reference groups to exchange views, was all that was sought. Others were seeking more permanent relationships that would serve to extend their range of social contacts. Several observed that interaction with non-familiar people was more likely. In some cases, social contact was initiated by children, who were a common ingredient shared by some parties. The physical planning of accommodations was also perceived to be an ameliorating factor, for if the accommodations were closely juxtaposed they facilitated interaction.

Although several respondents expressed a desire to interact with local people in the destination area, they reported that this was frequently difficult to achieve. Most interaction was with other tourists in the area. There was little common identity with local people who were serving as waitresses, and much more with other tourists who were also waiting in line or visiting a particular attraction for the first time. Some respondents suggested that travelling with others may inhibit opportunities for interacting with local people at the destination. The availability of companions provided built-in entertainment and removed the urge to visit with others outside of the group; the natural tendency was to turn inward rather than outward.

The organized tour was a preferred type of vacation for some respondents because it served as a vehicle for facilitating social intercourse as well as being financially expedient. The prime ingredients inducing the camaraderie which respondents reported from tour experiences appeared to be the sharing of many dimensions of the experience and close physical juxtaposition with others. Some participated regularly in group tours which were arranged locally and were comprised of people who knew others in the group from the outset. In essence, these people were taking some of their home social environment with them to a different location. The existence of a nucleus of known people provided a good foundation upon which to establish new social relationships through introductions. In addition, the group often had a common interest which facilitated social interaction. For example, it may be comprised of lawyers, teachers, doctors, rose growers, or home builders.

Cultural Motives

Motives located towards this end of the continuum were concerned with the destination rather than with the social and psychological status of the individual. Most respondents explained their reasons for going on pleasure vacations in terms of cultural motives. In many cases, cultural motives were more apparent than real. In other cases, the data suggested that many respondents did not receive socio-psychological satisfactions, but received almost exclusively cultural benefits.

Two primary cultural motives were expressed. They were novelty and education. These may be related since exposure to new destinations, sights, and experiences is presumably educational. However, respondents did not always perceive this relation ship and hence they are discussed separately.

Novelty

Novelty was defined by respondents in a variety of ways. Synonyms included curiosity, adventure, new and different. Novel meant new experience but it did not necessarily mean entirely new knowledge. Often respondents knew a lot about a place. The novelty resulted from actually seeing something rather than simply knowing of it vicariously.

A prefe*rence for going to a previously unvisited destination was a consistent factor. This* aspect had previously proved satisfactory, rather than to purchase a brand with which they have had no previous experience. Generally, this does not appear to apply to pleasure vacations.

Cultural disequilibrium appears to be an on-going state which requires a supply of fresh cultural stimuli to restore homeostasis. In most cases, respondents anticipated that re-experiencing known cultural stimuli would not contribute as much as experiencing new stimuli to reducing the tension state.

Hence, when the pleasure vacation product was purchased, a different destination brand was selected by respondents. At the same time, there were some respondents who returned to a previously visited vacation destination. In some cases, the same destination was selected each year. While the data did not enable the reasons for this to be identified, it may be speculated that three factors account for this phenomenon.

First, habitual destination respondents may be motivated primarily by socio-psychological rather than cultural motives. Second, they may have restricted knowledge of the want satisfying attributes of other places. Returning to a proven destination reduces the risk that an unfamiliar alternative may not be as satisfying as those previously experienced. The third factor may be fear, or anxiety of the unknown, which is removed by revisiting a destination.

The urge for new and adventurous experiences was frequently compromised by the felt need to minimize rises of exposure to novelty which may be threatening. One respondent, who was a travel agent, pointed out that for some people, it was a fearful experience to go into an unknown situation in a country where the people did not speak your language. These people "would like to go away from home but they also have the desire to be taken care of. That is why you get tours and tour conductors, because it is a security blanket." People used organized tours to introduce themselves to travel, its problems and associated fears. Organized tours served to remove any anxiety or exposure to unfamiliar situations that may have been threatening.

An alternative strategy to the organized tour for reducing anxiety and fear was to experience the unknown by starting with the known and using that as a base. For example, a number of respondents indicated that they had visited the Mexican border towns, but had no intention of going further into Mexico. The border towns were close to the perceived safety of the known United States and could thus be experienced relatively quickly with minimal anxiety. Similarly, some of the respondents who had visited Europe indicated that they started in the United Kingdom where they knew the language, or in a country that they had previously visited, so that there was some familiarity. From this relatively familiar base, sorties were made into new areas. When they felt comfortable there, the process was repeated and exploration extended to their new destinations.

Education

The positive influence of pleasure vacations on children's' education was exhorted by most respondents and in some cases was the primary consideration in the selection of a destination. Education was perceived as a means of developing a rounded individual. One respondent suggested, "As a generalization, those who have been on vacation, and have travelled, are usually more interesting to talk with than those who have not." It was perceived as almost a moral obligation to take the opportunity to visit a distinctive phenomenon, particularly if it was reasonably accessible. The sense of "ought" to see and experience a particular place frequently meant that circumstances, especially present location, had been the trigger which initiated selection of a destination. Cultural disequilibrium was not site or destination specific. It did not relate to one particular place, but it was generally applicable to all places. Hence, there was a feeling expressed by several respondents that, "I ought to go because I am here," particularly if it was anticipated that the present residential location was transitory. In this situation, it may have been perceived as the one opportunity in a lifetime to see particular cultural phenomena. If the opportunity was not grasped then educational benefits were lost.

Conclusions and Implications

Delineation of underlying motives offers useful insights into understanding the destination selection decision process. All else equal, preference is likely to be given to a destination which is perceived as most likely to service the dominant motive. Nine motives were identified. Seven of these were located towards the socio-psychological end of the disequilibrium continuum and two towards the cultural end. For ease of exposition, the motives were discussed as separate entities. However, they should not be considered as mutually exclusive, nor should any single tension state be selected as the determinant of behaviour. They operate in tandem or combination, for motives are multidimensional.

Thus, destination decisions were usually energized by several motives acting in tandem. The study suggested that any given destination can in principle attract customers whose motivations are neither homogeneous nor necessarily compatible. While the study gave no indication of the distribution of the two disequilibrium states in the population, it suggested that more attention usefully could be given by the tourist industry to socio-psychological disequilibrium in developing its product and promotion strategies than is presenting the case. The tourist industry's modus operandi is based upon the assumption that people go on vacation to do and see things. The data suggested that, for many respondents, this assumption is challengeable. They have been conditioned to thinking in terms of destination, but a number of motives emerged from the data which were not place specific. Consumers motivated by socio-psychological motives were not looking for uniqueness in the product. That is, some specific attribute it possessed which other destinations did not have. The pleasure vacation destination was not perceived by most respondents as a "speciality good."

There appear to be two directions which could usefully be pursued profitably by the tourist industry if it accepts the significance and role of socio-psychological tension states in pleasure vacation decisions suggested in this study. First, efforts are required to arouse people's awareness of their own real motives. The in-depth interviews caused many respondents to confront for the first time their real motives for going on a pleasure vacation. Several commented similarly to the respondent who stated, "This is interesting, I am learning all these things about myself." They expressed surprise at what they revealed, for the motives which ultimately emerged were often radically different from the reasons they were accustomed to giving for going on a vacation.

The interviews proved to be an exercise in self-discovery. The role of the travel agent may be a factor. These details were discovered through interviews, then the counsellor would be in a much better position to recommend the most appropriate type of pleasure vacation and destination. The second direction lies in the development of the destination product and its promotion.

The motives may be used as a basis for market segmentation. They provide cues and insights around which destinations can develop and promote their product to target segments. Supplier efforts have generally focused on unique amenities and facilities of the destination. Socio-psychological tension states suggest that this may not be the most appropriate strategy. For example, the escape from a mundane environment, exploration of self, and regression motives, require only a destination which is physically and socially different from the residential environment. Literally thousands of destinations could meet these criteria and thus serve as direct substitutes. The detailed cultural attractions of a destination are not important in this context. The best promotion strategies for this market segment may be to stress the contribution the destination can make to reducing these disequilibrium states and to stress price advantages.

Those destinations seeking to cater to the relaxation motive may stress familiarity and the availability of facilities to enjoy preferred activities rather than a radically different environment or new activities. Destinations targeting at the prestige market segment may emphasize their unique qualities as a destination, rather than the activities or facilities available. This uniqueness must be fairly widely disseminated so that it is known to peer groups in order that they are able to confer upon members appropriate prestige for visiting it. At the same time it should not be promoted as a popular mass destination. The social interaction motive may be accommodated by physical juxtaposition of parties and organized programming, while enhancement of kinship relationships may be a useful theme for promoting family pleasure vacations.

Cultural disequilibrium referred to the desire to see new places or do things in a different environment. It is this motive to which most tourist supplier effort is presently directed. Two culturally oriented motives were identified. These were novelty and education.

Novelty implied that there was no desire to return to a previously visited destination no matter how successful the vacation. This lack of "brand loyalty" may be ameliorated by establishing a network of cross recommendations. That is, agreement between destinations to recommend satisfied consumers to a destination with similar characteristics in a different location. Chain and franchise organizations offer illustration of this at the individual motel or fast-food facility level. For example, if the vacationer enjoyed Dade County, Florida, they may be recommended to try the Rio Grande Valley region of Texas, or Orange County, California. This offers the credibility accrued by the proven destination that there is a good probability of the vacationer enjoying a similarly satisfying experience in a different cultural context.

To remove the fear inhibition present for some in contemplating a novel pleasure vacation, the organized tour may more prominently promote its anxiety reducing potential, rather than concentrating exclusively on price advantage which is its present tendency. Similarly destinations may stress the attributes with which vacationers were likely to feel familiar, that is their recognizable cultural ties, before pointing out cultural differences. Establishing the known before proceeding to the unknown.

Educational prowess may be useful in attracting vacationers for whom the education motive is dominant. Finally, many respondents changed residential location frequently. Location appeared to be an important ingredient in bringing the education motive state to the head of the hierarchy of motives.

This suggests that people are likely to be susceptible to promotions reminding them that the opportunity to visit a destination in reasonable proximity may not arise again. People went on pleasure vacation to satisfy a variety of different motives. As a result, the attributes which might attract them to a destination differed. The implications suggested in the above paragraphs are intended to be illustrative of how these data may be applied rather than exhaustive. Specific implications appropriate to a particular destination will according to its attributes, environmental niche and goals.

Theoretical Aspects of the Sustainable Tourism Strategies

In order to identify the importance and appropriateness of the sustainable tourism strategy in the growth and development of the industry, it has to identify the theoretical support. The major tourism theories are discussed here for identifying how the CSR concept is relevant in the tourism development and growth.

Tourism theories: Travel and tourism theories are mostly based on travel motivation. The basic factors that influence the travelling decisions are tourist need satisfaction, customer satisfaction and destination loyalty. Tourist motivation factors have higher influence on the tourist behaviour of travellers with regard to their destination choice, needs, goals and preferences. In case of ecotourism, social psychological desire to break out from the habitual ordinary life is the primary push factor. The major pull factors which force travellers to take travel decisions are destination attributes such as natural attractions like wild life and immaculate environment.

As per the theory of Iso-Ahola interpersonal escape and interpersonal seeking motivate tourism and recreation among the individuals. In case of personal seeking and personal escape dimensions, tourism experiences have great role in motivation. Sporting events, beaches, amusement parks, and natural parks improves the motivational levels of tourism and recreational activities to a greater extent. Tourism motivation in holiday trips is the desire to travel for satisfying the internal needs and wants. Incentive tourism is a motivational tool among the employees as well as other organizational personnel.

Most of the weekend travel decisions are related to the intention to take rest and spend the weekend for relaxation. Travel behaviour among individuals can be described as a function of quantifiable aspects such as socio-demographic characteristics and physical characteristics of the region. Most of the travelling decisions are situational in nature.

Travel behaviour of individuals is influenced by individual personality, attitudes and perceptions. Attitude of travellers has influence on beliefs and behaviour in travel decision such as the frequency of use. Novelty seeking is the prime motivating factor that affects the travelling of most of the individuals. The positive and negative feed back from the travel affect their future decision to travel a particular destination.The motivational factors have a key role in the tourist decision making behaviour. In the motivational factors, push and pull concept was introduced by Crompton and Chon in 1979.

Push factors affect the desire for travel whereas pull factors affect the actual destination choice. In the concept of Crompton 1979, there are nine motive factors influencing the leisure travellers. Seven of them are socio psychological factors and two are cultural motives. Push factors are internal factors whereas pull factors are external The seven push factors include, making a change in the routine life environment, meeting self needs, relaxation, establishing social relationships, prestige and social interaction. Novelty and education are the pull factors. According to Iso-Ahola, 1980, there are mainly two motivational factors in tourist behaviour. The first feature is approach, focusing on recreational opportunities for intrinsic rewards, and the second feature is avoidance which is escape oriented. The increasing trend of shorter holiday breaks is a signal of escape dimension among the tourists behaviour.

The study by Teare (1994) on peoples' motives for selecting hotel leisure breaks in the UK states that there are six factors such as attending a pre arranged event, as a break from personal commitments, as well as employment pressures, to fulfil the desire of relaxation or visit a particular destination and to exploit the seasonal benefits of short breaks. The personal motivation factor may differ as per individual behaviour. When considering the theoretical concepts it revealed that protection of the natural environment is an essential factor for motivating the travellers to visit the destinations. Through the keeping of novelty of the destination environment, its attraction can be sustained over a longer period of time.

Thus the tourism theories better support the appropriateness of sustainable tourism strategy for the sustainable growth of the industry. Motivation for travel is a complex area of tourism research. Sharpley (1994) identifies many factors which motivate people to travel. These include a personal need to escape from daily routines, to visit friends and relatives or to learn about other cultures. To understand an individual's motivation to travel, it is necessary to examine their desires, needs, experience and preferences and social, economic and demographic circumstances as well as prevailing social norms and customs.

Although there is a large amount of literature on what motivates people to undertake travel and tourism, the quantity of research into cultural tourist motivation is limited. In particular, there are few studies or surveys of international visitors' motivations and attitudes to Australia's cultural attractions, events and products, despite considerable interest in the Australian cultural tourism industry. Some people, like the English elite who undertook the Grand Tour in the sixteenth and seventeenth centuries, are motivated to travel because of culture.

Such visitors, therefore, can be termed 'specific' cultural or culturally motivated visitors. However, for most people, culture is not a sole motive for travel. Rather, participation in cultural activities is one potential component of a travel itinerary and may occur if opportunities arise. Visitors for whom this is the case can be called 'general' cultural visitors.

Studies of the Motivations of Cultural Visitors

According to some tourist motivation theories, motivations are developed as a result of 'pull' and 'push' factors. Pull factors relate to the characteristics or attractions of a travel destination. For cultural tourists visiting Australia, they include attractions such as the Sydney Opera House and Aboriginal sites. Push factors relate to the needs and wants of individuals that lead them to 'buy' particular holidays. For cultural tourism and tourism as a whole, they include the desire for social interaction and relaxation, to experience something different and to learn about themselves and the places they visit for participating in cultural activities. Other researchers have identified more specific motivations.

Motivation Theory

"Crompton (1979) notes it is possible to describe the who, when, where, and how of tourism, together with the social and economic characteristics of tourist, but not to answer the question "why," the most interesting question of all tourist behaviour."

While motivation is only one of many variables in explaining tourist behaviour, it is nonetheless a very critical one, as it constitutes the driving force behind all behaviour. Motivation sets the stage for forming people's goals and is reflected in both travel choice and behaviour; as such it influences people's expectations, which in turn determine the perception of experiences. Motivation is therefore a factor in satisfaction formation.

Basic motivation theory suggests a dynamic process of internal psychological factors (needs, wants and goals), causing an uncomfortable level of tension within individuals' minds and bodies, resulting in actions aimed at releasing that tension and satisfying these needs. Motives, implying such an action, require the awareness of needs, as well as objectives, promising to satisfy these now conscious needs in order to create wants and move people to buy. Objectives or goals are presented in the form of products and services, it is therefore the role of marketing to create awareness of needs and suggest appropriate objectives, promising the satisfaction of these.

Several authors suggest that in the Western World free time and holidays are connected to the concept of self-actualisation or self-realisation. The latter defined by Grunow-Lutter (1983.) as *"a person's dynamic relationship between the real and the ideal self, constituting a process of decreasing the distance between these two cognitive systems, themselves subject to continuous change."* It is the individual's aim to achieve a state of stability, or homeostasis, which is disrupted when the person becomes aware of the gap between real and ideal self, or as Goosens calls it a need deficiency.

The resulting need to self-actualise represents the motive, which under the constraints of the situation sets the stage for the process of motivation. But to what extent does tourism satisfy the intrinsic need for self-actualisation? Tinsley and Eldredge (1995) summarise 15 years of research into psychological needs, satisfied by leisure activities, and proposed leisure activities clusters such as novelty, sensual enjoyment, cognitive stimulation, self-expression, creativity, vicarious competition, relaxation, agency, belongingness and service. It is questioned however; whether these superficial needs are intrinsically motivated, suggesting that these motivations are merely culturally learned stereotypes or explanations for leisure behaviour. As Fodness (1994) states, a widely accepted integrated theory for needs and goals behind motivation is lacking. The question is of course why this is the case.

Research into motivation can be distinguished into two categories, the behaviourist and the cognivist approach. The discussion has therefore traditionally revolved around either push or pull factors influencing tourist behaviour. Push factors represent lasting dispositions, as they are internally generated drives. The individual, energised by such drives, will then search objects for the promise of drive reduction and develop a motive.

The behaviourist view thus emphasises the emotional parameter of decision-making, while the cognivist approach focuses on situational parameters in which motives are expressed, consequently encompassing a certain knowledge which the tourist holds about goal attributes as well as a rational weighing up of situational constraints. This cognitive process results in motivations, which are more object specific than motives, as these only imply a class of objects and may result in a range of different behaviours, depending on the situation.

This unidimensional approach has been criticised however, as push and pull factors influence the consumer simultaneously, integrated by the concept of involvement, an unobservable state of motivation, arousal, or interest, which is evoked by stimulus or situations.

This is the case, since pull factors such as marketing stimuli as well as the destination's and service's attributes respond to and reinforce push factors. Consequently research increasingly seeks to integrate emotions and cognition in the individual's decision-making process, indicating a more holistic approach.

As a result it became evident that people's intrinsic needs are influenced by external factors. Rojek (1990) asserts that in post-modern society the superstructure of advertising, television, fashion, lifestyle magazines and designer values increasingly take the role of forming knowledge and beliefs. People's needs are neutral, as motives however, they require an object towards which the need is directed, and when linked to actual situations, cultural and social impacts are also applied. Situations raise motives to the level of values, as such they are evaluations based on learned behaviour and perception.

If a drive is reduced satisfactorily the individual is likely to remember the behaviour and employ the same behaviour again, thus acquiring habits. Tourism experiences may therefore become learned behaviour and acquire the role of habit enforcers. Cognivists argue that knowledge and beliefs in future rewards, anticipatory in nature, are equally a product of formerly encountered situations, and external formation.

It may be concluded that motives merely represent learned behaviour, which are influenced by offered objects or tourism activities, while motivations represent knowledge and beliefs formed by society and culture or tourism marketers. The psychogenic need for self-actualisation, abstract in nature, is therefore operationalised in a learned and practical manner and expressed in values, which are learned strategies to either adapt one's environment to one's needs or adapt one's self to a given environment. Such values equally include effects of enculturation and socialisation. Furthermore the perceived gap between real and ideal self, may indicate both externally and internally controlled evaluations. McCabe therefore asks what researchers can expect to know about individuals' drives, by asking them about their motivations and needs as these may not be available to individuals as part of their consciousness (2000a,).

Iso-Ahola (1982) states that *"people do not walk around with numerous leisure needs in their minds and do not rationalise specific causes of participation if their involvement is intrinsically motivated"* (cited in Goosens 2000). Hence it may be assumed that needs are suggested by immediate social peers, and the wider context of particular social realities as well as the influence of the media. Yet as Weissinger and Bandalos (1995) stress, intrinsic leisure motivation, which is a global disposition and describes a tendency to seek intrinsic rewards, is characterised by self-determination, an awareness of internal needs and a strong desire to make free choices based on these needs.

While self-actualisation may be accepted as a need intrinsic to all individuals, society exercises a great deal of influence on the formation of the ideal self and thus perceived needs. However the notion of authentic or true self, determined by way of experience, offers a solution to the predicament. According to Waterman (1984), individualism symbolises four psychological qualities, the first one is a sense of individual identity, based on the knowledge of who one is and what one's goals and values are, as such it is related to the philosophical concept of true self, which indicates what an individual reckons personally expressive and what it is to be actualised. The second is Maslow's self-actualisation, which is the driving to be one's true self. The third quality is Rotter's (1966) internal locus of control, which reflects a willingness to accept personal responsibility for one's life, and finally principles (postconventional), moral reasoning, which involves consistency with general abstract principles.

Consequently, only if tourists become more autonomous and thus aware of intrinsic needs and motives are they able to self-actualise. As McIntosh and Goeldner (1990) explained, order is becoming less important in Western society and a desire for disorder in the tourism experience is becoming more important. Kim and Lee point out that *"opportunities for unplanned action and freedom from institutionalised regulations are distinctive of Western tourists"* (2000). This indicates that tourists exhibit a certain desire to liberate their identities. According to Krippendorf (1984), in order for tourists to cease being just users of holidays, they must come to know themselves, their motives and other cultures.

It may therefore be assumed that self-actualisation is an intrinsic need, characteristic of any tourist, but must be understood in terms of true self as opposed to ideal self and as such is independent of societal pressures and involves the transcendence of habitual behaviours and mindstates. This proposition requires further elaboration and must be viewed in the context of modernity, which hinders this process but at the same time brought about its awareness.

The Escape Motivation

Recently, means-end theory has been applied to recreation and leisure settings by using the laddering method to investigate activities such as ski destination selection, spring break destination choice, nature park interpretation and marketing for urban tourism what a product is, what it does and what people get from it.

These form the three main elements of focus in means-end theory, starting with the physical, observable *attributes* (the "means"), *consequences* (benefits or costs) that follow from the attributes, which further lead to personal *values* (the "ends"). Means-end theory focuses on why and how product attributes are important. Attributes! Consequence (benefits or costs)! Value different) at either end based on personal values.

Individuals are attracted to a particular destination based on a variety of factors such as one's personal traits and leisure and travel motivation grounded within a broad conceptual push-pull scenario. Leisure and recreation are important motives for amenity migrants.

This model contends that motivation to reside specific to the Bow Valley include a desire to balance a mountain recreation lifestyle with work, to be with a friend or partner, to escape, to purchase a second home, to be in a place suits one's values, to be next to the (aesthetic lifestyle) mountains and to pursue a career in tourism or parks. Factor analysis results revealed two factor components labelled To Live and To Escape. The former included to pursue a career in tourism, hospitality or parks, to start a business, to balance work with a mountain recreation lifestyle and just to be with a friend or partner while the former included to own a second home and to escape.

Lived Experience of Negotiated Leisure. The leisure negotiation process is framed by the human-environment relationship and remains dynamic due to constant evaluations of the one's ability to negotiate aspects of a changing environment with one's personal resources. The lived experience component of the model includes the element of leisure and recreation behaviour. Behaviour is important as it is postulated here that leisure/recreation behaviour imprints the destination through the expression of demand. For example, the persistent behaviour of mountain biking may result in the development of additional mountain trails, a built mountain bike park, or even the banning of mountain biking from certain or all trails.

Likewise, the presence of upper middle class urban dwellers may bring about a perceived demand for up-scale restaurants and cafes. Or the presence of families with children may bring increased demand for traditional recreation facilities such as pools and ice arenas. Recreation behaviour is an expression of demand which is likely to impact supply thereby altering the environment.

Environment: The environment within a high recreation amenity destination can be characterized as having significant natural and cultural resources. It involves a strong social component of community and reference groups. The social element can also include detractions such as crowding, congestion and other forms of conflict such as with recent and long time residents. It also includes structural components such as the economy, housing, roads and health and educational infrastructure which all contribute to the negotiation. Physical, social and structural aspects of the environment are assumed to act both as a facilitator to one's leisure goals, and constraint or stressor at different times. It is also assumed that over time the nature and character of the Environment evolves (dotted line) as the physical and social aspects of the destination evolve.

***Negotiation and Coping Strategies*:** From a leisure and recreation perspective negotiation with one's internal and external constraints is widely understood within the Leisure Constraints model which includes three basic levels of leisure constraint of intra-personal, interpersonal and structural. The Leisure Constraints model is perhaps best suited to understanding what aspect of the internal (personal traits and motivation) and external (physical, social and structural) environments are being negotiated and how. The Recreation Coping model is used to understand the way in which people respond to stressors within a recreation setting.

The Recreation Coping model posits that individuals will respond using one of more of four possible responses to stress within a recreation environment they include two cognitive based responses of rationalization and product shift and two behavioural based responses of displacement and direct action. It is postulated that an individual will begin leisure and recreation negotiations relying on typical leisure constraint negotiations for the selection and pursuit of activities and behaviours. With increased time at the site it is believed that an individual will rely more heavily on recreation coping strategies as various types of stressors persist and complimentary strategies are found. However, it is assumed that despite the shift in emphasis over time both leisure constraint and recreation coping negotiation strategies may be present at any one time.

***Amenity Migrant Typology*:** Resulting from Motivation and the dynamic of the leisure centred human-environment negotiation is a typology of amenity migrants based on the findings of this investigation. The typology is primarily based on the qualitative data analysis and appears in Box A. The typology is a result of different types (what is being negotiated) and levels (intensity) of negotiation within the human environment. Various amenity migrant typologies appear in the literature. Factor analysis results revealed four distinct factor components based on importance of recreation amenities they include; back country, culture, recreation and entertainment.

Amenity Migrant Typology

1. Those who wish to pursue a mountain recreation lifestyle in the Bow Valley rely on it for their livelihood but can not negotiate the costs over the benefits and decide to leave;
2. Those who wish to pursue a mountain recreation lifestyle in the Bow Valley and rely on it for their livelihood but negotiate to overcome the costs for the benefit;

3. Those who live in the Bow Valley to pursue more urban recreation and hospitality & tourism careers within the area;
4. Those who wish to pursue a mountain recreation lifestyle but do not rely on the Bow Valley for their livelihood directly (commute or remote work situations); and
5. Those who wish to escape to the Bow Valley part-time (second home) and do not rely on the valley for their livelihood.

Place Attachment, Dependence, and Identity. The relationship the individual recreationist develops with the place over time can be understood using the concept of place attachment including underlying concepts of place dependence and identity.

Together, as place attachment, it is used to characterize the continuous manifestation of the human-environment negotiation as a relationship with the place. Place attachment, dependence and identity are assumed to be strong predictors of whether an individual will stay or leave a destination. Some will leave and others will remain. Even those who leave the site impact the evolution of the destination as was their behaviour an expression of demand for the tenure of their residency. Those who leave may be seeking other destinations more supportive of their identity, goals and personal resources. Those who remain impact the destination through their behaviour, and in other ways such as policy development, and through on-going, shared discourse that creates a collective understanding of place. Place attachment loops back (dotted line) to motivation as the individual's relationship with the place will be affected by the continuous negotiation process which is assumed to influence one's motivation to engage in future negotiations and in what manner. Place attachment loops back as an antecedent to the continuous negotiation process.

Affect on Destination and Recreation Supply. The final component of the models seeks to provide insight into how the leisure based human-environment relationship physically affects a high recreation amenity destination. It is postulated here that as population increases urban-type recreation supply increases and backcountry (outside of the townsite) generally remains stagnant or decreases. This general pattern has been previously observed. For example Glorioso & Moss (2006) discuss the rapid increase of urban amenities in the Santa Fe region during the 1980s to present in association with amenity migration. Moore, Williams & Gill (2006) report loss of recreation land adjacent to Whistler BC townsite as a result of residential and golf course development coupled with increased urbanization. As the destination evolves including the quantity and quality of urban and recreation supply this will result in an equally evolving image of the destination that will serve to attract different types of individuals.

This is a simple displacement process similar the Plog's (2002) model, however based on tourists, whereby a destination evolves and as it does it attracts 'venturerers' at first then 'dependables' later on. Similarly, early, density-crowding-satisfaction models realized that within any one site varying conditions would attract different groups of people more or less comfortable with crowding conditions. The quantitative survey included a 27-item scale to assess whether residents perceived change in their recreation and structural environment in the form of increases or decreases in urban-type recreation, backcountry recreation, tourism activity, and structural elements such as jobs, housing and cost of living.

Factor analysis on the scale revealed seven factor components in accordance to where most change has been perceived (no particular direction of change) they were labelled as crowding, backcountry, urbane, town, outdoor recreation, and urban. A five-cluster solution revealed that overall some factor components were perceived to have increased and others decreased. More specifically, overall factor components 'crowding' (seven crowding related items) and 'urbane' (four items related to cafes, restaurants, and bars) were perceived to have increased while 'outdoor' (four items related to trails, ski areas, festivals), 'backcountry' (four items related to more remote outdoor activity), was perceived to have decreased while 'town' (five items related to structural aspects and public recreation) has remained about the same.

The quantitative results generally support the final component of the model whereby in-town recreation supply increases while backcountry recreation increases. The results of cluster analysis on one of the four measures contained within the questionnaire. The sub-scale means for each of the clusters, the composite mean for each cluster, a cluster label and the results of the Scheffe test. The scale for Q8 was a six point scale with the final scale item of 'don't know' recoded as missing therefore it is based on a five point scale whereby 1 has increased greatly 3 is has not changed and 5 is has decreased greatly.

An ANOVA was conducted to determine if there were differences among the means of the clusters which yielded value of for each of the subscale items. A post hoc analysis of a Scheffe Test was conducted to determine which clusters are significantly different from which and in what direction. Numerous significant tests (p=.05) were reported with the direction of difference indicated by the arrow. Additionally Classification Results(a) test reported that 97.2% of the originally grouped cases were classified correctly.

Relaxation

How Motivations, Constraints, and Demographic Factors Predict Seniors' Overseas Travel Propensity

As the trend in aging societies is growing all over the world, the travel and tourism market for senior citizens has attracted much attention recently from both practitioners and academics. The market shows great potential, not only because of its considerable population proportion, but also because of senior citizens' great contribution to a tourism economy. It is generally accepted that seniors in developed countries on average possess a relatively large share of discretionary income and time and are still in good health. These characteristics enable them to travel more, and many seniors have the time to travel and are willing to spend a significant amount of their savings on travel. In addition, the travel behaviour of seniors is characterized as travelling more frequently, going longer distances, staying away longer, spending more money, and relying more on travel agents. Hence, senior travellers are important to the tourism industry and will grow in importance as their segment grows in size and wealth. Understanding seniors' travel decision behaviour is a crucial issue to travel marketers who compete for this important market.

The theory of tourism demand states that it is influenced by three major determinants: economic factors, socio-psychological factors, and exogenous factors. The economic factors include per capita income, cost of living, exchange rate, tourism prices, and transportation costs, among others. The social-psychological factors are associated with the decision-making of travellers such as demographic factors, travel motivations, constraints, images of destinations, and travel preferences, among others.

The exogenous factors are associated with the business environment. The psychological determinants of demand in explaining some reasons why tourists travel and select particular destinations. Motivation is defined as the 'driving force behind all behaviour'. From the perspective of the traveller's decision-making process, travel motivations are seen as the energizers of demand that promote an individual to decide on a holiday. Travel behaviour can be predicted by underlying motivations.

Hence, those who are highly motivated might be those who are most likely to overcome constraints and participate in more leisure activities. The concept of travel motivations is based on the existence of "push" and "pull" factors. This has been extensively discussed and is a generally accepted concept. Push motivation refers to an individual's internal energy and an increase in the desire for people to travel, while pull motivation refers to a force external to an individual that influences where people travel, given the initial desire to travel. Ryan (1991) finds that tourist travel motivations could be identified as wish fulfilment, shopping, escaping from a mundane environment, rest and relaxation, an opportunity for play, strengthening family bonds, prestige, social interaction, and educational opportunities.

The most common motivations identified by related research regarding seniors' travel motivation are rest and relaxation, escaping from a mundane environment, social interaction, physical exercise, learning, nostalgia, visiting friends and relatives, and excitement. Shoemaker (1989) notes that among fourteen motivations, rest and relaxation as well as escaping from a mundane environment are the most salient two motivations, while knowing friends of a different gender and playing golf are the least important two motivations for senior travellers in Pennsylvania.

Interestingly, after ten years, Shoemaker (2000) finds that the main motivations of senior travellers shifted to visiting new places and experiencing new things. Regarding seniors' travel motivation, some main classifications can be identified in the literature such as rest/relaxation, social interaction, health, learning, seeking, escaping, attracting, cost, nostalgia and visiting historical sites.

Huang and Tsai (2003) reported that 'Get rest and relaxation' (35.6%) and 'Meet people and socialization' (20.1%) are found as the main travel motivation of Taiwanese seniors. In addition, considering both push and pull dimensions of Taiwanese senior travel motivations, Jang and Wu (2006) found the push motivations include 'ego-enhancement', 'self-esteem', 'knowledge seeking', 'relaxation', and 'socialization' while the pull motivations encompass 'cleanliness and safety', 'facility, event and cost', and 'natural and historical sites'.

6

Integrated Marketing Communications

Integrated Marketing Communications (IMC) is the coordination and integration of all marketing communication tools, avenues, functions and sources within a company into a seamless program that maximizes the impact on consumers and other end users at a minimal cost.

What is IMC?

- Process for managing customer relationships that drive brand value.
- Its foundation is communication
- Cross-functional process for creating and nourishing profitable relationships with customers and other stakeholders by strategically controlling or influencing all messages sent to these groups and encouraging data-driven, purposeful dialog with them.
- Integrated marketing communications (IMC) is the coordination and integration of all marketing communication tools, avenues, and sources within a company into a seamless program that maximizes the impact on consumers and other end users at a minimal cost. This integration affects all firm's business-to-business, marketing channel, customer-focused, and internally directed communications.

IMC Components

- The Foundation-corporate image and brand management; buyer behaviour; promotions opportunity analysis.

- Advertising Tools-advertising management, advertising design: theoretical frameworks and types of appeals; advertising design: message strategies and executional frameworks; advertising media selection. Advertising also reinforces brand and firm image.
- Promotional Tools-trade promotions; consumer promotions; personal selling, database marketing, and customer relations management; public relations and sponsorship programs.
- Integration Tools-Internet Marketing; IMC for small business and entrepreneurial ventures; evaluating and integrated marketing program.

Marketing Mix Component

The Internet has changed the way business is done in the current world. The variables of segmentation, targeting and positioning are addressed differently. The way new products and services are marketed have changed even though the aim of business in bringing economic and social values remain unchanged. Indeed, the bottom line of increasing revenue and profit are still the same. Marketing has evolved to more of connectedness, due to the new characteristics brought in by the Internet. Marketing was once seen as a one way, with firms broadcasting their offerings and value proposition. Now it is seen more and more as a conversation between marketers and customers.

Marketing efforts incorporate the "marketing mix". Promotion is one element of marketing mix. Promotional activities include advertising (by using different media), sales promotion (sales and trades promotion), and personal selling activities. It also includes Internet marketing, sponsorship marketing, direct marketing, database marketing and public relations. Integration of all these promotional tools, along with other components of marketing mix, is a way to gain an edge over a competitor.

The starting point of the IMC process is the marketing mix that includes different types of marketing, advertising, and sales efforts. Without a complete IMC plan there is no integration or harmony between client and customers. The goal of an organization is to create and maintain communication throughout its own employees and throughout its customers.

Integrated marketing is based on a master marketing plan. This plan should coordinate efforts in all components of the marketing mix. A marketing plan consists on the following steps:

1. Situation analysis
2. Marketing objectives
3. Marketing budget.

Integrated marketing communications aims to ensure consistency of message and the complementary use of media. The concept includes online and offline marketing channels. Online marketing channels include any e-marketing campaigns or programs, from search engine optimization (SEO), pay-per-click, affiliate, email, banner to latest web related channels for webinar, blog, micro-blogging, RSS, podcast, Internet Radio, and Internet TV. Offline marketing channels are traditional print (newspaper, magazine), mail order, public relations, industry relations, billboard, traditional radio, and television. A company develops its integrated marketing communication programmer using all the elements of the marketing mix (product, price, place, and promotion). Integrated marketing communications plans are vital to achieving success. The reasons for their importance begin with the explosion of information technologies. Channel power has shifted from manufacturers to retailers to consumers.

Using outside-in thinking, Integrated Marketing Communications is a data-driven approach that focuses on identifying consumer insights and developing a strategy with the right (online and offline combination) channels to forge a stronger brand-consumer relationship. This involves knowing the right touch points to use to reach consumers and understanding how and where they consume different types of media. Regression analysis and customer lifetime value are key data elements in this approach.

Importance of IMC

Several shifts in the advertising and media industry have caused IMC to develop into a primary strategy for marketers:

1. From media advertising to multiple forms of communication.
2. From mass media to more specialized (niche) media, which are centered on specific target audiences.
3. From a manufacturer-dominated market to a retailer-dominated, consumer-controlled market.
4. From general-focus advertising and marketing to data-based marketing.
5. From low agency accountability to greater agency accountability, particularly in advertising.

6. From traditional compensation to performance-based compensation (increased sales or benefits to the company).
7. From limited Internet access to 24/7 Internet availability and access to goods and services.

4 P's vs. 4 C's

- Not PRODUCT, but CONSUMER.

You have to understand what the consumer's wants and needs are. Times have changed and you can no longer sell whatever you can make. The product characteristics have to match the specifics of what someone wants to buy. And part of what the consumer is buying is the personal "buying experience."

- Not PRICE, but COST.

Understand the consumer's cost to satisfy the want or need. The product price may be only one part of the consumer's cost structure. Often it is the cost of time to drive somewhere, the cost of conscience of what you buy, the cost of guilt for not treating the kids, etc.

- Not PLACE, but CONVENIENCE.

As above, turn the standard logic around. Think convenience of the buying experience and then relate that to a delivery mechanism. Consider all possible definitions of "convenience" as it relates to satisfying the consumer's wants and needs. Convenience may include aspects of the physical or virtual location, access ease, transaction service time, and hours of availability.

- Not PROMOTION, but COMMUNICATION.

Communicate, communicate, and communicate. Many mediums working together to present a unified message with a feedback mechanism to make the communication two-way. And be sure to include an understanding of non-traditional mediums, such as word of mouth and how it can influence your position in the consumer's mind. How many ways can a customer hear the same message through the course of the day, each message reinforcing the earlier images?

Effective Communications Elements

The goal of selecting the elements of proposed integrated marketing communications is to create a campaign that is effective and consistent across media platforms. Some marketers may want only ads with greatest breadth of appeal: the executions that, when combined, provide the greatest number of attention-getting, branded, and motivational moments. Others may only want ads with the greatest depth of appeal: the ads with the greatest number of attention-getting, branded, and motivational points within each.

Although integrated marketing communications is more than just an advertising campaign, the bulk of marketing dollars is spent on the creation and distribution of advertisements. Hence, the bulk of the research budget is also spent on these elements of the campaign. Once the key marketing pieces have been tested, the researched elements can then be applied to other contact points: letterhead, packaging, logistics, customer service training, and more, to complete the IMC cycle.

One common type of integrated marketing communication is personal selling. Personal selling can be defined as "face to face selling in which a seller attempts to persuade a buyer to make a purchase."

Promotions Opportunity Analysis

A major task that guides the way in creating an effective Integrated Marketing Communications plan is the promotions opportunity analysis. "A promotions opportunity analysis is the process marketers use to identify target audiences for a company's goods and services and the communication strategies needed to reach these audiences." A message sent by a marketer has a greater likelihood of achieving the intended results if the marketer has performed a good analysis and possesses accurate information pertaining to the target audience. There are five steps in developing a promotions opportunity analysis:

Conduct a communication market analysis;

- Competitors
- Opportunities
- Target markets
- Customers
- Product positioning.

Establish communication objectives;

- Develop brand awareness
- Increase category demand
- Change customer belief or attitude
- Enhance purchase actions
- Encourage repeat purchases
- Build customer traffic
- Enhance firm image

- Increase market share
- Increase sales
- Reinforce purchase decisions.

Create communications budget Several factors influence the relationship between expenditures on promotions and sales:

- The goal of the promotion
- Threshold effects
- Carryover effects
- Wear-out effects
- Decay effects
- Random events.

Prepare Promotional Strategies

Match Tactics with Strategies: Throughout these steps, marketers should consistently review and analyse the actions and tools that major competitors are utilizing.

Marketing Effectiveness

Marketing effectiveness is the quality of how marketers go to market with the goal of optimizing their spending to achieve good results for both the short-term and long-term.

It is also related to Marketing ROI and Return on Marketing Investment (ROMI).

Marketing effectiveness has four dimensions:

- Corporate – Each company operates within different bounds. These are determined by their size, their budget and their ability to make organizational change. Within these bounds marketers operate along the five factors described below.
- Competitive – Each company in a category operates within a similar framework as described below. In an ideal world, marketers would have perfect information on how they act as well as how their competitors act. In reality, in many categories have reasonably good information through sources, such as, IRI or Nielsen. In many industries, competitive marketing information is hard to come by.
- Customers/Consumers – Understanding and taking advantage of how customers make purchasing decisions can help marketers improve their marketing effectiveness. Groups of consumers

act in similar ways leading to the need to segment them. Based on these segments, they make choices based on how they value the attributes of a product and the brand, in return for price paid for the product. Consumers build brand value through information. Information is received through many sources, such as, advertising, word-of-mouth and in the (distribution) channel often characterized with the purchase funnel, a McKinsey & Company concept. Lastly, consumers consume and make purchase decisions in certain ways.

- Exogenous Factors – There are many factors outside of our immediate control that can impact the effectiveness of our marketing activities. These can include the weather, interest rates, government regulations and many others. Understanding the impact these factors can have on our consumers can help us to design programs that can take advantage of these factors or mitigate the risk of these factors if they take place in the middle of our marketing campaigns.

There are five factors driving the level of marketing effectiveness that marketers can achieve:

1. Marketing Strategy – Improving marketing effectiveness can be achieved by employing a superior marketing strategy. By positioning the product or brand correctly, the product/brand will be more successful in the market than competitors' products/brands. Even with the best strategy, marketers must execute their programs properly to achieve extraordinary results.
2. Marketing Creative – Even without a change in strategy, better creative can improve results. Without a change in strategy, AFLAC was able to achieve stunning results with its introduction of the Duck (AFLAC) campaign. With the introduction of this new creative concept, the company growth rate soared from 12% prior to the campaign to 28% following it.
3. Marketing Execution – By improving how marketers go to market, they can achieve significantly greater results without changing their strategy or their creative execution. At the marketing mix level, marketers can improve their execution by making small changes in any or all of the 4-Ps (Product, Price, Place and Promotion) (Marketing) without making changes to the strategic position or the creative execution

marketers can improve their effectiveness and deliver increased revenue. At the program level marketers can improve their effectiveness by managing and executing each of their marketing campaigns better. It's commonly known that consistency of a Marketing Creative strategy across various media (e.g. TV, Radio, Print and Online), not just within each individual media message, can amplify and enhance impact of the overall marketing campaign effort. Additional examples would be improving direct mail through a better call-to-action or editing web site content to improve its organic search results, marketers can improve their marketing effectiveness for each type of program. A growing area of interest within (Marketing Strategy) and Execution are the more recent interaction dynamics of traditional marketing (e.g. TV or Events) with online consumer activity (e.g. Social Media). Not only direct product experience, but also any stimulus provided by traditional marketing, can become a catalyst for a consumer brand "groundswell" online as outlined in the book Groundswell.

4. Marketing Infrastructure (also known as Marketing Management) – Improving the business of marketing can lead to significant gains for the company. Management of agencies, budgeting, motivation and coordination of marketing activities can lead to improved competitiveness and improved results. The overall accountability for brand leadership and business results is often reflected in an organization under a title within a (Brand management) department.
5. Exogenous Factors-Generally out of the control of marketers, external or exogenous factors also influence how marketers can improve their results. Taking advantage of seasonality, interests or the regulatory environment can help marketers improve their marketing effectiveness.

Return on Marketing Investment

Return on Marketing Investment (ROMI) and Marketing ROI are defined as the optimization of marketing spend for the short and long term in support of the brand strategy by building a market model using valid, objective marketing metrics.

Improving ROMI leads to improved marketing effectiveness, increased revenue, profit and market share for the same amount of marketing spend.

Metrics

There are two forms of the Return on Marketing Investment (ROMI) metric.

- short term ROMI
- long term ROMI.

Short Term

The first, short term ROMI, is also used as a simple index measuring the dollars of revenue (or market share, contribution margin or other desired outputs) for every dollar of marketing spend.

For example, if a company spends $100,000 on a direct mail piece and it delivers $500,000 in incremental revenue then the ROMI factor is 5.0. If the incremental contribution margin for that $500,000 in revenue is 60%, then the margin ROMI (the amount of incremental margin for each dollar of marketing spent is 3.0 (= 5.0 x 60%).

The value of the first ROMI is in its simplicity. In most cases a simple determination of revenue per dollar spent for each marketing activity can be sufficient enough to help make important decisions to improve the entire marketing mix.

Long Term

In a similar way the second ROMI concept, long term ROMI, can be used to determine other less tangible aspects of marketing effectiveness. For example, ROMI could be used to determine the incremental value of marketing as it pertains to increased brand awareness, consideration or purchase intent. In this way both the longer term value of marketing activities (incremental brand awareness, etc.) and the shorter term revenue and profit can be determined. This is a sophisticated metric that balances marketing and business analytics and is used increasingly by many of the world's leading organizations (Hewlett-Packard and Procter & Gamble to name two) to measure the economic (that is, cash-flow derived) benefits created by marketing investments. For many other organizations, this method offers a way to prioritize investments and allocate marketing and other resources on a formalized basis.

Criticism and Defence of Marketing Effectiveness

Direct measures of the short term variant of ROMI are often criticized as only including the direct impact of marketing activities without including the long-term brand building value of any communication inserted into the market.

Short term ROMI is best employed as a tool to determine marketing effectiveness to help steer investments from less productive activities to those that are more productive. It is a simple tool to gauge the success of measurable marketing activities against various marketing objectives (e.g., incremental revenue, brand awareness or brand equity). With this knowledge, marketing investments can be redirected away from under-performing activities to better performing marketing media.

Long term ROMI is often criticized as a 'silo-in-the-making"-it is intensively data driven and creates a challenge for firms that are not used to working business analytics into the marketing analytics that typically determine resource allocation decisions. Long term ROMI, however, is a sophisticated measure used by a number of forward thinking firms interested in getting to the bottom of value for money challenges often posed by competing brand managers.

Marketing Research Association

Founded in 1957, the Marketing Research Association, Inc. is one of the largest trade associations of market research and polling professionals. MRA has more than 3,000 members worldwide, representing all segments of the research industry. MRA advances, protects and promotes knowledge, standards, excellence, ethics, professional development and innovation for the global market and opinion research profession.

MRA Activities

MRA is in the information business, providing members with information through:

- Educational Programs: Webinars, Education-on-Demand, and a comprehensive Research Library
- Training
- Networking Opportunities
- Publications: *Alert!* magazine (monthly) and bi-weekly e-newsletter *eNews*
- Conferences: MRA's Annual Conference and MRA's First Outlook Conference.

MRA publishes the annual Blue Book Research Services Directory, which is used extensively by market research and opinion polling firms.

The Blue Book is the market research industry's most comprehensive and easy-to-use reference guide, listing thousands of experienced professionals in marketing research and related fields. The Blue Book comes out annually in February, so the information it contains is always current.

MRA also offers researchers the Professional Research Certification (PRC). PRC was developed as a powerful tool for researchers of all levels of work experience and education. Researchers who earn the prestigious PRC designation have established an objective measure of their knowledge and proficiency. Additionally, professionals with PRC are expected to increase consumer understanding of research and foster exceptional professional standards in the market research industry.

Marketing Research Mix

The term Marketing research mix (or the "Mr. Mix") was created in 2004 and published in 2007. It was designed as a framework to assist researchers to design or evaluate marketing research studies. The name was deliberately chosen to be similar to the Marketing Mix-it also has four Ps. Unlike the marketing mix these elements are sequential and they match the main phases that need to be followed. These four Ps are: Purpose; Population; Procedure and Publication.

Purpose

The purpose of the research is the reason why it is being done. The word "purpose" is useful because it has a wide coverage. It can be specifically defined or it can be loosely explained. The wide term also embraces studies to gather marketing intelligence, where the manager's role is to scan the environment for useful data, and there may be no specific objective.

Many marketers avoid the term hypothesis entirely and tend to use the words "research objective" or "aim". The word hypothesis (plural, hypotheses) is quite different from the terms mentioned above. It is an essential starting point for quantitative researchers, but takes a lesser role for qualitative researchers. The term is deeply rooted in the history of scientific thought. In statistics we expend much time and energy to generate hypotheses, to test hypotheses, and to reject them. Some people argue that we should only test one hypothesis; others say we should test several. In hypothesis testing we create a statement, which may be true or false, this statement is a "proposition"-we propose that something may be the case. If it is right then we accept it. If it is not right, if it is "wrong" then we reject it.

The first step is to formulate the null-hypothesis, abbreviated to Ho. This is usually intended to be rejected. Another carefully constructed hypothesis is the alternative hypothesis or the H1; this is actually called the 'research hypothesis'. After these have been articulated the researcher can design a research programme to test the hypotheses.

When the results are received, they are examined against the prediction of the null hypothesis. The basic idea is to use this possible explanation and then look for data to support the explanation (or not). It is best to spend as much time as possible on the hypothesis: it is the research question, and it determines how the study is carried out. It determines the design because it defines the problem.

The subject of hypothesis testing has been debated heavily for many years and there are suggestions that misuse of null hypothesis significance testing is widespread and damaging (Finch et al. 2001), at least in psychological research. It is relevant to cite an article on hypothesis testing in marketing research by Lawrence (1982) who tells us: "Practical survey researchers (realise) that, in many cases, no adequate theory exists for setting up hypotheses in advance". The article continues: "Drawing one-off hypotheses out of the air offers no solution to the problem. Researchers will be guided by their own ideas, experiences, hunches".

Population

When considering any market sector we need to ask "Who is involved in this marketplace?" Who are the players? Who should be the centre of the investigation and where are those subjects? This area considers the target audience, customer or player; the users or non-users. Who will become the respondent or informant? Should we contact all players or just some of them? Should we carry out a census or a sample: should respondents be selected by probability or non-probability methods? An important concept for primary research is sampling. We choose to interview or observe people who we think will give us the information that will solve our problems. So in choosing our research method, we need to consider whom we select and how we select.

This applies to qualitative research, with only a few people, and quantitative research with many people. Much emphasis in marketing research is on the end user, but "experts" can bridge the gap between primary and secondary data. An expert may be someone who has been in the business for many years. This part of the Mr. Mix involves identifying relevant sampling frames.

Procedure

When considering the procedure the key question is "How should the study be conducted?" Will it be qualitative or quantitative? This area also covers the question of timing: when will the fieldwork take place?

The best research starts by looking at secondary data, this information already exists. The two basic sources: internal (within an organisation) and external, published by someone outside have become easier to access in recent years. Information Technology, with Intranets and the Internet, has improved our ability to find such data. If secondary data doesn't solve the problem then original data (primary data) is sought. It is useful to think of different primary methods in these terms: we can ask people what they are doing; we can watch them or detect what they have done by counting or we can manipulate some variables to discover the effect. This creates three categories: questioning; observation and experimentation.

Primary data collection techniques can be subdivided into: interviewer-administered or respondent-administered; direct or indirect; personal or impersonal. Processing data, analysis and interpretation are essential parts of the procedure. Detailed examination of the appropriate tools used in the data collection needs to take place.

Publication

Under the heading of "Publication" the key questions are: Who is the audience for the results? What should be communicated? When and how should they be communicated? Research is of no use if findings are kept within the research team; similarly commercially sensitive information will have no competitive advantage if placed in the public domain. Choices need to be made on how publication takes place. Will a written report be created? Will tabulations be provided? Will a personal presentation take place? Who should be allowed sight of the results?

There are many different readers of research reports and these audiences all have very different expectations. Reporting must be personalised, writing and presentation style must be customised and adapted to the user. At one extreme there is the general public. There are many reasons why research is reported to the "mass consumer".

It may be a government report that has been commissioned to be in the public interest: concerning health, welfare, transport and so on. It may be a consumer report: consumer watchdog reports are of great interest to the man on the street, so we find the Which? Magazine and similar bodies have enabled the layman appreciate survey findings.

Editors of periodicals regularly commission research for editorial reasons, so the results may become part of an article for mass consumption. The research agency may report directly to the public on web pages, by email or by post, this is because it is now common to offer a short summary report to a respondent as a gesture of goodwill, an incentive, a thank you for co-operating in the research. Research findings may appear as part of a promotional campaign, appealing to the consumer's need to know that indeed this is a best seller ("nine out of ten cat-owners prefer...").

Then there are smaller audiences such as managers who are anxious to receive a report in order to make instant decisions. Additionally there are managers who will benefit from the information much later when the report is consulted as secondary data in the future.

Mystery Shopping

Mystery shopping or a mystery consumer is a tool used by Mystery Shopping Providers and market research companies to measure quality of retail service or gather specific information about products and services. Mystery Shopping should be performed by a person, so called Mystery Shopper, who is unknown to the establishment she/he is evaluating.

Mystery shoppers posing as normal customers perform specific tasks—such as purchasing a product, asking questions, registering complaints or behaving in a certain way—and then provide detailed reports or feedback about their experiences. Mystery shopping was standard practice by the early 1940s as a way to measure employee integrity.

Tools used for mystery shopping assessments range from simple questionnaires to complete audio and video recordings. Mystery shopping can be used in any industry, with the most common venues being retail stores, hotels, movie theatres, restaurants, fast food chains, banks, gas stations, car dealerships, apartments, health clubs and health care facilities. In the UK mystery shopping is increasingly used to provide feedback on customer services provided by local authorities, and other non-profit organizations such as housing associations and churches.

Methodology

When a client company hires a company providing mystery shopping services, a survey model will be drawn up and agreed to which defines what information and improvement factors the client company wishes to measure. These are then drawn up into survey instruments and assignments that are allocated to shoppers registered with the mystery shopping company.

The details and information points shoppers take note of typically include:

- number of employees in the store on entering
- how long it takes before the mystery shopper is greeted
- the name of the employees
- whether or not the greeting is friendly, ideally according to objective measures
- the questions asked by the shopper to find a suitable product
- the types of products shown
- the sales arguments used by the employee
- whether or how the employee attempted to close the sale
- whether the employee suggested any add-on sales
- whether the employee invited the shopper to come back to the store
- cleanliness of store and store associates
- speed of service
- compliance with company standards relating to service, store appearance, and grooming/presentation.

Shoppers are often given instructions or procedures to make the transaction atypical to make the test of the knowledge and service skills of the employees more stringent or specific to a particular service issue (known as scenarios). For instance, mystery shoppers at a restaurant may pretend they are lactose-intolerant, or a clothing store mystery shopper could inquire about gift-wrapping services. Not all mystery shopping scenarios include a purchase. While gathering information, shoppers usually blend in to the store being evaluated as regular shoppers. They may sometimes be required to take photographs or measurements, return purchases, or count the number of products, seats, people during the visit. A timer or a stopwatch may be required. In some states in the USA, mystery shoppers must also be licensed as private investigators in order to perform some of the tasks.

After the visit the shopper submits the data collected to the mystery shopping company, which reviews and analyses the information, completing quantitative or qualitative statistical [analysis] reports on the data for the client company. This enables measurement against the previously defined criteria.

Statistics

The mystery shopping industry had an estimated value of nearly $600 million in the United States in 2004, according to a 2005 report commissioned by the Mystery Shopping Providers Association (MSPA). Companies that participated in the report experienced an average growth of 11.1 percent from 2003 to 2004, compared to an average growth of 12.2 percent. The report estimates more than 8.1 million mystery shops were conducted in 2004. The report represents the first industry association attempt to quantify the size of the mystery shopping industry. Similar surveys are available for European regions where mystery shopping is becoming more embedded into company procedures. As a measure of its importance, customer/patient satisfaction is being incorporated more frequently into executive pay. A study by a U.S. firm found more than 55% of hospital chief executive officers surveyed in 2005 had "some compensation at risk," based on patient satisfaction, up from only 8% to 20% a dozen years ago."

CBC Television's news magazine program Marketplace *ran a segment on this topic during a January 2001 episode.*

Ethics

The Trade Organization for Mystery Shopping Providers, MSPA has defined a Code of Professional Standards and Ethics Agreement for Mystery Shopping Providers and for Mystery Shoppers. MSPA has also defined Standards for Mystery Shopping. The Standard is available in a full version and an Abstract version. The Abstract is available in 32 languages. Other organizations that have defined standards for Mystery Shopping are; ESOMAR, MRS and MRA.

USA

In June 2008 the American Medical Association's Council on Ethical and Judicial Affairs released a recommendation on the use of "secret shopper patients". The Recommendation: "Physicians have an ethical responsibility to engage in activities that contribute to continual improvements in patient care. One method for promoting such quality improvement is through the use of secret shopper 'patients' who have been appropriately trained to provide feedback about physician performance in the clinical setting." The most widely used set of professional guidelines and ethics standards for the Market Research industry is ISO 20252 ratified in 2006.

Scams

There is a fraudulent confidence trick (a form of advance fee fraud) perpetrated on people in several countries who wish to be mystery shoppers. A person is sent a money order, often from Western Union, or check for a larger sum than a mystery purchase they are required to make, with a request to deposit it into their bank account, use a portion for a mystery purchase and their fee, and wire the remainder through a wire transfer company such as Western Union or MoneyGram; the money is to be wired immediately as response time is being evaluated. The check is fraudulent, and is returned unpaid by the victim's bank, after the money has been wired. One scam involved fraudulent websites using a misspelled URL to advertise online and in newspapers under a legitimate company's name.

Valid mystery shopping companies do not normally send their clients a check prior to work being completed, and their advertisements usually include a contact person and phone number. Some fraudulent checks can be identified by a financial professional. On February 3, 2009 The Internet Crime Complaint Center issued a warning on this scam. A legitimate company that occasionally sends prepayment for large transactions says "We do occasionally fund upfront for very large spend purchases but we use cheques or direct bank transfers which should mean you can see when they are cleared and so can be sure you really do have the money."

European Society for Opinion and Marketing Research

The European Society for Opinion and Market Research (ESOMAR) is the world association for market, social and opinion researchers.

Founded in 1948, ESOMAR began as a regional association within Europe. Currently, with more than 5000 individual members in over 120 countries, ESOMAR's global membership brings together professionals in market and opinion research, marketing, advertising, business, public affairs and media from across the world. ESOMAR currently does not offer corporate membership. ESOMAR's mission is to be the essential organisation for encouraging, advancing and elevating market research worldwide. It's stated goal is to promote the highest standards in market research for improving decision making in the public and private sectors, by :

- safeguarding the interests of the Market, Social and Opinion Research industries globally
- improving and promote international best practice
- promoting the value of the industry to commerce and society.

ESOMAR, in collaboration with the International Chamber of Commerce, has established a world-wide code of ethical practice, the ICC/ESOMAR International Code on Market and Social Research, for its members and actively advocates self-regulation by promoting industry standards. All individual members agree to abide by these standards and codes of ethical practice while conducting market research. Additionally, the code has been adopted or endorsed by the major national professional bodies around the world.

Observational Techniques

In marketing and the social sciences, observational research (or field research) is a social research technique that involves the direct observation of phenomena in their natural setting. This differentiates it from experimental research in which a quasi-artificial environment is created to control for spurious factors, and where at least one of the variables is manipulated as part of the experiment.

Observational Techniques in Context

Compared with quantitative research and experimental research, observational research tends to be less reliable but often more valid. The main advantage of observational research is flexibility. The researchers can change their approach as needed. Also it measures behaviour directly, not reports of behaviour or intentions. The main disadvantage is it is limited to behavioural variables. It cannot be used to study cognitive or affective variables. Another disadvantage is that observational data is not usually generalizable.

Three Approaches

Generally, there are three types of observational research:

- Covert observational research-The researchers do not identify themselves. Either they mix in with the subjects undetected, or they observe from a distance. The advantages of this approach are: (1) It is not necessary to get the subjects' cooperation, and (2) The subjects' behaviour will not be contaminated by the presence of the researcher. Some researchers have ethical misgivings with the deceit involved in this approach.

- Overt observational research-The researchers identify themselves as researchers and explain the purpose of their observations. The problem with this approach is subjects may modify their behaviour when they know they are being watched. They portray their "ideal self" rather than their true self. The advantage that the overt approach has over the covert approach is that there is no deception.
- Researcher Participation-The researcher participates in what they are observing so as to get a finer appreciation of the phenomena. Researchers that participate tend to lose their objectivity.

7

Predictive Analytics

Predictive analytics encompasses a variety of techniques from statistics, data mining and game theory that analyse current and historical facts to make predictions about future events. In business, predictive models exploit patterns found in historical and transactional data to identify risks and opportunities. Models capture relationships among many factors to allow assessment of risk or potential associated with a particular set of conditions, guiding decision making for candidate transactions.

Predictive analytics is used in actuarial science, financial services, insurance, telecommunications, retail, travel, healthcare, pharmaceuticals and other fields. One of the most well-known applications is credit scoring, which is used throughout financial services. Scoring models process a customer's credit history, loan application, customer data, etc., in order to rank-order individuals by their likelihood of making future credit payments on time. A well-known example would be the FICO Score.

Definition

Predictive analytics is an area of statistical analysis that deals with extracting information from data and using it to predict future trends and behaviour patterns. The core of predictive analytics relies on capturing relationships between explanatory variables and the predicted variables from past occurrences, and exploiting it to predict future outcomes. It is important to note, however, that the accuracy and usability of results will depend greatly on the level of data analysis and the quality of assumptions.

Types

Generally, the term predictive analytics is used to mean predictive modelling, scoring of predictive models, and forecasting. However, people are increasingly using the term to describe related analytical disciplines, such as descriptive modelling and decision modelling or optimization. These disciplines also involve rigorous data analysis, and are widely used in business for segmentation and decision making, but have different purposes and the statistical techniques underlying them vary.

Predictive Models

Predictive models analyse past performance to assess how likely a customer is to exhibit a specific behaviour in the future in order to improve marketing effectiveness. This category also encompasses models that seek out subtle data patterns to answer questions about customer performance, such as fraud detection models.

Predictive models often perform calculations during live transactions, for example, to evaluate the risk or opportunity of a given customer or transaction, in order to guide a decision. With advancement in computing speed, individual agent modelling systems can simulate human behaviour or reaction to given stimuli or scenarios. The new term for animating data specifically linked to an individual in a simulated environment is avatar analytics.

Descriptive Models

Descriptive models quantify relationships in data in a way that is often used to classify customers or prospects into groups. Unlike predictive models that focus on predicting a single customer behaviour (such as credit risk), descriptive models identify many different relationships between customers or products. Descriptive models do not rank-order customers by their likelihood of taking a particular action the way predictive models do. Descriptive models can be used, for example, to categorize customers by their product preferences and life stage. Descriptive modelling tools can be utilized to develop further models that can simulate large number of individualized agents and make predictions.

Decision Models

Decision models describe the relationship between all the elements of a decision — the known data (including results of predictive models), the decision and the forecast results of the decision — in order to predict the results of decisions involving many variables. These models can be used in optimization, maximizing certain outcomes while minimizing others. Decision models are generally used to develop decision logic or a set of business rules that will produce the desired action for every customer or circumstance.

Applications

Although predictive analytics can be put to use in many applications, we outline a few examples where predictive analytics has shown positive impact in recent years.

Analytical Customer Relationship Management (CRM)

Analytical Customer Relationship Management is a frequent commercial application of Predictive Analysis. Methods of predictive analysis are applied to customer data to pursue CRM objectives.

Clinical Decision Support Systems

Experts use predictive analysis in health care primarily to determine which patients are at risk of developing certain conditions, like diabetes, asthma, heart disease and other lifetime illnesses. Additionally, sophisticated clinical decision support systems incorporate predictive analytics to support medical decision making at the point of care. A working definition has been proposed by Dr. Robert Hayward of the Centre for Health Evidence: "Clinical Decision Support systems link health observations with health knowledge to influence health choices by clinicians for improved health care."

Collection Analytics

Every portfolio has a set of delinquent customers who do not make their payments on time. The financial institution has to undertake collection activities on these customers to recover the amounts due. A lot of collection resources are wasted on customers who are difficult or impossible to recover. Predictive analytics can help optimize the allocation of collection resources by identifying the most effective collection agencies, contact strategies, legal actions and other strategies to each customer, thus significantly increasing recovery at the same time reducing collection costs.

Cross-sell

Often corporate organizations collect and maintain abundant data (e.g. customer records, sale transactions) and exploiting hidden relationships in the data can provide a competitive advantage to the organization. For an organization that offers multiple products, an analysis of existing customer behaviour can lead to efficient cross sell of products. This directly leads to higher profitability per customer and strengthening of the customer relationship. Predictive analytics can help analyse customers' spending, usage and other behaviour, and help cross-sell the right product at the right time.

Customer Retention

With the amount of competing services available, businesses need to focus efforts on maintaining continuous consumer satisfaction. In such a competitive scenario, consumer loyalty needs to be rewarded and customer attrition needs to be minimized. Businesses tend to respond to customer attrition on a reactive basis, acting only after the customer has initiated the process to terminate service. At this stage, the chance of changing the customer's decision is almost impossible.

Proper application of predictive analytics can lead to a more proactive retention strategy. By a frequent examination of a customer's past service usage, service performance, spending and other behaviour patterns, predictive models can determine the likelihood of a customer wanting to terminate service sometime in the near future.

An intervention with lucrative offers can increase the chance of retaining the customer. Silent attrition is the behaviour of a customer to slowly but steadily reduce usage and is another problem faced by many companies. Predictive analytics can also predict this behaviour accurately and before it occurs, so that the company can take proper actions to increase customer activity.

Direct Marketing

When marketing consumer products and services there is the challenge of keeping up with competing products and consumer behaviour. Apart from identifying prospects, predictive analytics can also help to identify the most effective combination of product versions, marketing material, communication channels and timing that should be used to target a given consumer. The goal of predictive analytics is typically to lower the cost per order or cost per action.

Fraud Detection

Fraud is a big problem for many businesses and can be of various types. Inaccurate credit applications, fraudulent transactions (both offline and online), identity thefts and false insurance claims are some examples of this problem. These problems plague firms all across the spectrum and some examples of likely victims are credit card issuers, insurance companies, retail merchants, manufacturers, business to business suppliers and even services providers. This is an area where a predictive model is often used to help weed out the "bads" and reduce a business's exposure to fraud.

Predictive modelling can also be used to detect financial statement fraud in companies, allowing auditors to gauge a company's relative risk, and to increase substantive audit procedures as needed.

The Internal Revenue Service (IRS) of the United States also uses predictive analytics to try to locate tax fraud.

Portfolio, Product or Economy Level Prediction

Often the focus of analysis is not the consumer but the product, portfolio, firm, industry or even the economy. For example a retailer might be interested in predicting store level demand for inventory management purposes. Or the Federal Reserve Board might be interested in predicting the unemployment rate for the next year. These type of problems can be addressed by predictive analytics using Time Series techniques.

Underwriting

Many businesses have to account for risk exposure due to their different services and determine the cost needed to cover the risk. For example, auto insurance providers need to accurately determine the amount of premium to charge to cover each automobile and driver. A financial company needs to assess a borrower's potential and ability to pay before granting a loan. For a health insurance provider, predictive analytics can analyse a few years of past medical claims data, as well as lab, pharmacy and other records where available, to predict how expensive an enrollee is likely to be in the future. Predictive analytics can help underwriting of these quantities by predicting the chances of illness, default, bankruptcy, etc. Predictive analytics can streamline the process of customer acquisition, by predicting the future risk behaviour of a customer using application level data. Predictive analytics in the form of credit scores have reduced the amount of time it takes for loan approvals, especially in the mortgage market where lending decisions are now made in a matter of hours rather than days or even weeks. Proper predictive analytics can lead to proper pricing decisions, which can help mitigate future risk of default.

Statistical Techniques

The approaches and techniques used to conduct predictive analytics can broadly be grouped into regression techniques and machine learning techniques.

Regression Techniques

Regression models are the mainstay of predictive analytics. The focus lies on establishing a mathematical equation as a model to represent the interactions between the different variables in consideration. Depending on the situation, there is a wide variety of models that can be applied while performing predictive analytics. Some of them are briefly discussed below.

Linear Regression Model

The linear regression model analyses the relationship between the response or dependent variable and a set of independent or predictor variables. This relationship is expressed as an equation that predicts the response variable as a linear function of the parameters. These parameters are adjusted so that a measure of fit is optimized. Much of the effort in model fitting is focused on minimizing the size of the residual, as well as ensuring that it is randomly distributed with respect to the model predictions. The goal of regression is to select the parameters of the model so as to minimize the sum of the squared residuals. This is referred to as ordinary least squares (OLS) estimation and results in best linear unbiased estimates (BLUE) of the parameters if and only if the Gauss-Markov assumptions are satisfied.

Once the model has been estimated we would be interested to know if the predictor variables belong in the model – i.e. is the estimate of each variable's contribution reliable? To do this we can check the statistical significance of the model's coefficients which can be measured using the t-statistic. This amounts to testing whether the coefficient is significantly different from zero.

How well the model predicts the dependent variable based on the value of the independent variables can be assessed by using the R^2 statistic. It measures predictive power of the model i.e. the proportion of the total variation in the dependent variable that is "explained" (accounted for) by variation in the independent variables.

Discrete Choice Models

Multivariate regression (above) is generally used when the response variable is continuous and has an unbounded range. Often the response variable may not be continuous but rather discrete. While mathematically it is feasible to apply multivariate regression to discrete ordered dependent variables, some of the assumptions behind the theory of multivariate linear regression no longer hold, and there are other techniques such as discrete choice models which are better suited for this type of analysis. If the dependent variable is discrete, some of those superior methods are logistic regression, multinomial logit and probit models. Logistic regression and probit models are used when the dependent variable is binary.

Logistic Regression

In a classification setting, assigning outcome probabilities to observations can be achieved through the use of a logistic model, which is basically a method which transforms information about the binary dependent variable into an unbounded continuous variable and estimates a regular multivariate model. The Wald and likelihood-ratio test are used to test the statistical significance of each coefficient b in the model. A test assessing the goodness-of-fit of a classification model is the:

Multinomial Logistic Regression

An extension of the binary logit model to cases where the dependent variable has more than 2 categories is the multinomial logit model. In such cases collapsing the data into two categories might not make good sense or may lead to loss in the richness of the data. The multinomial logit model is the appropriate technique in these cases, especially when the dependent variable categories are not ordered (for examples colors like red, blue, green). Some authors have extended multinomial regression to include feature selection/importance methods such as Random multinomial logit.

Probit Regression

Probit models offer an alternative to logistic regression for modelling categorical dependent variables. Even though the outcomes tend to be similar, the underlying distributions are different. Probit models are popular in social sciences like economics.

A good way to understand the key difference between probit and logit models, is to assume that there is a latent variable z. We do not observe z but instead observe y which takes the value 0 or 1. In the logit model we assume that y follows a logistic distribution. In the probit model we assume that y follows a standard normal distribution. Note that in social sciences (example economics), probit is often used to model situations where the observed variable y is continuous but takes values between 0 and 1.

Logit Versus Probit

The Probit model has been around longer than the logit model. They look identical, except that the logistic distribution tends to be a little flat tailed. One of the reasons the logit model was formulated was that the probit model was difficult to compute because it involved calculating difficult integrals. Modern computing however has made this computation fairly simple. The coefficients obtained from the logit and probit model are also fairly close. However, the odds ratio makes the logit model easier to interpret. For practical purposes the only reasons for choosing the probit model over the logistic model would be:

- There is a strong belief that the underlying distribution is normal
- The actual event is not a binary outcome (e.g. Bankrupt/not bankrupt) but a proportion (e.g. Proportion of population at different debt levels).

Time Series Models

Time series models are used for predicting or forecasting the future behaviour of variables. These models account for the fact that data points taken over time may have an internal structure (such as autocorrelation, trend or seasonal variation) that should be accounted for. As a result standard regression techniques cannot be applied to time series data and methodology has been developed to decompose the trend, seasonal and cyclical component of the series. Modelling the dynamic path of a variable can improve forecasts since the predictable component of the series can be projected into the future.

Time series models estimate difference equations containing stochastic components. Two commonly used forms of these models are autoregressive models (AR) and moving average (MA) models. The Box-Jenkins methodology (1976) developed by George Box and G.M. Jenkins combines the AR and MA models to produce the ARMA (autoregressive moving average) model which is the cornerstone of stationary time series analysis. ARIMA (autoregressive integrated moving average models) on the other hand are used to describe non-stationary time series. Box and Jenkins suggest differencing a non stationary time series to obtain a stationary series to which an ARMA model can be applied. Non stationary time series have a pronounced trend and do not have a constant long-run mean or variance. Box and Jenkins proposed a three stage methodology which includes: model identification, estimation and validation. The identification stage involves identifying if the series is stationary or not and the presence of seasonality by examining plots of the series, autocorrelation and partial autocorrelation functions. In the estimation stage, models are estimated using non-linear time series or maximum likelihood estimation procedures. Finally the validation stage involves diagnostic checking such as plotting the residuals to detect outliers and evidence of model fit.

In recent years time series models have become more sophisticated and attempt to model conditional heteroskedasticity with models such as ARCH (autoregressive conditional heteroskedasticity) and GARCH (generalized autoregressive conditional heteroskedasticity) models frequently used for financial time series. In addition time series models are also used to understand inter-relationships among economic variables represented by systems of equations using VAR (vector autoregression) and structural VAR models.

Survival or Duration Analysis

Survival analysis is another name for time to event analysis. These techniques were primarily developed in the medical and biological sciences, but they are also widely used in the social sciences like economics, as well as in engineering (reliability and failure time analysis).

Censoring and non-normality, which are characteristic of survival data, generate difficulty when trying to analyse the data using conventional statistical models such as multiple linear regression. The normal distribution, being a symmetric distribution, takes positive as well as negative values, but duration by its very nature cannot be negative and therefore normality cannot be assumed when dealing with duration/survival data. Hence the normality assumption of regression models is violated.

The assumption is that if the data were not censored it would be representative of the population of interest. In survival analysis, censored observations arise whenever the dependent variable of interest represents the time to a terminal event, and the duration of the study is limited in time. An important concept in survival analysis is the hazard rate, defined as the probability that the event will occur at time t conditional on surviving until time t. Another concept related to the hazard rate is the survival function which can be defined as the probability of surviving to time t.

Most models try to model the hazard rate by choosing the underlying distribution depending on the shape of the hazard function. A distribution whose hazard function slopes upward is said to have positive duration dependence, a decreasing hazard shows negative duration dependence whereas constant hazard is a process with no memory usually characterized by the exponential distribution. Some of the distributional choices in survival models are: F, gamma, Weibull, log normal, inverse normal, exponential etc. All these distributions are for a non-negative random variable.

Duration models can be parametric, non-parametric or semi-parametric. Some of the models commonly used are Kaplan-Meier and Cox proportional hazard model (non parametric).

Classification and Regression Trees

Classification and regression trees (CART) is a non-parametric Decision tree learning technique that produces either classification or regression trees, depending on whether the dependent variable is categorical or numeric, respectively. Decision trees are formed by a collection of rules based on values of certain variables in the modelling data set

- Rules are selected based on how well splits based on variables' values can differentiate observations based on the dependent variable
- Once a rule is selected and splits a node into two, the same logic is applied to each "child" node (i.e. it is a recursive procedure)
- Splitting stops when CART detects no further gain can be made, or some pre-set stopping rules are met.

Each branch of the tree ends in a terminal node;

- Each observation falls into one and exactly one terminal node
- Each terminal node is uniquely defined by a set of rules.

A very popular method for predictive analytics is Leo Breiman's Random forests or derived versions of this technique like Random multinomial logit.

Multivariate Adaptive Regression Splines

Multivariate adaptive regression splines (MARS) is a non-parametric technique that builds flexible models by fitting piecewise linear regressions.

An important concept associated with regression splines is that of a knot. Knot is where one local regression model gives way to another and thus is the point of intersection between two splines.

In multivariate and adaptive regression splines, basis functions are the tool used for generalizing the search for knots. Basis functions are a set of functions used to represent the information contained in one or more variables. Multivariate and Adaptive Regression Splines model almost always creates the basis functions in pairs. Multivariate and adaptive regression spline approach deliberately overfits the model and then prunes to get to the optimal model. The algorithm is computationally very intensive and in practice we are required to specify an upper limit on the number of basis functions.

Machine Learning Techniques

Machine learning, a branch of artificial intelligence, was originally employed to develop techniques to enable computers to learn. Today, since it includes a number of advanced statistical methods for regression and classification, it finds application in a wide variety of fields including medical diagnostics, credit card fraud detection, face and speech recognition and analysis of the stock market. In certain applications it is sufficient to directly predict the dependent variable without focusing on the underlying relationships between variables. In other cases, the underlying relationships can be very complex and the mathematical form of the dependencies unknown. For such cases, machine learning techniques emulate human cognition and learn from training examples to predict future events.

A brief discussion of some of these methods used commonly for predictive analytics is provided below. A detailed study of machine learning can be found in Mitchell (1997).

Neural Networks

Neural networks are nonlinear sophisticated modelling techniques that are able to model complex functions. They can be applied to problems of prediction, classification or control in a wide spectrum of fields such as finance, cognitive psychology/neuroscience, medicine, engineering, and physics.

Neural networks are used when the exact nature of the relationship between inputs and output is not known. A key feature of neural networks is that they learn the relationship between inputs and output through training. There are two types of training in neural networks used by different networks, supervised and unsupervised training, with supervised being the most common one. Some examples of neural network training techniques are backpropagation, quick propagation, conjugate gradient descent, projection operator, Delta-Bar-Delta etc. Some unsupervised network architectures are multilayer perceptrons, Kohonen networks, Hopfield networks, etc.

Radial Basis Functions

A radial basis function (RBF) is a function which has built into it a distance criterion with respect to a center. Such functions can be used very efficiently for interpolation and for smoothing of data. Radial basis functions have been applied in the area of neural networks where they are used as a replacement for the sigmoidal transfer function. Such networks have 3 layers, the input layer, the hidden layer with the RBF non-linearity and a linear output layer. The most popular choice for the non-linearity is the Gaussian. RBF networks have the advantage of not being locked into local minima as do the feed-forward networks such as the multilayer perceptron.

Support Vector Machines

Support Vector Machines (SVM) are used to detect and exploit complex patterns in data by clustering, classifying and ranking the data. They are learning machines that are used to perform binary classifications and regression estimations. They commonly use kernel based methods to apply linear classification techniques to non-linear classification problems. There are a number of types of SVM such as linear, polynomial, sigmoid etc.

Naïve Bayes

Naïve Bayes based on Bayes conditional probability rule is used for performing classification tasks. Naïve Bayes assumes the predictors are statistically independent which makes it an effective classification tool that is easy to interpret. It is best employed when faced with the problem of 'curse of dimensionality' i.e. when the number of predictors is very high.

K-nearest Neighbours

The nearest neighbour algorithm (KNN) belongs to the class of pattern recognition statistical methods. The method does not impose a priori any assumptions about the distribution from which the modelling sample is drawn. It involves a training set with both positive and negative values. A new sample is classified by calculating the distance to the nearest neighbouring training case. The sign of that point will determine the classification of the sample. In the k-nearest neighbour classifier, the k nearest points are considered and the sign of the majority is used to classify the sample. The performance of the kNN algorithm is influenced by three main factors: (1) the distance measure used to locate the nearest neighbours; (2) the decision rule used to derive a classification from the k-nearest neighbours; and (3) the number of neighbours used to classify the new sample. It can be proved that, unlike other methods, this method is universally asymptotically convergent, i.e.: as the size of the training set increases, if the observations are independent and identically distributed (i.i.d.), regardless of the distribution from which the sample is drawn, the predicted class will converge to the class assignment that minimizes misclassification error.

Geospatial Predictive Modelling

Conceptually, geospatial predictive modelling is rooted in the principle that the occurrences of events being modelled are limited in distribution. Occurrences of events are neither uniform nor random in distribution – there are spatial environment factors (infrastructure, sociocultural, topographic, etc.) that constrain and influence where the locations of events occur. Geospatial predictive modelling attempts to describe those constraints and influences by spatially correlating occurrences of historical geospatial locations with environmental factors that represent those constraints and influences. Geospatial predictive modelling is a process for analysing events through a geographic filter in order to make statements of likelihood for event occurrence or emergence.

Tools

There are numerous tools available in the marketplace which help with the execution of predictive analytics. These range from those which need very little user sophistication to those that are designed for the expert practitioner. The difference between these tools is often in the level of customization and heavy data lifting allowed.

In an attempt to provide a standard language for expressing predictive models, the Predictive Model Markup Language (PMML) has been proposed. Such an XML-based language provides a way for the different tools to define predictive models and to share these between PMML compliant applications. PMML 4.0 was released in June, 2009.

Brand Community

A brand community is a community formed on the basis of attachment to a product or marque. Recent developments in marketing and in research in consumer behaviour result in stressing the connection between brand, individual identity and culture. Among the concepts developed to explain the behaviour of consumers, the concept of a brand community focuses on the connections between consumers. A brand community can be defined as an enduring self-selected group of actors sharing a system of values, standards and representations (a culture) and recognizing bonds of membership with each other and with the whole. Brand communities are characterized in shared consciousness, rituals and traditions, and a sense of moral responsibility.

The term "brand community" was first presented by Albert Muniz Jr. and Thomas C. O'Guinn in a 1995 paper for the Association for Consumer Research Annual Conference in Minneapolis, MN.

In a 2001 article titled " Brand Community", published in the Journal of Consumer Research (SSCI), they defined the concept as "a specialized, non-geographically bound community, based on a structured set of social relations among admirers of a brand." This 2001 paper recently has been acknowledged by Thomson Scientific & Healthcare to be one of the most cited papers in the field of economics and business.

Many brands provide examples of brand communities. In computers and electronics: Apple Inc. (Macintosh, iPod, iPhone), Holga and LOMO cameras, and Palm and Pocket PC Ultra-Mobile PCs. In vehicles: Ford Bronco, Jeep, Miata, Mini Cooper, Saab, Saturn and Subaru automobiles, and Royal Enfield and Harley-Davidson motorcycles. In toys: Barbie and Lego.

Brand Engagement

Brand Engagement is a term loosely used to describe the process of forming an attachment (emotional and rational) between a person and a brand. It comprises one aspect of brand management. What makes the topic complex is that brand engagement is partly created by institutions and organizations, but is equally created by the perceptions, attitudes, beliefs and behaviours of those with whom these institutions and organizations are communicating or engaging with.

As a relatively new addition to the marketing and communication mix, brand engagement sits in the space between marketing, advertising, media communication, social media, employer branding, organizational development, internal communications and human resource management.

There is still lack of clarity and debate about whether this is a "soft" or hard measure, and whether it can be linked to any consumer or employee behaviour change – e.g. sales activity, trial, or recommendation.

External Brand Engagement

Brand engagement between a brand and its consumers/potential consumers is a key objective of a brand marketing effort. In general, the ways a brand connects to its consumer is via a range of "touchpoints" — that is, a sequence or list of potential ways the brand makes contact with the individual. Examples include retail environments, advertising, word of mouth, online, and the product/service itself.

Internal ("Close Stakeholder") Brand Engagement

There are two broad areas where brand engagement is relevant within an organization (employees and close stakeholders such as franchise staff, call centres, suppliers or intermediaries).

The first area is ensuring that the employer brand promised to employees is delivered upon once employees join the firm. If the employee experience is not what is promised, this could result in increased employee turnover and/or decreased performance.

The second area is ensuring employees and close stakeholders of an organization completely understand the organization's brand, and what it stands for—and to make sure that their activities on a day to day basis are contributing to expressing that brand through the customer experience.

In general, this requires an ongoing effort on the part of the organization to ensure that its employees and close stakeholders understand what the brand is promising to its customers, and to help all employees clearly understand how their actions and behaviours, on a day to day basis, either support or undermine the effort.

This often raises the issue of the value of investment in "brand engagement." It is a discretionary expense on the part of the organization. Proponents of brand engagement would argue that this is an investment—that is, the benefits to the organization outweigh the cost of the program.

Within any organization there is competition for resources, so there is a significant need to demonstrate Return on Investment in employee engagement/internal communications. While it is generally accepted that it is important for internal communications professionals to demonstrate the value this function delivers to the organization, it is difficult to place a discrete figure on this contribution.

Best practice in internal communications generally adheres to certain principles:

- Understanding the stakeholder (audiences)
- Knowing what messages and information is appropriate for each audience
- Ensuring that there is a feedback mechanism in place so communication is a dialogue
- Measuring effectiveness
- Enhancing participation and collaboration.

An aspect of internal brand engagement is Brand orientation which refers to "the degree to which the organization values brands and its practices are oriented towards building brand capabilities."

Thought leaders are increasingly placing employee engagement at the forefront of the fight for greater authenticity in the workplace, increased employee satisfaction and ultimately greater retention and improved customer service. They are passionate about the link to bottom line benefits and strongly advocate working on brands from the inside out. There are a range of experts and service providers who have created offers to bring the brand to life—all agree that the employee side of the equation is far more important than has been historically acknowledged.

The Measurement Angle

Much internal communication and employee engagement practice is based on measurement of effectiveness or business contribution. The key elements in creating a model of employee engagement is the measurement of "engagement drivers" — that is, what are the factors or combinations of factors which have an impact on productivity and commitment and can be monitored and addressed through people, process or technology changes?

Many of the "engagement drivers" currently in use internally are HR focused, and in many cases do not delve deeply into the employee's role in delivering the brand/customer experience as a distinct element.

Example

Probably the most compelling example of this is the service-profit chain. The first real case study of this appeared in "The Service Profit Chain" (the so-called Sears Model, Harvard Business Review, 1997). This statistical model tracks increases in employee "engagement drivers" to correlated increases in customer satisfaction and loyalty, and then correlates this to increases in Total Shareholder Return (TSR), revenue and other financial performance measures.

Since the service-profit chain emerged, it's been developed, and criticized, but the general consensus is that employee engagement can contribute roughly 20% to an organization's TSR (various Vivaldi, Watson Wyatt, Towers Perrin studies 2004, 2005, 2006).

Collaboration and Connectivity vs. Content Management

While some organizations are realizing the benefits of collaboration and work flow online, there appears to be significant focus on publishing and managing content, generally via Content Management Systems. There is an emerging school of thought that organizational perspectives on technology are frequently misaligned with the actual requirements and desires of the users of the technology. That is, the nature (or intention) of a technology may not always determine the nature of its use – the telephone, for example, was originally intended as a broadcast medium. Its designers were focused on delivering content, while its users sought – and still value – connectivity.

The social media phenomenon presents emerging evidence that this quest for connectivity is rapidly becoming a core focus of communication technology within organizations. This potentially creates a disconnect with more traditional content-driven models of internal communication—delivering (or making easily available) the right content at the right time to the right people using the right media. Therefore, there could be a great deal of potential within organisations, using their existing technologies, to derive cultural and performance benefits from re-thinking how they communicate, make decisions and work virtually.

Brand Implementation

Brand implementation refers to the physical representation and consistent application of brand identity across visual and verbal identity carriers. In visual terms, this can include signage, uniforms, liveries, interior design and branded merchandise. Brand implementation encompasses facets of architecture, product design, industrial design, quantity surveying, engineering, procurement, project management and retail design.

Background

Brand implementation emerged as a discipline in the 1990s when brand owners recognized the need for consistency across branded estates. Traditionally, brand implementation was handled by various parties, including shop-fitters, interior designers and sign companies. Lack of centralized project management led to inconsistencies, while information dissymmetry meant suppliers had too much control over brand issues. Brand implementation was thus coined as an umbrella term for all aspects of the application and maintenance of physical brand assets.

Today

Brand implementation is now a critical discipline focused on binding the relationship between the target audience and the brand. This allows brand implementation firms to identify the best possible manufacturing solution for each project.

Beyond having an impactful, consistent, and meaningful design, environmental branding must also have functional value to aid in brand identification, day and night visibility, merchandising and traffic flow.

Magic and Logic

Brand implementation does not involve the design or creation of brand identity. Instead, brand implementation agencies work closely with branding agencies to ensure that the latter's work is applied accurately and consistently. This relationship is referred to as Magic and Logic (RTM of Marketing Supply Chain International). Branding agencies look after the Magic (creative) and brand implementation agencies look after the Logic (implementation).

8

Promotions Through Advertisement

Tourism is the fastest growing industry internationally with destinations not only in industrialised countries, but also in less developed countries in East Africa, Central America and South East Asia. Developing countries which were previously seen as less likely destinations or were closed to tourism altogether are now considering the marketing of their natural and/or cultural attractions to receive a share of this global industry. Adventure tourism, and cultural tourism take advantage of this development.

Each year more exotic places are offered on the tourism market for those who have seen everything else, or prefer destinations 'off the beaten track'. The close contact with locals in isolated areas and their customs seems to be one of the main attractions of developing countries, and this is used extensively in marketing strategies. At the same time, the scientific study of tourism has developed such that tertiary education institutions worldwide offer degree courses in tourism studies. The perspectives and approaches one can adopt to study the topic are as diverse as tourism itself. Jafari (1990) presented an overview of disciplines and approaches in the study of tourism. The disciplines offered are of considerable diversity but 'health' does not rate a mention in this model of approaches.

Tourism and Health

Literature dealing with the combination of tourism and health abundantly covers health aspects of travellers to particular locations, health education, medical aspects of travel preparation, health problems in travellers or in returning tourists, and economic or administrative consequences of tourists' ill health. In short, 'Tourism and Health' usually focuses on the travellers' wellbeing. However, despite this necessary and applaudable development in protecting travellers from health problems, one needs to consider that there are people on the other end of the journey who may be subjected to a change in their health status as well, due to visiting fellow humans. 'Tourism and Health' rarely includes the hosts in its consideration.

Tourism's potential impact on the health of the local host communities can be direct or indirect. One example of direct impact is the possible transmission of diseases from travellers to locals. Nowadays, the emergence of new infectious diseases or the reemergence of diseases thought to be eradicated are causing great concern, and travel is a major contributor to their spread. Lea (1988) rightly pointed out that tourism has the dual effect of promoting the provision of improved health care in Third World destinations but, in addition, acts as a vehicle to spread some forms of disease.

Other possible direct health impacts are chronic diseases or disabilities, and accidents causing injuries or deaths of local tourist guides in the course of their employment in tourism. Indirect impacts can be attributed to the social, cultural, environmental and economic impacts which are the usual focus of accounts on tourism impact.

Methodology

Aim of the Study: The aim of this study was to ascertain the current knowledge on health impacts of tourism in developing countries, to provide information on gaps in this knowledge as a baseline for future research, to identify research topics which could be investigated by researchers from health, tourism and other disciplines, and to propose elements of a framework for the assessment of health impacts of tourism.

Design of the Study: First, a literature review was conducted. Publications related to the topic were identified in the fields of health and tourism. A few sources were located through networking with people working in disciplines pertinent to the subject. The key areas for the search were: travellers' health; tourism and health; tourism in developing countries; economic, environmental, sociocultural impacts of tourism; public health; and tropical medicine. The literature was reviewed to identify any references made in relation to the topic under study to recognise unresearched issues and, if possible, to obtain ideas for an innovative approach of investigation. Only publications in English, German and Spanish were sought and utilised.

Second, a field trip was undertaken to test the findings from the literature analysis against fieldwork in Easter Island/Chile and Peru. First, a range of tourism destinations (including some very popular and others only visited by few individual travellers) were examined with the aim of detecting evidence of positive or negative impacts of tourism on the health of the local population.

The emphasis here was on potential environmental impacts; potential health hazards due to running a tourism destination, e.g., construction, equipment, transport; and possible transmission of diseases. Second, semi-structured interviews were conducted with health practitioners, tour operators and conservationists to elicit their assessment of tourism's health impacts. Discussions centred around medical aspects, such as changes in disease pat terns, introduction of previously nonendemic infectious diseases, and work place health and safety aspects; tour operators' recollection of possible anecdotal evidence of health impacts; and conservationists' views on tourism in environmentally fragile destinations.

Tourism's Health Impact- a Review of the Literature

The Impact of Travel on the Health of the Hosts: An Historical Overview

Travel is inseparably linked with human existence. Historical accounts of travel and migrations as the main source of epidemics are numerous. The Roman Empire was struck by the bubonic plague, spread along the trade routes of the time, leading eventually to the dramatic and largest epidemic of the 'Black Death' in the 14th century. It had started in the Gobi desert in 1320 and reached Europe 30 years later, where it is estimated to have killed one-third to half of the population in some European countries.

Venetian authorities who observed outbreaks after the arrival of ships from the East assumed that travel may have to do with the spread of the plague. The first regulations governing the arrival of ships were introduced in Venice and Rhodos in 1377, detaining ship, passengers, crew and cargo at a distance for 40 days ('quaranta giorni' became quarantine) before being allowed into the harbour.

The conquest of the 'New World' is probably the best known event in history which has been linked to the spread of fatal diseases to non-immune peoples. It was clear from the first written accounts of the Spanish invasion of the Americas in the 15th century that the native peoples were not only killed in battle and through hard labour or physical punishment but also succumbed to a great extent to introduced infectious diseases to which they lacked immunity. In some parts of the New World, infections such as smallpox and influenza reduced the native population dramatically. When this lead to an acute shortage in the work force, the ensuing slave trade from West Africa lead to an even greater range of diseases. The arriving ships, for example, not only brought the yellow fever virus but also its vector *Aedes aegypti*.

Similar transmissions occurred in the Pacific region some hundred years later. It is not clear from historic travel logs if early explorers were aware of their potential role in the transmission of diseases. Beaglehole (1934) in his account of the exploration of the Pacific clearly focused on the exploratory aspect of journeys into the area with only one mention of "the visits of European ships destroyed utterly and horribly its primitive freedom from pestilence".

Captain James Cook seems to have been the first to actively at tempt the prevent ion of a transmission of infectious diseases from crew to native populations by confining any person found to be diseased to the ship while the rest of the crew was permitted to go ashore. Apart from syphil is, other often deadly diseases such as measles and dysentery were transmitted from Europeans to native people.

Uncertainty about the transmission of diseases did not seem to exist 100 years later when it was purposefully employed as the following excerpt illustrates. In 1860, three captains arrived at Port Resolution on Tanna (Vanuatu) to occupy the island. Alexander (1895) cited Rev. John Paton reporting: Our watchword is, "Sweep these creatures away and let white men occupy the soil". They then invited a chief by the name of Kapuku on board one of their vessels, promising him a present, and confined him for twenty-four hours without food in the hold among natives ill with measles, and finally sent him ashore without a present to spread the disease.

The measles thus introduced spread fearfully, and decimated the *population of the island.* Epidemics occurring in isolated 'virgin' populations, i.e., populations without immunity to a certain disease, are not confined to the Middle Ages. Forty years ago on Easter Island, Heyerdahl (1958) observed the influenza epidemic which accompanied the arrival of the yearly supply ship from the Chilean mainland:

The conongo *was the natives'* great terror- the annual influenza epidemic which always accompanied contact with the mainland. It came and went with the regularity of clockwork. After the ship's visit it always raged through the village for a month or two. It got into chests, heads, and stomachs: everyone was ill, and there was always a toll of *human lives before the* conongo passed and left the people in peace for the rest of the year.

A mumps epidemic in 1957 on St. Lawrence Island (Alaska) was started by a boy returning from the mainland after undergoing surgery. Similar outbreaks on other 'virgin' island populations in Alaska occurred in 1965 and 1967-68. Although it is generally argued that it is unlikely that there are any 'virgin' populations left due to the contacts of people around the world, partial or selective immunity still allows the transmission of diseases by people on the move. Today, business and leisure travel is claimed to be the driving force in the spread of disease and the (re)emergence of infectious diseases.

Potential Indirect Impacts of Tourism on the Health of the Host Community

The impacts of tourism are a popular topic in the literature, usually covering the economic, environmental and social aspects. However, few discourses are based on research evidence. Cater (1987) attributed this to the difficulty of studying impacts due to their complexity. An additional problem is that social and cultural dimensions are difficult to quantify and, therefore, out of reach of most researchers employing conventional methods. Using the tourism literature as a baseline, one can develop the arguments further and identify ways in which these impacts can affect health in positive or negative ways.

Economic impacts affecting health Economic benefits are certainly the primary cause for the promotion of tourism in developing countries. The benefits are mainly seen in the gain of (often desperately needed) term problem is water pollution. The following examples are taken from a compilation by Maurer (1992). Frequently, tourism developments in developing countries do not have an appropriate system for sewage and waste management and they use rivers and the sea for disposal. This can pose two problems. First, fish and molluscs eaten by the local population as a source of protein may be unsuitable for consumption due to pollutants deposited in these animals. Second, swimming in polluted water can lead to ear, eye, skin and gastrointestinal infections in even epidemic proportions. Herbicides used on golf courses have been shown to pollute the freshwater supply and impact on health directly or through food obtained from the water. The pollution of waterholes in deserts through the tourists' use of soap and shampoo poses another problem.

Redirection and overuse of freshwater for hotels, swimming pools and landscaping purposes in tourism facilities can lead to the local population having less or no clean drinking water which in turn puts them at risk of contracting diseases. Lack of water also impacts on the local agriculture leading to poor crops and a scarcity of food.

There is a need to substantiate examples such as those mentioned above. Very little research evidence supports numerous anecdotal accounts of environmental problems caused, at least partially, by tourism. More specific investigations into pollution and redirect ion of drinking water need to be carried out.

Also, resulting health problems need to be documented carefully to support strategies for improvement.

Garbage generated by tourists poses another public health hazard for host communities as, apart from its unaesthetic appearance, it creates breeding tourist areas in Argentina, 96.3% of respondents to a survey claimed that tourism was to blame for increasing costs, but the results have to be treated cautiously as the study had only a return rate of 23%. There seems to be a paucity of research supporting anecdotal accounts of economic impacts of tourism. Research needs to be conducted into changes of living costs and their effect on locals. For example, D'Sousa (1985) reported from Goa that, in addition to a lack of improved health, local tax payers paid for tourists' free medical care.

A different type of negative economic impact on health was reported by Loval and Feuerstein (1992): "There is said to be a drain of trained nurses away from the health sector in some Pacific areas as they seek jobs in tourism". No other reference could be found supporting this claim. Considering the expenses of training health personnel, it is important to know if this is a common trend in developing countries where salaries of health professionals are known to be very low. The problem of locals leaving their traditional activities of fishing or farming for seemingly more lucrative work in the tourism industry has been presented in the literature.

Environmental Impacts Affecting Health

Unfortunately, tourism seems to be the culprit for a number of environmental problems that pose health hazards to local communities. A serious longforeign exchange and the creation of employment. Archer (1986) claimed that "tourism generates a considerable secondary economic activity in a destination country" with income percolating to the public sector, business and private households. Consequently, locals' possession of foreign or local currency earned in the tourism industry enables them to purchase more or better food leading to a better health status (although more money may also mean more junk food).

It also allows them access to better health facilities if earnings from tourism have been used to improve the services. Hundt (1996) presented Jamaica as an example where tourism development has lead to prosperity and improved health of the population.

However, the same author admitted that "more important is the realisation that the profits of tourism generally are not used to improve the health status of the poor, marginalised natives in host countries". The following example from Peru may illustrate this statement. In 1995, the country received almost half a million tourists.

The area around Cusco is certainly one of the main attractions of the country and the majority of foreign tourists include a visit in their itinerary. Tourism generated income, however, does not seem to percolate to everybody in the general population in the area if the nutritional status of children in the Cusco Health District (as investigated by Wolff, Pérez, Gibson, Lopez, Peniston and Wolff, 1985) is taken as one outcome criterion. Tourism development may eventually lead to increasing living costs.

In two sites for disease-carrying arthropods and rodents. Harrington (1993) reports the pollution of the Amazon through tourists. In 1980, the South American Explorers Club collected approximately 400 kg of unburnable garbage on the Inka trail in Peru. An aspect not yet located in the literature is the possible danger of injuries (cuts, lacerations) caused by garbage. This may be of particular concern if people contract infections but are unable to access or pay for the treatment required.

Clearing for tourism developments or sports facilities causes serious ecological changes and can lead to flooding or landslides destroying crops, homes and lives. Apart from that, mosquitos which are potential vectors for diseases tend to move into cleared areas. When people (locals and tourists) move in to utilise the cleared land, they are at risk of contracting serious diseases such as malaria or yellow fever if the mosquitos are infected. The cutting of firewood along the world's trekking routes adds to the deterioration of forest already damaged due to cutting of wood for domestic purposes as can easily be seen in Nepal or Peru. At present, no statistics could be found indicating the exact extent of destruction of forest or bushland for tourism purposes.

On the other hand, tourism can have positive environmental effects, when generated income is used for environmental planning and education, or for the construct ion of appropriate sewage systems. Investing in the conservation of natural areas and safe tourist facilities in these areas ultimately benefits the physical and mental well-being of locals and visitors alike. Hellen (1995) argued that research into tourism in the developing world "opens up the prospect that global tourism may itself become a vehicle for investment in environmental health programs and securing improved health for all". So far, there is a striking paucity of examples supporting this vision.

Socio-cultural Impacts Affecting Health

This third major category of impacts is similarly widely discussed in the literature. Generally, it is stated that tourist-host encounters may lead to better understanding between cultures, remove prejudices and promote cultural pride eventually leading to the preservation or a renaissance of the local art/craft. Despite these positive arguments, it seems that tourism's impact on society and culture in developing countries is mainly perceived as negative. It is acknowledged that social and cultural change is a phenomenon attributed to modernisation in general but it seems that the frequent and fast exchange of encounters of people from different backgrounds accelerates this change at a rate not always favourable for the host communities. Obvious health problems accompanying these changes originate in the appearance or increase of prostitution, alcoholism, drug use and violence.

Also, lifestyle and food preferences of visitors seem to be imitated often leading to higher body weight, greater percentage of body fat, and high blood pressure, conditions previously unknown in these communities. Farrell (1982) named Hawaii and other areas in the Pacific as an example of areas where these changes occurred. Little additional research evidence on unhealthy lifestyles due to the influence of tourism could be located.

Mental health problems are less frequently discussed. Changes in the traditional lifestyle or loss of identity through changes in social and cultural values can put a considerable mental strain on people. Negative implications through changes in social and cultural values include potential mental health problems. Currently, it is unclear how many confirmed diagnoses of mental alterations could be attributed to long-term impacts of tourism. Physical and mental health problems caused by the forceful removal of peoples to make way for tourism are equally neglected in the literature.

Examples of this practice can be found around the globe. A more recent case was reported from Botswana where Kalahari Bushmen appealed to the UN to save them from being evicted from their ancestral lands which were to be used for tourism purposes. Forced relocations of indigenous people in the Peruvian Amazon area are a common method to make space for tourist lodges. Research into changes of locals' health status is very scarce.

Numerous questions arise when evaluating anecdotal evidence on sociocultural impacts. An important issue that needs investigation is if changes to lifestyle, the adoption of unhealthy food preferences, increase in prostitution, alcohol and drug use, and violence can clearly be attributed to tourism, or if they are symptoms of 'development' and modernisation. It is also of interest to ascertain if tourists engage in activities contradicting local rules and taboos, and of what type and frequency these actions are. Additionally, there has to be a closer investigation into the occurrence of people's forceful removal from their home and land for tourism purposes.

Potential Direct Impacts of Tourism on the Health of the Host Community

Health conditions which can affect local people directly and not as secondary implications of other impacts of tourism, are diseases, accidents, and conditions related to employment in tourism. The potential direct health impacts of tourism are mainly those occurring through the spread of infections by travelling individuals. These infections can be imported from the tourists' country of origin, or they could be contracted while travelling. The main infection risks for travellers in developing countries as compiled by Warren and Mahmoud. All of those can be transmitted to local individuals. There are diseases that are easily spread and are common, others require a range of factors and circumstances to be transmitted and are less common. Some diseases may have a minor impact on the individual and/or can be treated easily, others are difficult to treat and/or have serious impacts on the individual. The ease of spread of a range of diseases which can be transmitted from travellers to hosts and their level of impact on the host individual.

The mode of transmission of some conditions is common knowledge and well researched, the spread of others has not been discussed in the light of tourist-host transmission, possibly because some diseases are less common. Nevertheless, sometimes only one case of infection may be enough to introduce a virulent agent to people without the necessary immunity and lead to a major epidemic. This potential risk warrants the consideration of all possibilities of disease transmission. An additional factor needs to be addressed when discussing the potential spread to people in developing countries, and here particularly indigenous communi ties. Poor hygiene, unfavourable economic conditions, inadequate housing and nutrition predispose people already to a range of diseases such as tuberculosis, parasitic infections or hepatitis, with individuals often having several acute and chronic conditions at the same time. It is obvious that an additional load of pathogenic agents, especially when the immune system is compromised, can only aggravate health problems.

Field Studies on Tourism's Health Impact

One objective of this study was to test if the findings of the analysis of published material applied to real situations in developing countries.

Health Problems Linked to Tourism in Easter Island and Peru

On Easter Island it was found that the (only) campground on the island at Anakena Beach had no fresh water supply, and the sanitary facilities provided, according to the locals, had been locked for a long time. On weekends, hundreds of locals and tourists gather at the beach usually staying the whole day. This was discussed with staff at the hospital who reported a relatively high prevalence of diarrhoea on the island but had attributed this to vegetables imported from the Chilean mainland. After discussing the lack of sanitary facilities which becomes even more obvious with the added tourists, they agreed that it was worthwhile to investigate this potential health hazard. Staff, however, saw the main problem regarding tourism and health as the transmission of Sexually Transmitted Infections (STIs) from tourists to locals.

This anecdotal evidence has not yet been systematically investigated. The issue of the availability of health facilities came up during conversations with locals in the market. It could be concluded that tourism on Easter Island has not improved the locals' health facilities. This may have to do with the fact that tourists generally stay only a short time, either because of the limited facilities on the island or because they are only having a brief stopover on the connection Tahiti- Santiago de Chile. If seriously ill, the people joked, they had "only two options, Santiago [some 3700 km away] or the cemetery". Health professionals in Peru also maintained that cases of STIs were increasing and tourism was seen as a major contributing factor to this development, but they were unable to substantiate these claims. Toonen *et al.* (1996) conducted a health baseline study in the Camisea area in the Amazonian jungle where the Shell Company is prospecting. The potential risk of the native population to contract STIs was seen as very high because of people coming from outside (here mainly oil workers). The study does not clarify if locals also spoke of tourists, the term 'visitadores' in the study refers to prostitutes. Other diseases repeatedly named as being spread by people moving around were malaria and leishmaniasis.

The important aspect of tourist-host encounters die each year in the Andes including mountain guides. The health of tourism workers, however, can also be in danger in the developed world. More than 50 climbers and guides died within a few weeks in the European Alps in the summer of 1997. Another form of 'occupational health hazard' has been observed on the Argentinian side of the Iguazu Falls where, at a certain point, locals drive tourists in an open boat equipped with a small engine close to the edge of the falls. The engine barely is able to get the boat out of the current and back to shore. A thin rope along the edge clearly is not sufficient to withstand a boat should the engine fail.

Increasingly, developing countries with access to spectacular reefs market their underwater attractions to encourage diving holidays.

When the income of a diving guide depends on the number of dives, the minimum surface interval that is required for health reasons may not always be observed, putting them under considerable health risks. A lack of decompression chambers in developing countries, partly due to the failure of enforcing their installation, as Rudkin and Hall (1996) reported from Pacific islands, is of concern not only to the visiting diver but also to the local guide.

In many areas in the developing world, customs prevent people's exposure to physical danger by placing a taboo over a certain area. If such an area happens to become of interest to tourism, the reluctance of locals to go to such places may be overcome by the need to earn money. Two guides together with one tourist died in January 1995 at Mt. Yasur on Tanna/Vanuatu, killed by falling rocks ejected from the volcano. This author has witnessed local guides refusing to accompany visitors to the summit of this volcano.

In tribal areas in the jungle could not be examined during this field trip but needs urgent attention. This is so because some villages now seem to contact tour operators suggesting cooperation, and operators sensitive to potential problems need to be provided with information to facilitate their decision making. Environmental impacts of tourism in trekking areas with problems due to unregulated garbage disposal and the lack of sanitary facilities were suggested in the literature and could be observed in reality.

The problem applies to areas with opportunities for short hikes as well as to trails representing major tourist attractions such as routes in the Cordillera Blanca/Huaraz or the Inka Trail near Cusco.

The need for urgent action has been recognised in both areas and plans are already under way to implement solutions to the problems. A program is currently being designed to install sanitary facilities along well-used trails. This is of particular importance when the areas represent the main water supply for a large region.

Implications for Local Tourism Employees' Health

The neglect of local tourism workers' health in the literature is obvious. The importance of the consideration of this topic became apparent during the field trip.

It seems that many tourism workers in Peru (and other developing countries) earn their living as tourist guides, often in destinations with little tourism infrastructure such as nature based adventure tours. Tourists are given advice about the dangers they may encounter on these trips. But tourists are only exposed to those hazards for a very short time compared to the guides. Their health risks increase through the frequency of exposure due to their job as well as the terrain they are working in.

Adventure tours to the Amazonian jungle are very popular. Like tourists, guides are exposed to health hazards such as snake and other animals' bites, diseases such as malaria or leishmaniasis, and car or boat accidents. Several cases of snake bites and accidents with boats and trucks were named by a tour operator in Cusco.

Probably the highest health risk exists for mountain guides who risk altitude sickness, injury or death in their attempt to lead tourists to spectacular summits. Peak season means a higher income but also a higher health risk. Shlim (1996) reported that in just one storm in the Nepal Himalayas on 10-11 November 1995, 22 foreigners and more than 45 Nepalese guides and porters died in different regions due to heavy snowfall, avalanches and mudslides. It was claimed that up to 30 people and porters should be assessed and monitored. The identification of potential occupational health problems and a documentation of the spread of diseases contracted during employment in tourism to family and community, would assist in strategies to minimise health hazards.

Towards a Framework for Understanding Tourism's Health Impacts

Anecdotal Versus Research Evidence

This study suggests that, at the moment, there is very little research based evidence on the impact of tourism on locals' health in developing countries. Sources that can be found related to the topic are mainly anecdotal, underline the need for further research. Diseases which had been reported as transmittable through people's movement, were found again in the field.

Also, the health problems of local tourism workers proved to be a reality, and research into this area appears to be overdue. Although their numbers may be small compared to the entire population who may be at risk of infectious diseases, the concern over their work safety warrants further investigations. A retrospective and ongoing documentation of illness/death of local tour guides classified into areas of expertise, such as mountain, scuba diving, jungle and so on, should be established and a data bank created with links to neighbouring countries which have similar problems. Also, the health status of guides Health hazards for white water rafting guides have been described in the literature.

Sisson, Nichols and Hopkins (1983) reported schistosomiasis (blood flukes) infections among US rafting guides on the Omo River/Ethiopia. A year later, Istre, Fontaine, Tarr, and Hopkins (1984) described an outbreak of acute schistosomiasis among rafters on the same river, pointing out that commercial organisations were about to start business. This means that local guides, although partially immune, are exposed to repeated infections. A different potential health problem was identified in porters. For example, on the Inka Trail (with the highest altitude above 4000m.) one can find children carrying backpacks considered too heavy for well nourished healthy adult tourists. This may cause problems in later life such as bone deformation and chronic backpain which can prevent the individual from pursuing regular work.

The examples mentioned give a little insight into this complex area. Unfortunately, no research on this topic could be found. This may be because accidents or other health problems affect individual people, not groups or whole communities, cases are dealt with individually but not linked with other similar events. Because of the absence of data on frequency/occurrence, it is also difficult to make a risk assessment based on assumptions alone. Considering the fact that in developing countries there is rarely any organised support for such workers, health insurance or compensation for themselves or their families, this matter needs urgent attention if tourism is not to be seen as yet another type of exploitation. On the other hand, however, it is to be expected that some local guides can indeed make a living without putting themselves at risk and, subsequently, even lead a much healthier life than before.

The findings of the field work e.g., Pryor's (1980) account of residents' attitudes in Rarotonga, Cook Islands, or the many accusations about the role of (Western) tourists as transmitters of STIs and AIDS. Although there is no doubt that tourism contributes to the spread of diseases, facts are hard to obtain. Using Doxey's (1975) index of tourist irritation as a framework, one has to assume that anecdotal negative evidence on health impacts may have a lot to do with locals' antagonism toward tourists for whatever reason.

Comments, therefore, should be (or should have been) examined from this perspective to allow for a more realistic interpretation. Antagonism may even lead to the perception of transmission of diseases with entirely different aetiology. In this connection, one also needs to consider the well known conflict between national park management and the needs of the locals living within a park or in close proximity. For example, the conservation of flagship species such as the tiger or rhinoceros has to be weighed against the loss of lives of locals caused by those animals. Likewise, loss of livestock and crop destruction have impacts on the population's health status. In the context of this report, it is necessary to identify what events occur within the framework of conservation and which ones can clearly be attributed to tourism.

Numerous gaps have been identified in the current body of knowledge on the impact of tourism on the health of the local population in developing countries and topics for research have been suggested. It has been established that research into potential indirect health impacts has to go beyond the economic, environmental and sociocultural impacts already widely discussed in the literature, and focus specifically on their health implications. Research into potential direct health impacts should concentrate on epidemiological studies into the transmission of diseases through travellers and on investigations into the work place health and safety aspects in relation to local tourism employees.

In addition, a wide range of general issues is the focus for basic and applied research providing additional information to achieve a more complete picture of health impacts. Examples are offered here to illustrate the variety of study topics available to researchers from different disciplines. Historians could explore how visitors in the past (invaders, explorers, missionaries) changed the local health status.

At present, it seems information on this topic can only be found by chance when studying old documents or travel diaries. Addressing present day concerns, social scientists should establish if there is indeed an association between locals' negative attitudes towards tourism and anecdotal evidence of negative impacts (and then test those claims through epidemiological research).

Another focus of interest is an examination of national and regional tourism strategies in developing countries with respect to the consideration of the local public health and specific strategic activities to prevent a deterioration of the health status.

Public health interests could lie in: the comparison of the impact of different levels of low, moderate, and high degrees of tourism in small/isolated communities; the investigation of advice given to tourists in their home country or at the destination regarding their impact on local health; an assessment of tourists' knowledge of their potential role as transmitters of diseases; the identification of services offered for tourists' health care and the examination of their utilisation and availability for locals; the documentation of tourists using local health care facilities; or a comparison of the distribution of health care professionals and health services in touristic and non-touristic areas within one country.

Finally, tourism education should be included in research on the topic and curricula in tourism degree courses examined regarding their inclusion of health aspects. These study topics can be researched not only in individual projects focusing on a particular geographic area but allow for comparison between areas with the aim of collaborative efforts in dealing with identified health problems linked to tourism.

The addition and consideration of country specific research needs which may be proposed by local health authorities will be of particular importance when deciding on a specific topic for research.

The Need for Research as a Basis for Tourism Planning

The goal of tourism planning is usually said to be economic, sociological, biological and cultural sustainability. Ethical concerns have been raised in connection with tourism development in the 'Third World'. The four goals in tourism development:

(1) enhanced visitor satisfaction,

(2) improved economy and business success,

(3) protected resource assets, and

(4) community and area integration clearly include participation of and approval by the local population. Any development that does not protect local people and environment could be classified as unethical.

It becomes clear when examining available tourism strategies and plans that tourism planning is an immensely complex activity. Publications on two areas visited during the field trip have been reviewed with respect to their coverage of issues which may directly or indirectly affect the health of local populations.

Aguilar, Hinojosa and Milla (1992) suggested a wide range of strategies and actions to develop tourism in the 'Inka Region', an area extending over the Departments of Cusco, Madre de Dios and Apurímac, but no reference relating to health could be found. The 'Plan for Touristic and Recreation Use of the Huascaran National Park' applies to the national park in the Cordillera Blanca/Huaraz which predicted 104,000 conventional tourists and 4,000 adventure tourists (mountain climbers) for the year 1996, and 320,000 conventional tourists and 12,000 adventure tourists for the year 2005. As this plan relates to a national park, it comes as no surprise that considerable emphasis is placed on the environmental impact of tourism (garbage, lack of toilets, water and sewage system). It also recommends that conditions are to be established "for the rural population to participate in tourism in a manner which permits sustainable development". Both aspects influence the local health status but health as such is not mentioned explicitly. The plan also suggests that local guides be registered in order to monitor uncontrolled activities in the park. Such a register, i f implemented, could be an excellent opportunity to monitor their health status.

Research is the basis to appropriate tourism planning. It is obvious that the lack of research into health issues has prevented their inclusion in tourism strategic plans.

Methodological Considerations

The benefit of studying a little investigated area is that there are few conceptual restrictions for the researcher but a great opportunity for creativity and innovative approaches when defining research topics. Research in some of the areas suggested, clearly poses enormous methodological challenges for the investigator, not least because of the transient character of tourism. Here again creativity is needed in employing a range of different research approaches, going beyond the conventional. Two will be mentioned here. For example, for some of these topics an action research approach based on Critical Social Theory could be adopted. The philosophy behind Critical Social Theory is that empowering people helps them to change their situation, to help themselves.

A classic text is Paolo Freire's (1972) *Pedagogy of the Oppressed* on the empowerment through education. In a similar way, communities affected by negative health impacts from tourism could work at overcoming these by adopting the problem solving approach based on empowerment. The core of action research is the employment of a problem solving approach whereby the researcher guides the representatives of a group/community (who also become part of the research team) through the process of change until a satisfactory outcome is achieved.

The usefulness of a Geographical Information System (GIS) for epidemiological purposes is now widely accepted. The inherent geographical element of tourism and the aspect of movement represent factors very suitable for the employment of GIS for research purposes on this topic. Furthermore, its use would allow the combination of epidemiological and tourism variables. At this stage, it could not be established if GIS has ever been used in this form. However, the combination of medicine and geography is not new. Hellen (1995) discussed the use of applied medical geography in, for example, disease hazard mapping, and emphasised the need for a "multidisciplinary approach to safeguarding the health of individuals and ensuring the sustainability of tourism to potentially hazardous areas", albeit from the perspective of travellers' health.

It is quite clear that the range of research questions suggested in this paper indicates that a lot of these need to be approached in a multidisciplinary fashion. This would also provide a unique opportunity to cooperate with local professionals and to train locals as research assistants to enable them to continue research and monitoring on a long-term basis.

The purpose of research is to generate and test theories. Applied research emphasises its practical applicability to the field of study. Consequently, research undertaken on this hitherto under- investigated topic will contribute to a body of knowledge which may eventually be expressed in a more abstract form as theories and represented as models for easier understanding. The theories, in turn, will have to be tested and refined.

Bushell and Lea (1996) quite rightly pointed out that there is more to 'tourism and health' than traveller illness and suggest a reorientation towards 'traveller and host wellness'. They then continue to present a tourism health model linked to the concept o f eco logical public health as a framework for research. It defines 'tourism and health' as the interface between (1) tourists, (2) hosts and (3) the natural environment. The model takes into account arguments by Brown (1985) supporting an epidemiology of health in contrast to the traditional epidemiology of diseases. Based on these arguments, the authors also propose a forced field approach considering the perspectives of promoting/preventing wellness/illness as a guideline for investigations, and request that a new public health framework be integrated in the existing field of 'tourism and health'. Without doubt, this is one possible avenue. However, it can be argued that this model is rather one-sided as it focuses on health with little evidence of including tourism aspects (apart from the tourists). The model may represent the broad field of tourism and health but it does not depict enough detail to accommodate attributing factors which are mentioned by Bushell and Lea, such as typology of tourists or destination categories.

It does not seem refined enough to offer directions for further research incorporating both fields (tourism and health) sufficiently. A framework can be seen as a system where all components are interdependent and interlinked in a way that variations in one component affect the rest of the system. Based on the results of this study, a framework for understanding tourism's health impacts in developing countries will most likely consist at least of the following major components: tourists, type of tourism, operators/developers, local population, local authorities, the environment, the level of tourism, and the country's current economic status.

Tourists (As Individuals/as Groups)

Tourists are probably the most active part in this framework as they are the ones actually moving around and coming into contact with places and people. A range of factors need to be considered as attributes of this constant visit or host encounter: tourist typology; tourists' health status and educational status; knowledge required for a particular trip; advice given; activities sought and their implications; speed of travel; size and numbers of groups; mode of transport chosen; accommodation (e.g., enclave vs homestay); travel patterns; travel corridors; travel seasons; and the degree of contact with the local population. Some of these factors are deliberately chosen by the individual, others occur unintentionally or have been decided for the tourist.

Type of Tourism

A further component is the type of tourism occurring in a particular location, from individual adventure travel to mass tourism. This has an effect on the degree of contact tourists have with locals as well as the potential of introducing diseases or causing other negative impacts, for example, on the environment. Although mass travel implies that large numbers of people travel, the accumulation of large numbers usually only occurs at very popular destinations, and these visitors may not come in contact with locals at all or rarely.

The impact of mass tourism on health is likely to be indirect, i.e. through economic, environmental or sociocultural affects. Adventure tourism is pursued by travelling individuals, alone or in very small groups, but their destinations are usually in more remote and isolated areas where they are also much more likely to come in c loser contact with local communities. These interactions most likely prepare the ground for potential direct impacts such as the transmission of diseases. Tourist activities are another dimension impacting on local destinations. Pearce and Moscardo (1989) developed a tool to investigate the Structure of Tourism Activities for Regions (STAR).

A list of attributes allows the classification of activities. Some of those at tributes are based on interactions between tourists and the environment (and hence important in relation to possible impacts), but no attribute is allocated to a possible interaction with the local population. As this interaction obviously does occur, on a continuum from very little to very close, not only should this dimension be added to the STAR (Structure of Tourism Activities for Regions) instrument, but it is an important factor in the assessment of health impacts of tourism. It may be useful to design a modified STAR tool that allows the creation of profiles of activities and their impact on host communities' health.

The dimensions of such a tool would be factors such as impact on the environment, degree of contact with locals, or potential risks to local employees.

Operators/developers A further important component are those individuals or companies/organisations who develop tourism destinations and provide services and facilities from travel agencies to transport companies and the accommodation industry. Clearly, the primary purpose of those businesses is to make a profit out of the tourism they promote. Ideally, operators should be mediators between tourists and hosts, if only to ensure sustainability of the operations. In reality, however, it seems that the links with the tourists are much closer, tourists and operator s are involved in a business transaction with one supplying what the other demands. Operators have a great responsibility when it comes to planning, developing and running tourism products as these rarely occur without impacts on the local populations. Very often, operators decide on activities offered, destinations visited, accommodation constructed and mode of transport provided. They, therefore, do represent a very important element in the health impact framework due to their intermediate position between visitors and hosts.

Local Population

Here, we are looking at the more passive, receiving end of the activity 'travel'. The following aspects are of importance: the geographical location; immunity and health status; level of education; previous contact with visitors; dependence on tourism; degree of contact with tourists; attitudes towards tourism; the difference between the cultural and social values of visitor and host; locals' involvement in tourism planning. Brown (1985) strongly emphasised that a suitable approach to an epidemiology of health "must take account of complexity, open-endedness, multiple interactions, value choices, social rules and types of personality...". Nothing less should be applied to the local host population.

Local authorities (health tourism) So far, little attention has been paid to the role of local health and tourism authorities in the protection of the health of the local population. It is important to recognise the role of these authorities. Although the aims of both authorities may not seem to have much common ground, with one developing and promoting tourism and the principles of business in mind, and the other in charge of the public health status, if they are to achieve sustainable tourism which benefits all parties involved, a close cooperation between both is necessary. This applies particularly to activities such as monitoring the local health status in tourism destinations and implementing strategies of improvement if necessary; investigating health impacts (in cooperation with other agencies, such as conservation groups); approving of tourism destinations only after a positive outcome of a health impact assessment; or terminating an operation when its impact is detrimental. In this respect, local authorities play a central role in the monitoring of tourists, locals, and operators as well as environmental issues.

Environment

The environment represents an essential resource for tourism. Budowski (1976) proposed three possible relationships between tourism and nature, *conflict, coexistence* and *symbiosis,* claiming that the majority of relationships are those of coexistence moving toward conflict. It seems not much has changed 20 years later. Changes in the environment affect humans' health as a short- or long-term consequence. It is, therefore, important that every effort is made to closely observe the environment for changes attributable to tourism to allow for timely act ion in order to reduce the health risks to locals and tourists.

Economic Status

In order to achieve the required monitoring discussed above, not only is a substantial budget necessary but also professional expertise in fields such as health, tourism, and conservation.

The same requirements apply i f research is to be conducted into topics suggested throughout this paper. A lesser developed country may well recognise negative impacts of tourism on the health of its people but may be in no position to do anything about it, not least because it is desperately dependent on tourism and foreign currency. Therefore, ways will have to be designed that allow countries with little expertise and economic abilities to still have strategies at hand to minimise a decrease in the local health status attributable to tourism.

These components and their relationships with each other can be seen as starting points for investigations A growth of research based knowledge on tourism's health impacts (as well as putting this area on priority lists of funding bodies) will allow the generation of theoretical frameworks in a reasonably near future. Such frameworks are necessary for applying this knowledge to practice, particularly for assessing health impacts. The ultimate goal will be to conduct such an assessment for prospective or current tourism developments in the same way as is already done for economic, environmental or, to a lesser extent, sociocultural impacts as, literally, prevention is better than cure.

Lacking such an assessment framework at the moment, other solutions have to be employed. Short-term solutions may centre around creating an awareness in tourists, locals and operators. In the longer term, other interventions may be necessary. Simmons' (1996) advice was meant for the protection of the environment but is equally applicable to health when he suggests the provision of 'honeypots' to draw people away from vulnerable spots. In practice, this could mean, rather than searching for isolated tribes in a rainforest, providing tourists with high quality interpretation centres.

The increase in tourism worldwide is likely to continue and the positive aspects of tourism in developing countries are acknowledged. However, it seems that health is being ignored in the process of tourism development, both "in terms of the local people and in the potential impact of travellers on the already scarce health resources" as Rudkin and Hall reported from the South Pacific.

If visitor-host encounters lead to a decreasing health status of the hosts, action needs to be taken in order to promote people's well-being and, consequently, the sustainability of tourism destinations for the benefit of the visitor *and* the host. Otherwise, the World Tourism Organization's objective" to accelerate and enlarge the contribution of tourism (international and domestic) to peace, understanding, *health,* and prosperity throughout the world" cannot be met

Medical Tourism and its Negative Impact on the Rural Primary Health Care to the Poor Families in Rural India

Medical tourism refers to the practice of people travelling abroad to obtain medical care and services. In the past medical tourism has mainly consisted of wealthy people travelling to countries such as the United States and paying for the use of advanced medical facilities. Nowadays, there is an increasing trend whereby patients are travelling to middle and low-income countries to obtain low-cost health services with short waiting times. Medical and surgical procedures can cost between five to ten times less in India than the United States.

Some destination countries such as India have actively promoted medical tourism. This is because it can bring about benefits including increases in revenue, foreign exchange reserves and tourism. It is estimated that medical tourism generates over US$60 billion in business. In addition, it has led to the creation of high-tech private medical facilities in India.

Questions remain about whether local populations actually benefit from these facilities and national health systems from the revenues that they generate. Experience from India suggests that private hospitals attract health professionals away from the public health sector and rural areas in India. This internal brain drain creates shortages of trained health workers, thus reducing access to healthcare for local populations in rural India and exacerbating inequalities.

In India some private hospitals agreed to provide services to poor people for no costs and in turn received government subsidies in the form of land, tax breaks and medical equipment. However, the facilities oriented towards medical tourism (technology intensive tertiary services) do not meet the health needs of the average poor rural Indian and evidence suggests that few poor people have benefited from such care. It is important that the government does not overlook the negative impacts that health tourism can have on local populations, in particular on access to services and availability of public health professionals. They should also find ways of ensuring that the revenues accrued from health tourists are channelled into the public sector through national laws and regulations.

The article describes a trend, where large numbers of patients from wealthy countries, such as America, are travelling abroad to diverse countries including India, in search of less expensive health care. The article uses examples of India and Thailand to examine the implications of medical tourism in these countries. It shows that in both countries medical tourism has caused private hospitals to emphasise treatment over prevention, and promote technology-intensive tertiary services at the expense of primary health care. This has created distortions in the allocation of resources and spending that doesn't match the needs of local people.

UK conference discusses 'disastrous' impact of the myth of 'HIV health tourism' HIV health tourism is one of the Government's main justifications for "a harmful, costly and inhumane charging policy." The UK Government's policy of charging so-called 'health tourists' for HIV treatment and care is a "public health disaster" based on myth not fact, Yusef Azad, Director of Policy and Campaigns for the National AIDS Trust (NAT) told last week's British HIV Association (BHIVA)

Autumn Conference during a session on treating migrant populations and their eligibility for care.

HIV health tourism is one of the Government's main justifications for "a harmful, costly and inhumane charging policy," according to a new NAT report, *The myth of HIV health tourism*. The results of that policy were highlighted at the conference by a panel consisting of an HIV clinician, a human rights lawyer, a GP who has cared for many asylum seekers with HIV, an HIV-positive migrant advocate, and Mr. Azad.

Since April 2004, overseas visitors, refused asylum seekers, undocumented migrants and visa overstayers have no longer been entitled to HIV treatment and care from the National Health Service (NHS) in England, although treatment for all other infectious diseases and sexually transmitted infections continues to be free to everyone on public health grounds irrespective of residency status. (The NHS in Scotland and Wales have different policies.)

Earlier this year, a High Court ruling resulted in HIV-positive refused asylum seekers being entitled to free HIV treatment and care for as long as they remained in the UK. But the judge refused a claim that there was a human right to NHS treatment, saying that any discrimination in the rules was justifiable so as to discourage 'health tourism'.

Yet a new NAT report that "separates facts and evidence around migration from fears and misinformation", argues that there is no evidence to demonstrate that HIV health tourism to the UK exists. Allegations of 'HIV health tourism', says the report, "make a serious charge against the integrity and truthfulness of many HIV-positive migrants to the UK, effectively alleging that stated reasons for migration to the UK are at best a pretext and at worst totally untrue. Given the discrimination and marginalisation experienced by many migrants we must question very carefully any claim which might add to social hostility".

The report also notes, "the claim of health tourism has been central to the Government's policy of charging refused asylum seekers and other migrants without lawful residency status for healthcare. The Government argues that free NHS care for those without what they deem to be a legitimate reason to migrate to the UK acts as a 'pull factor', encouraging illegal immigration and discouraging refused asylum seekers from leaving. Charges for NHS care for certain categories of migrant were introduced to end the 'pull' of free NHS care and address the so-called problem of 'health tourism'.

"Is there really evidence of HIV health tourism which would justify on grounds of immigration policy the singling out of HIV for NHS charges alone amongst all serious or sexually transmitted infections?" asks NAT. Over the course of twelve pages, the paper robustly argues that there is no evidence to demonstrate that 'HIV health tourism' is "a significant or real motivation for migration to the UK" and considerable evidence to demonstrate otherwise, "in particular the lower rates of HIV prevalence compared with country of origin, the long average delays [an average of five years] between arrival in the UK and accessing HIV testing and care, and the evidence available on the actual motivations of migrants coming to the UK".

Dr. Le Feuvre, a Kent GP, told the conference that NAT's conclusions match his own experience. "We had tens of thousands of [refugees and asylum seekers] coming through East Kent in the last ten years. I only personally remember one person amongst those tens of thousands who seemed to be coming here for medical treatment and the majority of people diagnosed with HIV, and who left the, left with it being diagnosed after their arrival and not before."

One of the paper's recommendations is that "since the provision of free HIV treatment has no bearing on migration trends, the basis for the Government's policy of charging for HIV treatment is wholly undermined. It has been demonstrated elsewhere that the policy actually increases costs to the NHS and endangers public health.

The Government must review its policy on NHS charging so as to exempt HIV treatment from charges."

The impact of this policy was brought into sharp focus at the BHIVA conference by Professor Jane Anderson of Homerton University Hospital, east London, who provided a case study to illustrate the desperation faced by HIV-positive undocumented migrants in England.

She told the conference about a 35 year-old East African woman who was refused a prescription by a medical team outside of London when she had only three days supply of antiretrovirals left and no means to return to her country of origin. "We gave her an immediate prescription for antiretroviral drugs...and gave her a travelcard from our charitable fund so she could get food and support from other charitable sources," she said.

She argued that HIV care in the UK should be for everyone. She noted that the new UK HIV testing guidelines, which include a list of 'indicator diseases' prompting the offer of opt-out testing "is only ethically acceptable if positive individuals are immediately linked into appropriate HIV treatment and care. Yet," she asked, "we are meant to send them to a place where they're going to get a big bill. Is this appropriate practice?"

Adam Hundt, a human rights lawyer provided an overview of the complex rules and regulations governing access to secondary NHS treatment and care, which he described as "a bit of a minefield". He noted that there are situations, people, and diseases exempted from the charging regulations including treatment given at an emergency department, 34 infectious diseases (including TB and viral hepatitis) and all sexually transmitted infections apart from HIV which he said, "is a policy decision".

There is also an exemption for continuing a course of treatment, including treatment for HIV, as long as someone has lawfully entered the UK. "Unhelpfully," he noted, "there's no definition of what 'a course of treatment' is."

The Government recently clarified that 'treatment' does not necessarily mean antiretroviral therapy, but in fact, can mean continued monitoring of immune and clinical status due to an HIV diagnosis. He noted that there is also much confusion amongst clinicians over what constitutes 'immediately necessary treatment' which should be provided to anyone regardless of their ability to pay. "It basically specifies that if someone requires treatment because their condition is life threatening, or because if treatment is not given immediately it will become life threatening, or because permanent and serious damage would be caused by any delay then they must be given treatment regardless of whether they can pay or not and then be charged for it later," he said.

Dr. Ian Williams, BHIVA's Chair, recently wrote to the Department of Health to argue that HIV care should be considered immediately necessary in the same way as maternity care. "I think the most important thing to remember," noted Mr. Hundt, "is that it's a matter of clinical judgment which should not be second-guessed by administrative staff." In the discussion that followed, Prof. Anderson pointed out the paradox of one Government department, the Department for International Development, supporting universal access to HIV treatment and care overseas, but another two Government departments, the Department of Health and the Home Office "denying that care free here and also sending people back through various legislation and legal decisions to places where there's no care. Why can't we have domestic policies that are the same as foreign policy?" she asked.

9

Branding Faith

Faith branding is the concept of branding religious organizations, leaders, or media programming, in the hope of penetrating a media-driven, consumer-oriented culture more effectively. Essentially, faith branding treats faith as a product and attempts to apply the principles of marketing in order to "sell" the product. Faith branding is a response to the challenge that religious organizations and leaders face today regarding how to express their faith in a media-dominated culture.

History

The idea of branding has been around since the 1400s, back then the most prominent book that was being sold was in fact the (Bible Einstein 67). The advertising strategy was to be up front and frank about what it was that the individual was trying to sell.

For instance they would say what the produce was, that people could buy that product right that moment, and how much it cost, these series of statements became known as direct sale messages (Einstein 67). As centuries past by the direct sale messages were used up until the industrial revolution of the 1800s and the marketing chain began to expand and change to adapt to the revolution.

Companies and manufactures began to change the way that they advertised their products to the consumers, they now talk about the physical features and how the product will benefit the consumer as they said that it would "make things simpler" (Einstein 67). In today's media driven society these same procedures have lived and are becoming more apparent with each and every new product that is released to the public.

Usage

This process has been refined to meet several different applications from religious groups to non-profit organizations that need help to become publicized and gain a voice of who they are and what their goals are. By utilizing commercial and advertising organizations to help promote the "product" (for example their Faith) they can make themselves known to the local area and even to the world. Due to the big media biz of the twenty first century, many people are not aware of how often the process of Faith Branding is used and how it affects them day to day.

Contributors

Mara Einstein, the author of Brands of Faith and Phil Cooke, the author of Branding Faith both describe the ways that faith branding is used throughout the world and how successful this type of marketing can be when you do the steps correctly and follow the plan. These two authors teach the subject of how faith branding can be used to break through the media that dominates most of the world's lives and how it can be exploited.

Examples of Faith Branding

Since society is so caught up in media today many have become distracted from other important issues. Another example of mass media taking over the lives of everyday people including Christians who according to the standards set by their worldview chooses to place priorities out of religious order, and even non-believers who choose to live by the standards that are set forth by the media and accept that as their life style. Take the major companies that dominate the shopping industry and look closely at their marketing techniques they use to advertise their products. During a religious holiday is when they are at their worst, in this case look at the Christian holiday known as Christmas. Ever since the man in a big red suit and a white beard started appearing in story time, Companies have taken this time to pull all of the stops out to sell their products in large scale by telling every individual that they deserve bigger and better things. This is not what Faith branding is used for at all.

Negative Aspects and Precautions

Faith Branding doesn't always work the way that we intend it to work and it does oppose some opinions to the way that it should work. Branding in general does throw up some red flags especially when the topic of branding is about faith or even culture. Most people believe that the procedure of making something more apparent in the media would be solely for the corporations that produce and sell consumer goods that would be purchased and used by an individual, and the subject would develop a "bad reputation" (Cooke 160).

In Cooke's book he states that there are three dangerous areas that need to be revealed when it comes to the process of faith branding, they are "technology, chasing relevance, and conflict with the concept of marketing" (Cooke 160). Cooke discovered these issues so that when organizations are faith branding then they know what they should be cautious when they use the techniques for breaking through the ever evolving media age of the twenty first century.

Designer Label

The term designer label refers to clothing and other personal accessory items sold under an often prestigious marque which is commonly named after a designer. The term is most often only applied to luxury items. Examples includes labels such as Burberry, Gucci, Armani, Calvin Klein, Versace, Shiatzy Chen, Louis Vuitton, Cartier SA, Dolce & Gabbana, Polo Ralph Lauren, Prada, Valentino, Chanel and others which are derived from the company's founder and most iconic designer.

Other clothing (and accessories) marquee names do not directly refer to the company's founder: for example, Dooney & Bourke, United Colors of Benetton, and L.L.Bean may be referred to as designer labels. While members of the upper middle class, or the mass affluent, are perhaps the most commonly targeted customers of these designer labels, some marquees—such as Cartier—tend to a wealthier customer base.

While a relationship between consumer products and social class may exist to some extent, any notion connecting consumer products to class status is of highly subjective and vague nature.

Branding Strategy

Branding is an important decision designed to enhance the identity of the product through the use of unique brand names, symbols and other distinctive measures. With competition growing more intense in almost all industries, establishing a strong brand allows an organization's products to stand out and avoid potential pitfalls, such as price wars, that have befallen many products. Therefore, a clear understanding of branding strategy is essential in order to build solid products and product lines. In particular, marketers should be aware of various branding approaches that can be pursued.

By branding approach we are referring to different product identification strategies that can be deployed to establish a product within the market. As we will see, the purpose of these approaches is to build a brand that will exist for the long term. Making smart decisions up front is crucial since a company may have to live with the decision for a long time.

Approaches to Branding

Branding approaches include the following:

- Individual Product Branding – Under this branding approach new products are assigned new names with no obvious connection to existing brands offered by the company. Under individual product branding the marketing organization must work hard to establish the brand in the market since it cannot ride the coattails of previously introduced brands. The chief advantage of this approach is it allows brands to stand on their own thus lessening threats that may occur to other brands marketed by the company. For instance, if another company brand receives negative publicity this news is less likely to rub off on the company's other brands that carry their own unique names. Additionally, as mentioned in the Product Decisions tutorial, brands can create financial gains through the concept known as brand equity. Under an individual branding approach, each brand builds its own separate equity which allows the company, if they choose, to sell off individual brands without impacting other brands owned by the company. The most famous marketing organization to follow this strategy is Procter and Gamble, which has historically introduced new brands without any link to other brands or even to the company name.
- Family Branding – Under this branding approach new products are placed under the umbrella of an existing brand. The principle advantage of this approach is that it enables the organization to rapidly build market awareness and acceptance since the brand is already established and known to the market. But the potential disadvantage is that the market has already established certain perceptions of the brand. For instance, a company that sells low-end, lower priced products may have a brand that is viewed as an economy brand. This brand image may create customer confusion and hinder the company if they

attempt to introduce higher-end, higher priced products using the same brand name. Additionally, with family branding any negative publicity that may occur for one product within a brand could spread to all other products that share the same name.

- Co-Branding – This approach takes the idea of individual and family branding a step further. With co-branding a marketer seeks to partner with another firm, which has an established brand, in hopes synergy of two brands on a product is even more powerful than a single brand. The partnership often has both firms sharing costs but also sharing the gains. For instance, major credit card companies, such as Visa and Master Card, offer co-branding options to companies and organizations. The cards carry the name of a co-branded organization (e.g., University name) along with the name of the issuing bank (e.g., Citibank) and the name of the credit card company. Besides tapping into awareness for multiple brands, the co-branding strategy is also designed to appeal to a larger target market, especially if each brand, when viewed separately, does not have extensive overlapping target markets with the other brand. Thus, co-branding allows both firms to tap into market segments where they did not previously have a strong position.
- Private or Store Branding – Some suppliers are in the business of producing products for other companies including placing another company's brand name on the product. This is most often seen in the retail industry where stores or online sellers contract with suppliers to manufacture the retailer's own branded products. In some cases the supplier not only produces product for the retailer's brand but also markets their own brand so that store shelves will contain both brands.
- Brand Licensing – Under brand licensing a contractual arrangement is created in which a company owning a brand name allows others to produce and supply products carrying the brand name. This is often seen when a brand is not directly connected with a product category. For instance, several famous children's characters, such as Sesame Street's Elmo, have been licensed to toy and food manufacturers who market products using the branded character's name and image.

Developing New Products

By its nature marketing requires new ideas. Unlike some organizational functions, where basic processes follow a fairly consistent routine (e.g., accounting), successful marketers are constantly making adjustments to their marketing efforts. New ideas are essential for responding to changing demand by the target market and by pressure exerted by competitors. These changes are manifested in decisions in all marketing areas including the development of new products.

In addition to being responsive to changing customer tastes and competitive forces, there are many other reasons why new product development is vital. These include:

- Many new products earn higher profits than older products. This is often the case for products considered innovative or unique which, for a period of time, may enjoy success and initially face little or no competition.
- New products can help reposition the company in customer's minds. For instance, a company that traditionally sold low priced products with few features may shift customers' perceptions about the company by introducing products with more features and slightly higher pricing.
- Fierce global competition and technological developments make it much easier for competitors to learn about products and replicate them. To stay ahead of competitors marketers must innovate and often create and introduce new products on a consistent schedule.

Generic Brand

Generic brands of consumer products (often supermarket goods) are distinguished by the absence of a brand name. It is often inaccurate to describe these products as "lacking a brand name", as they usually are branded, albeit with either the brand of the store in which they are sold or a lesser-known brand name which may not be aggressively advertised to the public. They are identified more by product characteristics.

They may be manufactured by less prominent companies, or manufactured on the same production line as a 'named' brand. Generic brands are usually priced below those products sold by supermarkets under their *own* brand (frequently referred to as "store brands" or "own brands"). Generally they imitate these more expensive brands, competing on price. Generic brand products are often of equal quality as a branded product, however, the quality may change suddenly in either direction with no change in the packaging if the supplier for the product changes.

Comparison with Store Brands

Today, such stark package design is rarely used. Lower priced products today usually bear the name of the store or supermarket where it is sold, or the name of the distribution company that supplies that store. A variation on this that is common in the United States is private labelling: brand names owned by the store that sells the product, that are not the same as the name of the store. For example, supermarket chain Safeway, Inc. sells dairy products under the Lucerne brand, while the Kroger's line of supermarkets sells products under several names, ranging from the top quality Private Selection down to the budget-driven line Kroger Value.

Membership-based "warehouse club" stores have begun their own contract-packed brands. The Wal-Mart owned Sam's Club sells products under the name Member's Mark, Costco sells products under the name Kirkland Signature (a reference to former corporate home office location, Kirkland, Washington), and BJ's Wholesale Club sells products branded Berkley & Jensen.

Generic branded food, as well as being cheaper than branded food products, may be a healthier alternative with independent research finding supermarket own-brand cereals containing less salt, and saturated fat than the branded equivalent.. In addition to price and nutrition, evidence suggests that quality is equal to, if not better than established brands and in the 2007 Whisky Bible several supermarket single malts were rated higher than top-brand distilleries with Tesco the highest rating own-brand..

Premium and Value Generic Brands

Rather than offering a single own-brand alternative supermarkets have in recent years introduced 'premium' and 'value' ranges offering varying quality and price. Some supermarkets advertise the quality of their premium own-brands for example Sainsbury's television commercial featuring celebrity chef Jamie Oliver. Value supermarket brands are sold at considerably less than known brands, sometimes even below cost price, to entice the shopper into the store. Despite perceived lower quality supermarket own-brands continue to sell and a trading standards investigation found that there was little nutritional or taste difference between value and regular products.

Generic Drugs: When patent protection expires on a drug it may be sold generically at a considerable discount, less both patent royalties and marketing expenses.

Name Generator

A name generator is a program that uses language rules or word combining techniques to generate a list of names.

Name Domains

According to verisign, the.name top-level domain name (TLD) is designed for individuals to create a presence and make online communications easy and accessible. Not exclusive to registrars, social networking and community sites may also offer.name registration to their members and customers as a value-added service to help establish an individual identity online.

Ethnic Names

- Arabic name
- Bulgarian name
- Chinese name
- Dutch name
- Family name
- French name
- German name
- Germanic name
- Greek name
- Hebrew name
- Hungarian name
- Icelandic name
- Indian name
- Indonesian name, including single-word names
- Japanese name
- Javanese name
- Korean name
- Mongolian name
- Pakistani name
- Polish name
- Russian name
- Saint Thomas Christian names
- Slavic names

- Spanish name
- Vietnamese name.

Brands and Branding

An essential issue in product management is branding. Different firms have different policies on the branding on their products. While 3M puts its brand name on a great diversity of products, Proctor & Gamble, on the opposite extreme, maintains a separate brand name for each product. In general, the use of *brand extensions* should be evaluated on the basis of the compatibility of various products—can the same brand name represent different products without conflict or confusion?

Coca Cola for many years resisted putting its coveted brand name on a diet soft drink. In the old days, available sweeteners such as saccharin added an undesirable aftertaste, implying a clear sacrifice in taste for the reduction in calories.

Thus, to avoid damaging the brand name Coca Cola, Coke instead named its diet cola Tab. Only after NutraSweet was introduced was the brand extension allowed. Research shows that consumers are more receptive to brand extensions when (1) the company appears to have the expertise to make the product [McDonald's was not thought as credible as a photo-finishing service], (2) the products are congruent (compatible), and (3) the brand extension is not seen as being exploitative of a high quality brand name [e.g., one should not use a premium brand name like Heineken to make a trivially easy product like popcorn]. In many markets, brands of different strength compete against each other. At the top level are *national* or *international* brands. A large investment has usually been put into extensive brand building—including advertising, distribution and, if needed, infrastructure support. Although some national brands are better regarded than others—e.g., Dell has a better reputation than e-Machines—the national brands usually sell at higher prices than to *regional* and *store* brands.

Regional brands, as the name suggests, are typically sold only in one area. In some cases, regional distribution is all that firms can initially accomplish with the investment capital and other resources that they have. This means that advertising is usually done at the regional level.

This limits the advertising opportunities and thus the effect of advertising. In some cases, regional brands may eventually grow into national ones.

Trademark

A trademark or trade mark or trade-mark is a distinctive sign or indicator used by an individual, business organization, or other legal entity to identify that the products or services to consumers with which the trademark appears originate from a unique source, and to distinguish its products or services from those of other entities.

A trademark may be designated by the following symbols:

- ™ (for an unregistered trade mark, that is, a mark used to promote or brand goods)
- ! (for an unregistered service mark, that is, a mark used to promote or brand services)
- ® (for a registered trademark).

A trademark is typically a name, word, phrase, logo, symbol, design, image, or a combination of these elements. There is also a range of non-conventional trademarks comprising marks which do not fall into these standard categories, such as those based on colour, smell, or sound.

The owner of a registered trademark may commence legal proceedings for trademark infringement to prevent unauthorized use of that trademark. However, registration is not required. The owner of a common law trademark may also file suit, but an unregistered mark may be protectable only within the geographical area within which it has been used or in geographical areas into which it may be reasonably expected to expand.

The term *trademark* is also used informally to refer to any distinguishing attribute by which an individual is readily identified, such as the well known characteristics of celebrities. When a trademark is used in relation to services rather than products, it may sometimes be called a service mark, particularly in the United States.

Fundamental Concepts

The essential function of a trademark is to exclusively identify the commercial source or origin of products or services, such that a trademark, properly called, indicates source or serves as a badge of origin. In other words, trademarks serve to identify a particular business as the source of goods or services. The use of a trademark in this way is known as trademark use. Certain exclusive rights attach to a registered mark, which can be enforced by way of an action for trademark infringement, while unregistered trademark rights may be enforced pursuant to the common law tort of passing off. It should be noted that trademark rights generally arise out of the use or to maintain exclusive rights over that sign in relation to certain products or services, assuming there are no other trademark objections.

Different goods and services have been classified by the International (Nice) Classification of Goods and Services into 45 Trademark Classes (1 to 34 cover goods, and 35 to 45 services). The idea of this system is to specify and limit the extension of the intellectual property right by determining which goods or services are covered by the mark, and to unify classification systems around the world.

History

In trademark treatises it is usually reported that blacksmiths who made swords in the Roman Empire are thought of as being the first users of trademarks. Other notable trademarks that have been used for a long time include Lowenbrau, which claims use of its lion mark since 1383, and Stella Artois, which claims use since 1366.

Registered trademarks involve registering the trademark with the government. The oldest registered trademarks in various countries include:

- United Kingdom: 1876 – The Bass Red Triangle was the first trademark to be registered under the Trade Mark Registration Act 1875.
- United States: Picture of Samson wrestling a lion, to Samson Rope in 1884.

Symbols

The two symbols associated with U.S. trademarks ™ (the trademark symbol) and ® (the registered trademark symbol) represent the status of a mark and accordingly its level of protection. While ™ can be used with any common law usage of a mark, ® may only be used by the owner of a mark following registration with the relevant national authority, such as the U.S. Patent and Trademark Office (USPTO or PTO). The proper manner to display either symbol is immediately following the mark in superscript style.

Terminology

Terms such as “mark”, “brand” and “logo” are sometimes used interchangeably with “trademark”. “Trademark”, however, also includes any device, brand, label, name, signature, word, letter, numerical, shape of goods, packaging, colour or combination of colours, smell, sound, movement or any combination thereof which is capable of distinguishing goods and services of one business from those of others. It must be capable of graphical representation and must be applied to goods or services for which it is registered.

Specialized types of trademark include certification marks, collective trademarks and defensive trademarks. A trademark which is popularly used to describe a product or service (rather than to distinguish the product or services from those of third parties) is sometimes known as a genericized trademark. If such a mark becomes synonymous with that product or service to the extent that the trademark owner can no longer enforce its proprietary rights, the mark becomes generic.

Registration

The law considers a trademark to be a form of property. Proprietary rights in relation to a trademark may be established through actual use in the marketplace, or through registration of the mark with the trademarks office (or "trademarks registry") of a particular jurisdiction. In some jurisdictions, trademark rights can be established through either or both means. Certain jurisdictions generally do not recognize trademarks rights arising through use. If trademark owners do not hold registrations for their marks in such jurisdictions, the extent to which they will be able to enforce their rights through trademark infringement proceedings will therefore be limited. In cases of dispute, this disparity of rights is often referred to as "first to file" as opposed to "first to use." Other countries such as Germany offer a limited amount of common law rights for unregistered marks where to gain protection, the goods or services must occupy a highly significant position in the marketplace — where this could be 40% or more market share for sales in the particular class of goods or services.

In the United States the registration process entails several steps prior to a trademark receiving its Certificate of Registration. First, an Applicant, the individual or entity applying for the registration, files an application to register the respective trademark. The application is then placed in line in the order it was received to be examined by an examining attorney for the U.S. Patent and Trademark Office. Second, following a period of anywhere from three to six months the application is reviewed by an examining attorney to make sure that it complies with all requirements in order to be entitled to registration. This review includes procedural matters such as making sure the applicant's goods or services are identified properly.

It also includes more substantive matters such as making sure the applicant's mark is not merely descriptive or likely to cause confusion with a pre-existing applied-for or registered mark. If the application runs afoul of any requirement, the examining attorney will issue an office action requiring the applicant to address certain issues or refusals prior to registration of the mark. Third, and after the examination of the mark has concluded with no issues to be addressed or an applicant has responded adequately to an examining attorney's concerns, the application will be published for opposition. During this 30-day period third-parties who may be affected by the registration of the trademark may step forward to file an Opposition Proceeding to stop the registration of the mark. If an Opposition proceeding is filed it institutes a case before the Trademark Trial and Appeal Board to determine both the validity of the grounds for the opposition as well as the ability of the applicant to register the mark at issue. Fourth, provided that no third-party opposes the registration of the mark during the opposition period or the opposition is ultimately decided in the applicant's favour the mark will be registered in due course.

Outside of the United States the registration process is substantially similar to that found in the U.S. save for one notable exception in many countries: registration occurs prior to the opposition proceeding. In short, once an application is reviewed by an examiner and found to be entitled to registration a registration certificate is issued subject to the mark being open to opposition for a period of typically 6 months from the date of registration.

A registered trademark confers a bundle of exclusive rights upon the registered owner, including the right to exclusive use of the mark in relation to the products or services for which it is registered. The law in most jurisdictions also allows the owner of a registered trademark to prevent unauthorized use of the mark in relation to products or services which are identical or "colourfully" similar to the "registered" products or services, and in certain cases, prevent use in relation to entirely dissimilar products or services. The test is always whether a consumer of the goods or services will be confused as to the identity of the source or origin. An example may be a very large multinational brand such as "Sony" where a non-electronic product such as a pair of sunglasses might be assumed to have come from Sony Corporation of Japan despite not being a class of goods that Sony has rights in.

Once trademark rights are established in a particular jurisdiction, these rights are generally only enforceable in that jurisdiction, a quality which is sometimes known as territoriality. However, there is a range of international trademark laws and systems which facilitate the protection of trademarks in more than one jurisdiction.

Search

In the United States, the USPTO maintains a database of registered trademarks. The database is open to the public; however a licensed attorney may be required to interpret the search results. Furthermore as trademarks are governed by federal law, state law, and common law, a thorough search as to the availability of a mark is very important. In the United States, obtaining a trademark search and relying upon the results of an opinion issued by an attorney may insulate a trademark user from being required to pay treble damages and attorney's fees in a trademark infringement case as it demonstrates that the trademark user performed due diligence and was using the mark in good faith. The USPTO internally captures more information about trademarks than what they publicly disclose on their official search website. For example, the USPTO collects information about what exactly is shown inside every logo trademark filing.

Trademarks may also be searched on third-party databases, such as LexisNexis, Dialog and Compu-Mark.

In Europe and if a community trademark has to be filed, searches have to be conducted with the OHIM (Community Trademark Office) and with the various national offices. An alternative solution is to conduct a trademark search within private databases.

Ability to Register

In most systems, a trademark can be registered if it is able to distinguish the goods or services of a party, will not confuse consumers about the relationship between one party and another, and will not otherwise deceive consumers with respect to the qualities of the product.

Distinctive Character

Maintaining Rights

Trademarks rights must be maintained through actual lawful use of the trademark. These rights will cease if a mark is not actively used for a period of time, normally 5 years in most jurisdictions. In the case of a trademark registration, failure to actively use the mark in the lawful course of trade, or to enforce the registration in the event of infringement, may also expose the registration itself to become liable for an application for the removal from the register after a certain period of time on the grounds of "non-use".

It is not necessary for a trademark owner to take enforcement action against all infringement if it can be shown that the owner perceived the infringement to be minor and inconsequential. This is designed to prevent owners from continually being tied up in litigation for fear of cancellation. An owner can at any time commence action for infringement against a third party as long as it had not previously notified the third party of its discontent following third party use and then failed to take action within a reasonable period of time (called acquiescence). The owner can always reserve the right to take legal action until a court decides that the third party had gained notoriety which the owner 'must' have been aware of. It will be for the third party to prove their use of the mark is substantial as it is the onus of a company using a mark to check they are not infringing previously registered rights. In the US, owing to the overwhelming number of unregistered rights, trademark applicants are advised to perform searches not just of the trademark register but of local business directories and relevant trade press. Specialized search companies perform such tasks prior to application.

All jurisdictions with a mature trademark registration system provide a mechanism for removal in the event of such non use, which is usually a period of either three or five years. The intention to use a trademark can be proven by a wide range of acts as shown in the "Wooly Bull" and "Ashton v Harlee" cases. In the U.S., failure to use a trademark for this period of time, aside from the corresponding impact on product quality, will result in abandonment of the mark, whereby any party may use the mark. An abandoned mark is not irrevocably in the public domain, but may instead be re-registered by any party which has re-established exclusive and active use, and must be associated or linked with the original mark owner. If a court rules that a trademark has become "generic" through common use (such that the mark no longer performs the essential trademark function and the average consumer no longer considers that exclusive rights attach to it), the corresponding registration may also be ruled invalid.

Unlike other forms of intellectual property (e.g., patents and copyrights) a registered trademark can, theoretically, last forever. So long as a trademark's use is continuous a trademark holder may keep the mark registered with the U.S. Patent and Trademark Office by filing Section 8 Affidavit(s) of Continuous Use as well as Section 9 Applications for renewal, as required.

Specifically, once registered with the U.S. Patent and Trademark Office the owner of a trademark is required to file a Section 8 Affidavit of Continuous Use to maintain the registration between the 5th and 6th year anniversaries of the registration of the mark or during the 6-month grace period following the 6th-year anniversary of the registration. Note, if the Section 8 Affidavit is filed during the 6-month grace period additional fees to file the Affidavit with the U.S. Patent and Trademark Office will apply.

In addition to requirement above, U.S. trademark registrations are also required to be renewed on or about every 10-year anniversary of the registration of the trademark. The procedure for 10-year renewals is somewhat different from that for the 5th-6th year renewal. In brief, registrants are required to file both a Section 8 Affidavit of Continuous Use as well as a Section 9 Application for Renewal every ten years to maintain their registration.

Enforcing Rights

The extent to which a trademark owner may prevent unauthorized use of trademarks which are the same as or similar to its trademark depends on various factors such as whether its trademark is registered, the similarity of the trademarks involved, the similarity of the products or services involved, and whether the owner's trademark is well known or, under U.S. law relating to trademark dilution, famous.

If a trademark has not been registered, some jurisdictions (especially Common Law countries) offer protection for the business reputation or goodwill which attaches to unregistered trademarks through the tort of passing off. Passing off may provide a remedy in a scenario where a business has been trading under an unregistered trademark for many years, and a rival business starts using the same or a similar mark.

If a trademark has been registered, then it is much easier for the trademark owner to demonstrate its trademark rights and to enforce these rights through an infringement action. Unauthorized use of a registered trademark need not be intentional in order for infringement to occur, although damages in an infringement lawsuit will generally be greater if there was an intention to deceive.

For trademarks which are considered to be well known, infringing use may occur where the use occurs in relation to products or services which are not the same as or similar to the products or services in relation to which the owner's mark is registered. A growing area of law relating to the enforcement of trademark rights is secondary liability, which allows for the imputation of liability to one who has not acted directly to infringe a trademark but whose legal responsibility may arise under the doctrines of either contributory or vicarious liability.

Limits and Defenses to Claims of Infringement

Trademark is subject to various defenses, such as abandonment, limitations on geographic scope, and fair use. In the United States, the fair use defence protects many of the interests in free expression related to those protected by the First Amendment. Fair use may be asserted on two grounds, either that the alleged infringer is using the mark to describe accurately an aspect of its products, or that the alleged infringer is using the mark to identify the mark owner. One of the most visible proofs that trademarks provide a limited right in the U.S. comes from the comparative advertising that is seen throughout U.S. media. An example of the first type is that although Maytag owns the trademark "Whisper Quiet", makers of other products may describe their goods as being "whisper quiet" so long as these competitors are not using the phrase as a trademark.

An example of the second type is that Audi can run advertisements saying that a trade publication has rated an Audi model higher than a BMW model, since they are only using "BMW" to identify the competitor. In a related sense, an auto mechanic can truthfully advertise that he services Cadillacs, and a former *Playboy* Playmate of the Year can identify herself as such on her website.

Wrongful or Groundless Threats of Infringement

Various jurisdictions have laws which are designed to prevent trademark owners from making wrongful threats of trademark infringement action against other parties. These laws are intended to prevent large or powerful companies from intimidating or harassing smaller companies.

Where one party makes a threat to sue another for trademark infringement, but does not have a genuine basis or intention to carry out that threat, or does not carry out the threat at all within a certain period, the threat may itself become a basis for legal action. In this situation, the party receiving such a threat may seek from the Court a declaratory judgment; also known as a declaratory ruling.

10

Hologram Trademarks

A hologram trademark is a non-conventional trademark where a hologram is used to perform the trademark function of uniquely identifying the commercial origin of products or services. In recent times holograms have been increasingly used as trade marks in the marketplace. However, it has traditionally been difficult to protect holograms as trademarks through registration, as a hologram was not considered to be a 'trademark'. This issue was addressed by the World Trade Organization Agreement on Trade-Related Aspects of Intellectual Property Rights, which broadened the legal definition of trademark to encompass "any sign...capable of distinguishing the goods or services of one undertaking from those of other undertakings" (article 15(1)).

Despite the recognition which must be accorded to holograms trademarks in most countries in other fields of the art, the *graphical representation* of such marks sometimes constitutes a problem for trademark owners seeking to protect their marks, and different countries have different methods for dealing with this issue.

Registration of Hologram Marks in Different Jurisdictions

Canada: In Canada, hologram trademarks are generally not acceptable if they cannot be represented graphically or if they are regarded as more than one mark.

European Union: In the European Union, Article 4 of *Council Regulation (EC) No. 40-94* of 20 December 1993 ("signs of which a Community Trade Mark may consist") relevantly states that any CTM may consist of "any signs capable of being represented graphically...provided that such signs are capable of distinguishing the goods or services of one undertaking from those of other undertakings". In Sieckmann v German Patent Office (case C-273/00) the EcJ states that graphical representation, preferably means by images, lines or characters, and that the representation must be clear, precise, self-contained, easily accessible, intelligible, durable and objective.

This definition generally encompasses only very simply structured holograms, and therefore an applicant for a CTM may use one photograph or some views to graphically represent their trade mark.

United States

In the United States, the trademark manual for examination requires under 1202.14 that a hologram used in varying forms does not function as a mark in the absence of evidence that consumers would perceive it as a trademark. Where the Board held that a hologram used on trading cards in varying shapes, sizes, and positions did not function as a mark, because the record showed that other companies used holograms on trading cards and other products as anti-counterfeiting devices, and there was no evidence that the public would perceive applicant's hologram as an indicator of source. The Board noted that "the common use of holograms for non-trademark purposes means that consumers would be less likely to perceive applicant's uses of holograms as trademarks."

59 USPQ2d at 1693. Therefore, in the absence of evidence of consumer recognition as a mark, the examining attorney should refuse registration on the ground that the hologram does not function as a mark, under §§1, 2 and 45 of the Trademark Act, 15 U.S.C. §§1051, 1052 and 1127. Generally, if a hologram has two or more views, the examining attorney should also refuse registration under §§1 and 45 of the Trademark Act, 15 U.S.C. §§1051 and 1127, on the ground that the application seeks registration of more than one mark. In re Upper Deck, supra. Provided the applicant can demonstrate that the use of a hologram or moving image both serves as a mark and is not functional, an application for such a mark may be made to either register. That being said, Examining Attorneys are instructed to refuse an application for registration of a hologram if the applicant does not provide evidence of consumer recognition of the hologram as a mark. the applicant seeking registration of a hologram must submit a drawing of the mark that captures the dimensions thereof.

Further, Examiners are instructed to refuse registration of any holograms that show two different images on the grounds that the application is seeking protection for two separate marks. Further, the application must include detailed written description of the mark. During publication the drawing pages for these marks are published and thereafter the drawing page is incorporated into the registration certificate which is made available at the USPTO as well as the USPTO website.

List of Fictional Brands

A fictional brand is a non-existing brand used in artistic or entertainment productions — paintings, books, comics, movies, TV serials, etc. The fictional brand may be designed to imitate a real corporate brand, satirize a real corporate brand, or differentiate itself from real corporate brands. Such a device may be required where real corporations are unwilling to license their brand names for use in the fictional work, particularly where the work holds the product in a negative light. More recently, Muzellec and Lynn (2010) have shown that fictional brands my be used for commercial purposes through the process of reverse product placement. Their paper considers the case of Duff Beer and Bertie Bott's Every Flavour Beans and reveals that consumers'attachment to those brands in the fictional world may be leveraged through "defictionalisation" or "productisation" in the real world.

Why Create Fictional Brands?

Works of fiction often mention or show specific brands to give more realism to the plot or scenery. Specific brands provide descriptive details that the author can use to craft a plot: a character may own a factory that manufactures a popular product, or may make a scene by demanding a particular brand; a detective may get clues from the brand of cigarettes smoked by a suspect; a film may include a commercial poster on the background, or show a package of cereal in close-up.

However, unauthorized use of real trademarks for such purposes could trigger legal action by their owners — especially if the brands are referenced in a way that could be seen to have negative marketing impact. In general, the use of a real brand requires prior written consent by the brand's owner, who will typically demand some control on the brand's use. These hassles are probably the main reason for the use of fictitious brands.

Real brands are often used, of course. Sometimes a specific brand is needed because of its prior associations; e.g. the Coca-Cola machine scene in Kubrick's Dr. Strangelove would not work with any other real or fictitious brand (except possibly Pepsi). Sometimes the author will use a common brand only to make the scene more natural or create a specific ambience. More commonly, such uses are instances of product placement — the insertion of "casual" (but actually paid and intentional) positive references to brands in movies, television programming, games, and books. However, this practice is so widespread in the entertainment industry that it gives authors another reason to avoid the use of real brands: any such reference would be suspected by the public of being paid advertising, and could diminish the artistic or intellectual merit of the work.

Another advantage to a fictional brand is that all its specifications can be invented. In this sense, an author can invent a model or brand of car, for which he can make up details. That way, he doesn't have to go look up specifications on a car, which would take time and effort-he could just make them up. Sometimes, usually on television or movies, a real brand would not be permitted due to restrictions in advertising particular products, especially cigarettes and alcohol. Usually a fictional brand would be created that bears some resemblance to a real brand.

Television programs made in Canada for the Canadian market are not permitted to show or mention real brand names except in certain specific circumstances. The CRTC's prohibition of product placement exists primarily to prevent producers from accepting payola, especially if accepting it affects creative control or leads producers to attempt to deceive the audience (by, for instance, implying that X Brand Olive Oil is the best brand because the host uses it). In some instances (especially cooking and home improvement shows) brand names are merely inked, taped, or edited out; in dramatic presentations, however, fake brand names may be used. The restriction does not apply to news or current affairs programs when mention of the brand is necessary to fairly and fully present the subject matter, and it does not apply to televised sporting events, where branding may be beyond the station's control. Programs produced outside of Canada are not subject to these rules.

Yet another reason to use a fictional brand is that sometimes a product is itself a major "character" in the plot, and using a real brand would limit creativity as the author would be constrained by the actual attributes of that brand. A subset of this is comedic brands, the most famous being "Acme" for the maker of complicated gadgets that never quite work.

Finally, the use of a real brand may be excluded also when the plot is meant to develop in a time or place (e.g. in a distant future, or in a fictional universe) where the real brand would not have existed anyway. Alternately, made-up brands are often more humorous than real brands, which is why a lot of cartoons and sitcoms prefer them.

Sound Trademarks

A sound trademark is a non-conventional trademark where sound is used to perform the trademark function of uniquely identifying the commercial origin of products or services.

In recent times, sounds have been increasingly used as trademarks in the marketplace. However, it has traditionally been difficult to protect sounds as trademarks through registration, as a sound was not considered to be a 'trademark'.

This issue was addressed by the World Trade Organization Agreement on Trade-Related Aspects of Intellectual Property Rights, which broadened the legal definition of trademark to encompass "any sign...capable of distinguishing the goods or services of one undertaking from those of other undertakings". Despite the recognition which must be accorded to sound trademarks in most countries, the *graphical representation* of such marks sometimes constitutes a problem for trademark owners seeking to protect their marks, and different countries have different methods for dealing with this issue.

Registration of Sound Marks in Different Jurisdictions

Australia

Graphic Representation

In Australia, sound trademarks are generally acceptable if they can be represented by musical notation. According to the Australian trademarks Office, an application for a sound trademark which cannot be graphically represented with musical notation must include the following requirements.

- a graphic representation of the mark (e.g.. "CLIP CLOP MOO");
- a clear and concise description of the trademark (examples are given below);
  - o The trademark is a sound mark. It comprises the sound of dogs barking to the traditional tune "Greensleeves" as rendered in the audio tape accompanying the application.

- o The trademark consists of the sound of two steps taken by a cow on pavement, followed by the sound of a cow mooing (clip, clop, MOO) as rendered in the recording accompanying the application.
- o The trademark consists of the sound of a soprano voice singing wordlessly to the tune represented in the musical score attached to the application. The trademark is demonstrated in the recording accompanying the application form.
- o The trademark consists of a repeated rapid tapping sound made by a wooden stick tapping on a metal garbage can lid which gradually becomes louder over approximately 10 seconds duration. The sound is demonstrated in the recordings accompanying the application.

- a recording of the trademark which can be played back on media which is easily and commonly accessible.

Other requirements are set out in the *trademarks Office Manual of Practice and Procedure* issued by IP Australia.

European Union

In the European Union, Article 4 of *Council Regulation (EC) No. 40-94* of 20 December 1993 ("signs of which a Community trademark may consist") relevantly states that any CTM may consist of "any signs capable of being represented graphically...provided that such signs are capable of distinguishing the goods or services of one undertaking from those of other undertakings". In Shield mark B.V. v Joost Kist (case C-283/01) the EcJ basically repeats the criteria from Sieckmann v German Patent Office (case C-273/00) that graphical representation, preferably means by images, lines or characters, and that the representation must be clear, precise, self-contained, easily accessible, intelligible, durable and objective.

This definition generally encompasses sound marks, and therefore an applicant for a CTM may use musical notation to graphically represent their trademark. A piece of music—a tune, or a ring tone on a telephone, can they be easily registered as a trademark (provided, of course, that it meets the Community trademark tests for registrability and distinctiveness). While tunes are capable of registration, before 2005 noises were not. The sound of a dog barking or the crash of surf cannot be recorded in musical notation and sonagrams were not accepted by the OHIM trademark registry. A change in legislation occurred in 2005 so that now the Office accepts sonograms as a graphical representation of a trademark if they are accompanied by an MP3 sound file when filing a trademark electronically.

United States

In the United States, the test for whether a sound can serve as a trademark "depends on [the] aural perception of the listener which may be as fleeting as the sound itself unless, of course, the sound is so inherently different or distinctive that it attaches to the subliminal mind of the listener to be awakened when heard and to be associated with the source or event with which it struck".

This was the fairly strict test applied by the US Trademark Trial and Appeal Board in the case of General Electric Broadcasting Co., 199 USPQ 560, in relation to the timed toll of a ship's bell clock.

More famously, Harley-Davidson attempted to register as a trademark the distinctive "chug" of a Harley Davidson motorcycle engine. On 1 February 1994, the company filed its application with the following description: "The mark consists of the exhaust sound of applicant's motorcycles, produced by V-twin, common crankpin motorcycle engines when the goods are in use". Nine of Harley Davidson's competitors filed oppositions against the application, arguing that cruiser-style motorcycles of various brands use the same crankpin V-twin engine which produces the same sound. After six years of litigation, with no end in sight, in early 2000, Harley Davidson withdrew their application.

Other companies have been more successful in registering their distinctive sounds: MGM and their lion's roar; the NBC chimes; famous basketball team the Harlem Globetrotters and their theme song "Sweet Georgia Brown"; Intel and the three-second chord sequence used with the Pentium processor; THX and its "Deep Note"; Federal Signal Corporation and the sound of their "Q2B" fire truck siren; AT&T and the spoken letters "AT&T" accompanied by music; RKO with a combined moving image and sound mark depicting the RKO Pictures radio tower transmitting a Morse-code like signal; and 20th Century Fox with the very famous fanfare composed by Alfred Newman.

Corporate Identity

In marketing, a corporate identity is the "persona" of a corporation which is designed to accord with and facilitate the attainment of business objectives. It is usually visibly manifested by way of branding and the use of trademarks. Corporate identity comes into being when there is a common ownership of an organizational philosophy that is manifest in a distinct corporate culture — the corporate personality.

At its most profound, the public feel that they have ownership of the philosophy. Often referred to as organizational identity, corporate identity helps organizations to answer questions like "who are we?" and "where are we going?" Corporate identity also allows consumers to denote their sense of belonging with particular human aggregates or groups. In general, this amounts to a corporate title, logo (logotype and/or logogram), and supporting devices commonly assembled within a set of guidelines.

These guidelines govern how the identity is applied and confirm approved colour palettes, typefaces, page layouts and other such methods of maintaining visual continuity and brand recognition across all physical manifestations of the brand. These guidelines are usually formulated into a package of tools called corporate identity manuals.

Many companies, such as McDonald's and Electronic Arts, have their own identity that runs through all of their products and merchandise. The trademark "M" logo and the yellow and red appears consistently throughout the McDonald's packaging and advertisements. Many companies pay large amounts of money for the research, design and execution involved in creating an identity that is extremely distinguishable and appealing to the company's target audience.

Concept

Corporate identity is often viewed as being composed of three parts:

- Corporate design (logos, uniforms, corporate colours etc.)
- Corporate communication (advertising, public relations, information, etc.)
- Corporate behaviour (internal values, norms, etc.)

Corporate identity has become a universal technique for promoting companies and improving corporate culture. Most notable is the COCOMAS committee and company PAOS, both founded by Motoo Nakanishi in Tokyo, Japan in 1968. Nakanishi fused design, management consulting and corporate culture to revolutionize corporate identity in Japan. In the United States, graphic design firms such as Chermayeff & Geismar pioneered the application of modernist principles to corporate identity design.

Organizational Point of View

In a recent monograph on Chinese corporate identity (Routledge, 2006), Peter Peverelli, proposes a new definition of corporate identity, based on the general organization theory proposed in his earlier work, in particular Peverelli (2000). This definition regards identity as a result of social interaction:

- Corporate identity is the way corporate actors (actors who perceive themselves as acting on behalf of the company) make sense of their company in ongoing social interaction with other actors in a specific context. It includes shared perceptions of reality, ways-to-do-things, etc., and interlocked behaviour.
- In this process the corporate actors are of equal importance as those others; corporate identity pertains to the company (the group of corporate actors) as well as to the relevant others;
- Corporate actors construct different identities in different contexts.

Visual Identity

Corporate visual identity plays a significant role in the way an organization presents itself to both internal and external stakeholders. In general terms, a corporate visual identity expresses the values and ambitions of an organization, its business, and its characteristics. Four functions of corporate visual identity can be distinguished. Three of these are aimed at external stakeholders.

1. First, a corporate visual identity provides an organisation with visibility and "recognizability". For virtually all profit and non-profit organisations, it is of vital importance that people know that the organization exists and remember its name and core business at the right time.
2. Second, a corporate visual identity symbolizes an organization for external stakeholders, and, hence, contributes to its image and reputation (Schultz, Hatch and Larsen, 2000). Van den Bosch, De Jong and Elving (2005) explored possible relationships between corporate visual identity and reputation, and concluded that corporate visual identity plays a supportive role in corporate reputations.
3. Third, a corporate visual identity expresses the structure of an organization to its external stakeholders, visualising its coherence as well as the relationships between divisions or units. Olins (1989) is well-known for his "corporate identity

structure", which consists of three concepts: monolithic brands for companies which have a single brand, a branded identity in which different brands are developed for parts of the organization or for different product lines, and an endorsed identity with different brands which are (visually) connected to each other. Although these concepts introduced by Olins are often presented as the corporate identity structure, they merely provide an indication of the visual presentation of (parts of) the organization. It is therefore better to describe it as a "corporate visual identity structure".

4. A fourth, internal function of corporate visual identity relates to employees' identification with the organization as a whole and/or the specific departments they work for (depending on the corporate visual strategy in this respect). Identification appears to be crucial for employees, and corporate visual identity probably plays a symbolic role in creating such identification.

The definition of the corporate visual identity management is:

Corporate visual identity management involves the planned maintenance, assessment and development of a corporate visual identity as well as associated tools and support, anticipating developments both inside and outside the organization, and engaging employees in applying it, with the objective of contributing to employees' identification with and appreciation of the organization as well as recognition and appreciation among external stakeholders.

Special attention is paid to corporate identity in times of organizational change. Once a new corporate identity is implemented, attention to corporate identity related issues generally tends to decrease. However, corporate identity needs to be managed on a structural basis, to be internalized by the employees and to harmonize with future organizational developments.

Efforts to manage the corporate visual identity will result in more consistency and the corporate visual identity management mix should include structural, cultural and strategic aspects. Guidelines, procedures and tools can be summarized as the structural aspects of managing the corporate visual identity.

However, as important as the structural aspects may be, they must be complemented by two other types of aspects. Among the cultural aspects of corporate visual identity management, socialization

– i.e., formal and informal learning processes – turned out to influence the consistency of a corporate visual identity. Managers are important as a role model and they can clearly set an example. This implies that they need to be aware of the impact of their behaviour, which has an effect on how employees behave. If managers pay attention to the way they convey the identity of their organization, including the use of a corporate visual identity, this will have a positive effect on the attention employees give to the corporate visual identity.

Further, it seems to be important that the organization communicates the strategic aspects of the corporate visual identity. Employees need to have knowledge of the corporate visual identity of their organization – not only the general reasons for using the corporate visual identity, such as its role in enhancing the visibility and recognizability of the organization, but also aspects of the story behind the corporate visual identity. The story should explain why the design fits the organization and what the design– in all of its elements – is intended to express.

Visual Identity History

Nearly 7,000 years ago, Transylvanian potters inscribed their personal marks on the earthenware they created. If one potter made better pots than another, naturally, his mark held more value than his competitors'. Ancient religious sects created some of the most recognized logos: the Christian cross, the Judaic Star of David, and the Islamic crescent moon. In addition, Kings and nobles in medieval times had clothing, armor, flags, shields, tableware, entryways, and manuscript bindings that all bore coats of arms and royal seals. The symbols depicted a lord's lineage, aspirations, familial virtues, as well as memoirs to cavalry, infantry, and mercenaries of who they were fighting for on the battlefields.

A trademark became a symbol of individuals' professional qualifications to perform a particular skill by the 15th century. For example, the caduceus on a physician's sign signified that the doctor was a well-trained practitioner of the medical arts. Simple graphics such as the caduceus carried so much socioeconomic and political weight by the 16th century, that government offices were established throughout Europe to register and protect the growing collection of trademarks used by numerous craft guilds.

The concept of visually trademarking one's business spread heavily during the Industrial Revolution. The shift of business in favour of nonagricultural enterprise caused business, and corporate consciousness, to boom. Logo use became a mainstream part of identification, and over time, it held more power than being a simple identifier. Some logos held more value than others, and served more as assets than symbols.

Logos are now the visual identifiers of corporations. They became components of corporate identities by communicating brands and unifying messages. The evolution of symbols went from a way for a king to seal a letter, to how businesses establish their credibility and sell everything from financial services to hamburgers. Therefore, although the specific terms "corporate image" and "brand identity" didn't enter business or design vocabulary until the 1940s, within twenty years they became key elements to business success.

Visual Identity Designers

The visual identity design profession has substantially increased in numbers over the years since the rise of the Modernist movement in the United States in the 1950s. Three designers are widely considered the pioneers of that movement and of logo and corporate identity design (in the United States): The first is Chermayeff & Geismar, which is the firm responsible for a large number of iconic logos, such as PanAm (1957), Chase Bank (1964), Mobil Oil(1965), NBC(1984), PBS(1986), National Geographic(2003) and others.

Due to the simplicity and boldness of their designs, many of their logos are still in use today. The firm recently designed logos for the Library of Congress and the fashion brand Armani Exchange. Another pioneer of corporate identity design is Paul Rand, who was one of the originators of the Swiss Style of graphic design. He designed many posters and corporate identities, including the logos for IBM, UPS, and ABC. Rand died in 1996. The third pioneer of corporate identity design is Saul Bass. Bass was responsible for several recognizable logos in North America, including both the Bell Telephone logo (1969) and successor AT&T globe (1983). Other well-known designs were Continental Airlines (1968), Dixie (1969), and United Way (1972). Later, he would produce logos for a number of Japanese companies as well. He died in 1996.

Media and Corporate Identity

As technology and mass media have continued to develop at exponential rates, the role of the media in business increases as well. The media has a large effect on the formation of corporate identity by reinforcing a company's image and reputation. Global television networks and the rise of business news have caused the public representation of organizations to critically influence the construction and deconstruction of certain organizational identities more than ever before.

Many companies proactively choose to create media attention and use it as a tool for identity construction and strengthening, and also to reinvent their images under the pressure of new technology. The media also has the power to produce and diffuse meanings a corporation holds, therefore giving stakeholders a negotiation of the organizational identity.

Brand USA

Former United States Secretary of State Colin Powell once said, "We're selling a product. That product we are selling is democracy." Although the United States is not a corporation, it still has organizational components and has a certain image and identity. The US is founded on certain principles, values, and beliefs, and at the same time, has a diverse and widely recognizable popular culture. Because of distinct founding principles, and the way US culture operates, the US too can be observed as a "brand."

Images and identity do not always have to be planned and built by an organization, they also can be attributed to an organization by others' interpretations. During the Cold War, Coca-Cola, Marilyn Monroe, and Baywatch were booming in popularity and became obsessions of popular American culture.

These images portrayed confidence and superiority in American media, therefore the USA seemed more secure and superior during the war. With the growth of the media, popular culture and celebrities still seem to define America in certain ways. Images of Brad Pitt and Mickey Mouse are easily associated to the US. The US has evolved into a nation with industries focused solely on celebrity gossip, TV shows, music, and blockbuster hits, making the US a highly-mediated nation with a strong focus on celebrity.

In addition to the "celebrity" identity factor, there have been more strategic and patriotic images used to re-brand the country as well. After the September 11 attacks, Bush administration initiated the re-brand of the United States from "global bully" to a "compassionate hegemon." The vast majority of American citizens contributed to the act of patriotism by placing American flag bumper stickers on their cars, purple ribbons on trees in their yards, or hanging flags in their windows, all to recreate the feeling and image of nationwide pride and support.

List of Company Name Etymologies

This is a list of company names with their name origins explained. Some origins are disputed.

- 20th Century Fox – Film studio; formed in 1935 through the merger of William Fox's Fox Film, and Twentieth Century Pictures.
- 23andme – Using the 23 pairs of chromosomes that make up each person's genome, the company helps individuals make sense of their own genome.
- 27b/6 – The apartment where George Orwell wrote the novel Nineteen Eighty Four was number 27B on level 6.
- 37signals – Web development company; named for the 37 radiotelescope signals identified by astronomer Paul Horowitz as potential messages from extraterrestrial intelligence.
- 3Com – Network technology producer; the three *coms* are *computer*, *communication*, and *compatibility*.
- 3M – from the company's original name, Minnesota Mining and Manufacturing Company.
- 7-Eleven – Convenience stores; renamed from "U-Tote'm" in 1946 to reflect their newly extended hours, 7:00 a.m. until 11:00 p.m.
- A&M Records – named after founders Herb Alpert and Jerry Moss
- A&P – from Atlantic & Pacific in Great Atlantic and Pacific Tea Company, a U.S.-based supermarket chain.
- A&W Root Beer – named after founders Roy Allen and Frank Wright
- ABN AMRO – in the 1960s, the Nederlandsche Handel-Maatschappij (Dutch Trading Society; 1824) and De Twentsche Bank merged to form the Algemene Bank Nederland (ABN; General Bank of the Netherlands); in 1966, the Amsterdamsche Bank and the Rotterdamsche Bank merged to form the Amro Bank; in 1991, ABN and Amro Bank merged to form ABN AMRO.
- Accenture – from "Accent on the future". The name Accenture was proposed by a company employee in Norway as part of an

internal name finding process (*BrandStorming*). Before January 1, 2001, the company was called Andersen Consulting.

- Acer – Born as Multitech International in 1976, the company changed its name to Acer in 1987. The Latin word for "sharp, acute, able and facile"
- Adecco – named from the merger of Swiss staffing company Adia with French staffing company Ecco.
- Adidas – from the name of the founder Adolf (Adi) Dassler.
- Adobe Systems – from the Adobe Creek that ran behind the house of co-founder John Warnock.
- Ahold – a holding company of Albert Heijn and other supermarkets. For its 100th anniversary in 1987, Ahold was granted the title of *Koninklijke* ("Royal" in Dutch) by the Monarchy of the Netherlands, changing its name to Koninklijke Ahold (Royal Ahold).
- Ahlstrom-named after founder Antti Ahlstrom
- Akai – named for its founder, Masukichi Akai.
- Akamai – from the Hawaiian word *akamai* meaning smart or clever; the company defines it as "intelligent, clever and cool".
- AKZO – named from the 1969 merger of Algemene Kunstzijde Unie (AKU) and Koninklijke Zout Organon (KZO).
- AKG Acoustics – from the company's original name, Akustische und Kino-Gerate (Acoustic and Cinema Equipment)
- Alcatel-Lucent – Alcatel was named from Societe Alsacienne de Constructions Atomiques, de Telecomunications et d'Electronique. It took over Lucent Technologies in 2006.
- Alcoa – Aluminum Company of America.
- Aldi – portmanteau for Albrecht (name of the founders) and discount
- Alfa Romeo – the company was originally known as ALFA, an acronym for Anonima Lombarda Fabbrica Automobili. When Nicola Romeo bought ALFA in 1915, his surname was appended.
- Alstom – set up as Alsthom in 1928 by Societe Alsacienne de Constructions Mecaniques and Compagnie Française Thomson-Houston, it changed the spelling to Alstom in 1997.
- AltaVista – Spanish for "high view".
- ALZA – from the name of the founder Alex Zaffaroni.

- Amazon.com – founder Jeff Bezos renamed the company *Amazon* (from the earlier name of Cadabra.com) after the world's most voluminous river, the Amazon. He saw the potential for a larger volume of sales in an online (as opposed to a bricks and mortar) bookstore. (Alternative: Amazon was chosen to cash in on the popularity of Yahoo, which listed entries alphabetically.)
- AmBev – American Beverage Company, the largest Brazilian beverage company and fourth in the world. In 2004 it merged with Interbrew to create Inbev, which in turn purchased Anheuser-Busch in 2008 to form Anheuser-Busch InBev.
- AMC Theatres – American Multi-Cinema: the company pioneered multi-screen cinemas.
- AMD – Advanced Micro Devices
- AMKOR – AMericanKORea
- Amiga Corporation-The original developers of the 16-bit Amiga computer chose the name, which means a 'female friend' in Spanish and Portuguese, because it sounded friendly, and because it came before rivals (Apple Inc. and Atari) alphabetically.
- Amoco – AMerican Oil COmpany – now part of BP
- Amstrad – Amstrad Consumer Electronics plc was founded by Lord Alan Michael Sugar in the UK. The name is a contraction of Alan Michael Sugar Trading.
- Anheuser-Busch InBev – Formed by the 2008 purchase of Anheuser-Busch by InBev. Anheuser-Busch was named for the company's original founder, Eberhard Anheuser, and his later partner Adolphus Busch.
- Antrix Corporation Limited — The business and marketing arm of Indian Space Research Organization (ISRO). The name "Antrix" is an anglicized version of Antariksh, from the Sanskrit word for "space" or "sky".
- AOL – from America Online. The company was founded in 1983 as Quantum Computer Services.
- Apache – according to the project's 1997 FAQ: "The Apache group was formed around a number of people who provided patch files that had been written for NCSA httpd 1.3. The result after combining them was A PAtCHy server."

- Apple – For the favourite fruit of co-founder Steve Jobs and/ or for the time he worked at an apple orchard, and to distance itself from the cold, unapproachable, complicated imagery created by other computer companies at the time – which had names such as IBM, DEC, and Cincom
- Apricot Computers – early UK-based microcomputer company founded by ACT (Applied Computer Techniques), a business software and services supplier. The company wanted a "fruity" name (Apple and Acorn were popular brands) that included the letters A, C and T. Apricot fit the bill.
- Arby's – the enunciation of the initials of its founders, the Raffel Brothers. The partners wanted to use the name Big Tex, but were unsuccessful in negotiating with the Akron businessman who was already using the name. So, Forrest said, "We came up with Arby's, which stands for R.B., the initials of Raffel Brothers, although I guess customers might think the initials stand for roast beef."
- Arcelor – created in 2001 by a merger of Arbed (Luxembourg), Aceralia (Spain) and Usinor (France) with the ambition of becoming a major player in the steel industry.
- AREVA – named from the region of Avila in northern Spain, location of the Arevalo abbey. Arevalo was shorted to AREVA.
- Aricent – communications software company name created in 2006 by combining two words "arise" and "ascent".
- ARM Limited – named after the microprocessor developed by small UK company Acorn as a successor to the 6502 used in its BBC Microcomputer. ARM originally stood for Acorn Risc Machine. When the company was spun off with backing from Apple and VTI, this was changed to Advanced Risc Machines.
- Arm & Hammer – based on the arm and hammer of Vulcan, the Roman god of fire and metalworking. It was previously the logo of the Vulcan Spice Mills in Brooklyn. When James Church, the son of Church & Dwight founder Austin Church, came to Church and Dwight from Vulcan Spice Mills, he brought the logo with him.
- ARP – company that made analog synthesizers in the 1970s, named after founder Alan Robert Pearlman.
- Artis (zoo in Amsterdam) – from the Latin phrase, *Natura Artis Magistra*, or *Nature is Art's Teacher*

- Asda – Asda Stores Limited was founded as Associated Dairies & Farm Stores Ltd in 1949. However the formation of the Asda name occurred in 1965 with the merger of the Asquith chain of three supermarkets and Associated Dairies; *Asda* is an abbreviation of Asquith and Dairies, a large UK supermarket chain that is now a subsidiary of Wal-Mart.
- ASICS – an acronym for Anima Sana In Corpore Sano, which, translated from Latin, means "Healthy soul in a healthy body". Originally the citation is *mens sana in corpore sano*, but MSICS does not sound as good.
- Ask.com – search engine formerly named after Jeeves, the gentleman's gentleman (valet, *not* butler) in P. G. Wodehouse's series of books. Ask Jeeves was shortened to Ask in 2006.
- Asus – named after Pegasus, the winged horse of Greek mythology. The first three letters of the word were dropped to get a high position in alphabetical listings. An Asus company named Pegatron, using the spare letters, was spun off in 2008.
- Aston Martin – from the "Aston Hill" races (near Aston Clinton) where the company was founded, and the surname of Lionel Martin, the company's founder.
- AT&T – the American Telephone and Telegraph Corporation officially changed its name to AT&T in the 1990s.
- Atari – named from the board game Go. "Atari" is a Japanese word to describe a position where an opponent's stones are in danger of being captured. It is similar, though not identical, to "check" in chess. The original games company was American but wanted a Japanese-sounding name.
- ATI – Array Technologies Incorporated
- ATS – Auto Technik Spezialerzeugnisse, a German company producing light alloy wheels and motor parts, which ran its own Formula 1 racing team in the late 1970s and early 1980s.
- Audi – Latin translation of the German name "Horch". The founder August Horch left the company after five years, but still wanted to manufacture cars. Since the original "Horch" company was still there, he called his new company Audi, the Latin form of his last name. In English it is "hark".
- B&Q – from the initials of its founders, Richard Block and David Quayle

- Bahco-from the name B.A. Hjort & Company, who signed a deal to distribute the tools of inventor Johan Petter Johansson.
- Bang & Olufsen – from the names of its founders, Peter Bang and Svend Olufsen, who met at a School of Engineering in Denmark.
- Bally – originally Lion Manufacturing, the company changed its name to Bally after the success of its first popular pinball machine, *Ballyhoo.*
- Banesto – from Banco Español de Credito (*Spanish Credit Bank*)
- BAPE-A Bathing Ape is a cult clothing company founded by Tomoaki "Nigo" Nagao in 1993. The name is derived from a Japanese saying, "A Bathing Ape In Lukewarm Water", which Nigo says is "a reference to the young generation being spoiled, pampered and too complacent."
- BASF – from Badische Anilin und Soda Fabriken. Anilin and Soda were the first products. *Badisch* refers to the location in the state of Baden, Germany (Black Forest region).
- Bauknecht – founded as an electrotechnical workshop in 1919 by Gottlob Bauknecht, and now a Whirlpool brand.
- Bayer – named after Friedrich Bayer, who founded the company in 1863.
- BBC – British Broadcasting Corporation, originally British Broadcasting Company.
- BBVA – Banco Bilbao Vizcaya Argentaria.
- BCC Research – from the company's former name, Business Communications Company.
- BEA Systems – from the first initial of each of the company's three founders: Bill Coleman, Ed Scott and Alfred Chuang.
- Ben & Jerry's – named after Ben Cohen and Jerry Greenfield, who founded an ice cream parlor in 1978 after completing a correspondence course on ice cream making from Pennsylvania State University. The company, Ben & Jerry's Homemade Holdings, Inc. was later taken over by Unilever.
- BenQ – Bringing Enjoyment and Quality to life
- BHP – Broken Hill Proprietary, named after the town of Broken Hill, where BHP was founded (now BHP Billiton)

- BIC Corporation – the pen company was named after one of its founders, Marcel Bich. He dropped the final *h* to avoid a potentially inappropriate English pronunciation of the name.
- Black & Decker – named after founders S. Duncan Black and Alonzo G. Decker.
- Blaupunkt – Blaupunkt ("Blue dot") was founded in 1923 under the name "Ideal". Its core business was the manufacturing of headphones. If the headphones came through quality tests, the company would give the headphones a blue dot. The headphones quickly became known as the *blue dots* or *blaue Punkte*. The quality symbol would become a trademark and the trademark would become the company name in 1938.
- BMW – Bayerische Motoren Werke (*Bavarian Motor Works*).
- Boeing – named after founder William E. Boeing. It was originally called Pacific Aero Products Co.
- Bosch – named after founder Robert Bosch. *Robert Bosch GmbH* (full company name) is a German diversified technology-based corporation.
- Bose Corporation – named after founder Amar Bose.
- BSNL – from Bharat Sanchar Nigam Limited (India Communications Corporation Limited).
- BP – formerly British Petroleum, now BP. (The slogan "Beyond Petroleum" has incorrectly been taken to refer to the company's new name following its rebranding effort in 2000.)
- BRAC – Bangladesh Rural & Advancement Committee, world's largest NGO (non governmental organization).
- Bridgestone – named after founder Shojiro Ishibashi. The surname *Ishibashi* means "stone bridge", or "bridge of stone".
- Brine, Corp. – sporting goods company named after founder, W.H. Brine. It was taken over by New Balance in 2006.
- BSA-Birmingham Small Arms Company.
- BT – formerly British Telecom (from BT Group, formerly British Telecommunications plc.)
- Bull – *Compagnie des machines Bull* was founded in Paris to exploit the patents for punched card machines taken out by Norwegian engineer Fredrik Rosing Bull.
- Burroughs Corporation – founded in 1886 as the American Arithmometer Company and later renamed after the adding

machine invented by William Seward Burroughs. The company took over Sperry Corporation and became Unisys.

- Bultaco – Spanish company of motorcycles, which disappeared in the 1980s. Its name is based on the name of its founder, Paco Bultó.
- BHEL – Bharat Heavy Electricals Limited, a government of India company.
- CA – Computer Associates was founded in 1976 as Computer Associates International, Inc. by Charles Wang
- C&A – named after the brothers Clemens and August Brenninkmeijer, who founded a textile company called C&A in the Netherlands in 1841.
- Cadillac – named after the 18th century French explorer Antoine Laumet de La Mothe, sieur de Cadillac, founder of Detroit, Michigan. Cadillac is a small town in the South of France.
- CAE – originally Canadian Aviation Electronics
- Campagnolo – from the name of its founder, Tullio Campagnolo.
- Canon – Originally (1933) *Precision Optical Instruments Laboratory* the new name (1935) derived from the name of the company's first camera, the *Kwanon*, in turn named after the Japanese name of the Buddhist bodhisattva of mercy.
- Caprabo – Catalan supermarkets, founded by Carbó, Prats and Bonet.
- Carrefour – chain of supermarkets and hypermarkets which started with a store near a crossroads (carrefour in French) in Annecy.
- Caterpillar – Originally Holt Tractor Co, merged with Best Tractor Co. in 1925. A company photographer exclaimed aloud of a Holt tractor that the tracks' movement resembled a caterpillar moving along the ground. The name stuck.
- Cathay Pacific Airways Limited – The airline was founded on 24 September 1946 by American Roy C. Farrell and Australian Sydney H. de Kantzow, with each man putting up HK$1 to register the airline. They named it Cathay Pacific because Cathay was the ancient name given to China; and Pacific because Farrell speculated that they would one day fly across the Pacific.

- Casio – from the name of its founder, Kashio Tadao, who had set up the company Kashio Seisakujo as a subcontractor factory.
- CBS – Columbia Broadcasting System
- CDAC-Centre for Development of Advanced Computing, a government of India company.
- Celera – inspired by 'celerity' or swiftness (in decoding the human genome), with "era of the cell" a secondary meaning.
- Cenex – short for Central Exchange).
- CGI Group – from the first letters of Information Management Consultant in French (Conseillers en Gestion et Informatique).
- Chevrolet – named after company co-founder Louis Chevrolet, a Swiss-born auto racer. The company was merged into General Motors in 1917 and survives only as a brand name.
- Chello – a Dutch internet service provider, its name was originally pronounced 'say hello' (in Dutch the letter C at the beginning of a word is pronounced 'say'). This did not catch on and now it is pronounced "cello" (as in the stringed instrument).
- Chrysler – named after the company founder, Walter P. Chrysler.
- Ciba Geigy – CIBA, named from Chemical Industry Basel (after Basel in Switzerland), merged with a company named after its founder Johann Rudolf Geigy-Merian. It became Novartis after a merger with Sandoz.
- CiCi's Pizza – from the first letters of the last names of the founders of the franchise (Joe Croce and Mike Cole).
- Cigna – CIGNA was formed in 1982 through the combination of Insurance Company of North America (INA) and Connecticut General (CG). The name is combination of the letters of the predecessor companies, CG and INA.
- Cincom – originally called United Computer Systems, which was similar to several other software and services companies of the day. Two of the three founders visited Philco (Philadelphia Company), and this inspired them to create a new company name derived from Cincinnati (where it was based) and Computer (its business).
- Cisco – short for San Francisco.
- Citroen – named after Andre-Gustave Citroen (1878–1935), a

French entrepreneur of Dutch descent. He was the fifth and last child of the Dutch Jewish diamond merchant Levie Citroen and Mazra Kleinmann (of Warsaw, Poland). The Citroen family moved to Paris from Amsterdam in 1873 where the name changed to Citroen.

- Coca-Cola – derived from the coca leaves and kola nuts used as flavoring. Coca-Cola creator John S. Pemberton changed the 'K' of kola to 'C' to make the name look better.
- Coleco – began as the Connecticut Leather Company.
- Colgate-Palmolive – formed from a merger of soap manufacturers Colgate & Company and Palmolive-Peet. *Peet* was dropped in 1953. *Colgate* was named after William Colgate, an English immigrant, who set up a starch, soap and candle business in New York City in 1806. *Palmolive* was named for the two oils (Palm and Olive) used in its manufacture.
- COLT – from City Of London Telecom
- Comcast – from communications and broadcast.
- Compaq – from computer and "pack" to denote a small integral object; or: Compatibility And Quality; or: from the company's first product, the very *compact* Compaq Portable.
- COMSAT – a contraction of communications satellites. This American digital telecommunications and satellite company was founded during the era of U.S. President John F. Kennedy era to develop the technology.
- ConocoPhillips – formed from the merger of Conoco (from Continental Oil Company) and the Phillips Petroleum Company.
- Copersucar – Brazilian production cooperative in sugar and alcohol, its name is a contraction of Cooperativa de Açucar e Alcool.
- Corel – from Cowpland Research Laboratory, after the name of the company's founder, Dr. Michael Cowpland.
- Cosworth – automotive engineering company named after company founders Mike Costin and Keith Duckworth.
- CPFL – Companhia Paulista de Força e Luz (Sao Paulo Company of Light and Power), one of the largest in Brazil, based in Campinas.
- Crabtree & Evelyn – toiletry company named after gardener John Evelyn, and the tree that bears Crabapples

- Cray – supercomputer company named after its founder, Seymour Cray.
- CRC Press – originally Chemical Rubber Company
- Cromemco – early microcomputer company in Silicon Valley (circa 1975–198?) founded by two PhD students who once lived at Stanford University's Crothers Memorial Hall (a dormitory).
- Cutco – Cooking Utensils Company.
- CVS – originally Consumer Value Stores. CEO Tom Ryan has said he now considers 'CVS' to stand for "Customer, Value, and Service".
- Daewoo – company founder Kim Woo Chong called it Daewoo which means "Great House" or "Great Universe" in Korean.
- DAF Trucks – from 1932 the company's name was *Van Doorne's Aanhangwagen Fabriek* (Van Doorne's Trailer Factory). In 1949 the company started making trucks, trailers and buses and changed the name into *Van Doorne's Automobiel Fabriek* (Van Doorne's Automobile Factory).
- Daihatsu – the first kanji from "Osaka" ('YBW, the kanji is here pronounced *dai*) and "engine". Engine manufacturers were listed on the Tokyo and Osaka Stock Exchanges, and their names shortened to the first kanji. (The company listed on the Tokyo exchange is Tohatsu.)
- Danone (Dannon in the U.S.) – Isaac Carasso in Barcelona made his first yoghourts with the nickname of his first son Daniel (DAN-ONE)
- Datsun – first called DAT, from the initials of its financiers Den, Aoyama and Takeuchi. Soon changed to DATSON to imply a smaller version of their original car, then (as SON can mean "loss" in Japanese) again to DATSUN when they were acquired by Nissan.
- Debian – project founder Ian Murdock named it after himself and his girlfriend, Debra.
- DEC – Digital Equipment Corporation, a pioneering American minicomputer manufacturer founded by Ken Olsen and taken over by Compaq, before Compaq was merged into Hewlett-Packard (HP). It was generally called DEC ("deck"), but later tried to rebrand itself as Digital.
- DEKA – named after its founder Dean Kamen, developer of the Segway, iBOT, HomeChoice Dialysis and other products.

- Delhaize – named after its founders, Jules Delhaize and his brothers, who originated from Charleroi (Belgium). They opened the first European self-service "supermarket" in Ixelles/Elsene, a Brussels borough.
- Dell – named after its founder, Michael Dell. The company changed its name from Dell Computer in 2003.
- Denning & Fourcade, Inc. – interior designer company named after its founders Robert Denning and Vincent Fourcade in 1960.
- DHL – named after its founders, Adrian Dalsey, Larry Hillblom, and Robert Lynn.
- Dick's Sporting Goods-named after its founder, Dick Stack, who opened a bait and tackle shop in 1948 with a $300 gift from his grandmother.
- Digg, Inc.-Kevin Rose's friend David Prager (The Screen Savers, This Week in Tech) originally wanted to call the site "Diggnation", but Kevin wanted a simpler name. He chose the name "Digg", because users are able to "dig" stories, out of those submitted, up to the front page. The site was called "Digg" instead of "Dig" because the domain name "dig.com" was previously registered, by Walt Disney Internet Group. "Diggnation" would eventually be used as the title of Kevin Rose and Alex Albrecht's weekly podcast discussing popular stories from Digg.
- Digi-Key – electronic component distributor whose name is derived from founder Dr. Ronald Stordahl's amateur radio telegraphic keyer, the "IC Keyer Kit", which utilized digital integrated circuits.
- The Walt Disney Company, named for its co-founder Walt Disney.
- Dixons – commonly-used abbreviation for DSG International plc (Dixons Stores Group), a UK-based retailer. The company was founded in 1937 by Charles Kalms and Michael Mindel. When opening their first photographic shop in Southend, they only had room for six letters on the fascia, and chose the name Dixons from the phone book.
- DKNY – Donna Karan New York.
- Dow – named after its founder, Herbert Henry Dow.

- Duane Reade – named after Duane and Reade Streets in lower Manhattan, where the chain's first warehouse was located.
- Dynegy – the Natural Gas Clearinghouse changed its name in 1998 to reflect its self-described traits as a *dynamic energy* company. "Dynergy" had already been taken by a German health foods company.
- EA Games – EA is from Electronic Arts. The company was founded in May 1982 as Amazin' Software and changed its name to Electronic Arts in October the same year.
- eBay – Pierre Omidyar, who had created the Auction Web trading website, had formed a web consulting concern called Echo Bay Technology Group. "Echo Bay" did not refer to the town in Nevada, "It just sounded cool", Omidyar reportedly said. Echo Bay Mines Limited, a gold mining company, had already taken EchoBay.com, so Omidyar registered what (at the time) he thought was the second best name: eBay.com.
- EDS – Electronic Data Systems, founded in 1962 by former IBM salesman Ross Perot. According to the company history: "He chose Electronic Data Systems from potential names he scribbled on a pledge envelope during a service at Highland Park Presbyterian Church in Dallas."
- Eidos – named from a Greek word meaning "species". The company became well-known for its *Tomb Raider* series of games.
- Eletropaulo – One of the largest Brazilian companies in electricity generation and distribution, its name derives from Companhia de Electricidade de Sao Paulo.
- Embraer – Brazilian aircraft manufacturer, its name is an abbreviation of Empresa Brasileira de Aeronautica (Brazilian Aeronautics Company).
- EMBRAPA – Brazilian state agricultural research and development company, its name is an abbreviation of Empresa Brasileira de Pesquisa Agropecuaria (Brazilian Agriculture Research Company).
- EMBRATEL – an abbreviation of Empresa Brasileira de Telecomunicacoes (Brazilian Telecommunications Company). Brazil's largest telecommunications company, it was a state monopoly until 1992 when it was privatized and sold to MCI, then later resold to Telmex.

- EMC Corporation – named from the initials of the founders, Richard Egan and Roger Marino. There has long been a rumor that another partner provided the third letter (C). Other reports indicate the C stands for Company. EMC adopted the EMC^2 notation to refer to Einstein's famous equation, $E = mc^2$.
- EMI – formerly Electric and Musical Industries Ltd.
- Emporis – Empor comes from the German and means "aloft, rising". One of the world's largest providers of data concerning buildings.
- Equifax – Equitable and factual
- Ernst & Young – Named for the company's founders, A.C. Ernst and Arthur Young
- ESPN – Entertainment and Sports Programming Network
- ESRI – Environmental Systems Research Institute, the first geographic information system (GIS) software company founded by Jack and Laura Dangermond in Redlands, California, in 1969
- Epson – Epson Seiko Corporation, the Japanese printer and peripheral manufacturer, was named from "Son of Electronic Printer"
- Esso – the enunciation of the initials S.O. in Standard Oil of New Jersey.
- Exxon – a name contrived by Esso (Standard Oil of New Jersey) in the early 1970s to create a neutral but distinctive label for the company. Within days, Exxon was being called the "double cross company" but this eventually subsided. (Esso is a trademark of ExxonMobil.) Esso had to change its name in the U.S. because of restrictions dating to the 1911 Standard Oil antitrust decision.
- FAS – abbreviation for Foras Aiseanna Saothair (*Labour Facilities Foundation*). Fas means *grow* in Irish.
- Facebook – name stems from the colloquial name of books given to newly enrolled students at the start of the academic year by university administrations in the US with the intention of helping students to get to know each other better.
- Fair Isaac Corporation – named after founders Bill Fair and Earl Isaac.
- Fazer – Finnish food company named after its founder, Karl Fazer.

- FCUK – French Connection United Kingdom.
- FedEx – abbreviation of Federal Express Corporation, the company's original name.
- Fegime – abbreviation for "Federation Europeenne des Grossistes Independants" (European Federation of Independent Electrical Wholesalers).
- Ferodo – anagram of the name of its founder, Herbert Froode.
- Ferrari – from the name of its founder, Enzo Ferrari.
- Fiat – acronym of Fabbrica Italiana Automobili Torino (Italian Automobile Factory of Turin)
- Finnair – from "Finland" and "air". Originally called "Aero Osakeyhtio", which led to its international flight code, "AY".
- Firestone – named after its founder, Harvey Firestone.
- Five Guys – American restaurant chain founded by "five guys" — Jerry Murrell and his four sons. The "five guys" would later become the Murrell sons, after Jerry and his wife Janie had a fifth son two years after opening their first restaurant.
- Fluke – named after its founder, John Fluke, Sr.
- Ford Motor Company – named after its founder, Henry Ford, who introduced automobile mass production in 1914.
- Forrester Research – from the family name of the mother of the founder George Forrester Colony.
- FranklinCovey – named after Benjamin Franklin and Stephen Covey. The company was formed from the 1997 merger of FranklinQuest and the Covey Leadership Center.
- Fuji – named after Mount Fuji, the highest mountain in Japan.
- Garmin – named after its founders, Gary Burrell and Dr. Min Kao.
- Gartner – named after its founder, Gideon Gartner, who left the firm in 1992 to start Giga (named from Gideon Gartner).
- Gatti's Pizza – Gatti was the maiden name of Pat Eure, wife of company founder Jim Eure.
- GCap Media – named after the merger of the GWR Group and Capital Radio Group in May 2005. GWR was launched in 1985 after the merger of Radio West and Wiltshire Radio.
- Genentech – from Genetic Engineering Technology.
- GEICO – from Government Employees Insurance Company

- Gerdau – Largest producer of long steel in the Americas, named from the surname of the founder: Johannes Heinrich Kaspar Gerdau.
- Glaxo – a dried-milk company set up in Bunnythorpe, New Zealand, by Joseph Edward Nathan. The company wanted to use the name "Lacto" but it was similar to some already in use. Glaxo evolved and was registered on 27 October 1906. GlaxoSmithKline was a 2000 merger of Glaxo Wellcome and SmithKline Beecham.
- Glock Ges.m.b.H. – named after its founder, Gaston Glock.
- Goodyear – named after the founder of vulcanization, Charles Goodyear, the Goodyear Tire and Rubber company was founded by Frank Seiberling in 1898.
- Google – an originally accidental misspelling of the word googol and settled upon because google.com was unregistered. Googol was proposed to reflect the company's mission to organize the immense amount of information available online.
- Grey Global Group – an advertising and marketing agency supposed to have derived its name from the colour of the walls of its first office.
- Grundig – named after its founder, radio dealer-turned-manufacturer Max Grundig, in 1945.
- Gulfstream Aerospace – named after the Gulf Stream current that starts in the Gulf of Mexico and crosses the Atlantic. The company traces its origins to the Grumman Aircraft Engineering Corporation, which was sold and renamed in 1985.
- Haagen-Dazs – Name was invented in 1961 by ice-cream makers Reuben and Rose Mattus of the Bronx "to convey an aura of the old-world traditions and craftsmanship". The name has no meaning.
- H&M – named from Hennes & Mauritz. In 1947, Swedish businessman Erling Persson established *Hennes*, a ladies' clothing store, in Vasterås, Sweden. "Hennes" is Swedish for "hers". In 1968, Persson bought the Stockholm premises and inventory of a hunting equipment store called *Mauritz Widforss.* The inventory included a collection of men's clothing, which prompted Persson to expand into menswear.
- Haribo – from the name of the founder and the German home town of the company: Hans Riegel, Bonn.

- Harman Kardon – named after its founders Dr. Sidney Harman and Bernard Kardon.
- Harpo Productions – production company founded by Oprah Winfrey. Harpo is Oprah backwards.
- Hasbro – founded by Henry and Helal Hassenfeld, the Hassenfeld Brothers.
- HBOS – UK-based banking company formed by the merger of the Halifax and the Bank of Scotland.
- HCL – Hindustan Computers Ltd, Indian software company founded by Shiv Nadar.
- Hess Corporation – named after its founder Leon Hess.
- HP – Bill Hewlett and Dave Packard tossed a coin to decide whether the company they founded would be called Hewlett-Packard or Packard-Hewlett.
- Hispano-Suiza – a former Spanish luxury automotive and engineering firm; its name-literally meaning "Spanish-Swiss"-refers to Spanish origin of the company and Swiss origin of its head engineer Marc Birkigt
- Hitachi – old place name, literally "sunrise"
- HMV – from "His Master's Voice", which appeared in 1899 as the title of a painting of Nipper, a Jack Russell terrier, listening to a gramophone.
- Hoechst – from the name of a district in Frankfurt.
- Honda – from the name of its founder, Soichiro Honda.
- Honeywell – from the name of Mark Honeywell, founder of Honeywell Heating Specialty Co. It later merged with Minneapolis Heat Regulator Company and was finally called Honeywell Inc. in 1963.
- Hospira – the name, selected by the company's employees, is derived from the words hospital, spirit, inspire and the Latin word spero, which means hope. It expresses the hope and optimism that are critical in the healthcare industry.
- Hotmail – Founder Jack Smith got the idea of accessing e-mail via the web from a computer anywhere in the world. When Sabeer Bhatia came up with the business plan for the mail service he tried all kinds of names ending in 'mail' and finally settled for Hotmail as it included the letters "HTML" – the markup language used to write web pages. It was initially

referred to as HoTMaiL with selective upper casing. (At one time, if you clicked on Hotmail's 'mail' tab, you would have seen "HoTMaiL" in the URL, but since Hotmail is now Windows Live Mail, it is no longer there.)

- H&R Block – after the founders, brothers Henry W. and Richard Bloch (with "Bloch" changed to "Block" to avoid mispronunciation).
- HSBC – Hongkong and Shanghai Banking Corporation.
- HTC Corporation – A contraction of its original corporate name, High Tech Computer Corporation.
- Hudson's Bay Company – in 1670, a Royal Charter granted the lands of the Hudson Bay watershed to "the Governor and Company of Adventurers of England trading into Hudson Bay." The company ceded the territory to Canada in 1870.
- Hyundai – connotes the sense of "the present age" or "modernity" in Korean.
- IBM – named by Tom (Thomas John) Watson Sr, an ex-employee of National Cash Register (NCR Corporation). To one-up them in all respects, he called his company International Business Machines.
- ICL – abbreviation for International Computers Limited, once the UK's largest computer company but now a service arm of Fujitsu, of Japan.
- IG Farben – Interessen-Gemeinschaft Farbenindustrie AG was so named because the constituent German companies produced dyestuffs among many other chemical compounds. The consortium is most known today for its central participation in the World War II Holocaust, as it made the Zyklon B gas used in the gas chambers.
- Iiyama – manufacturer of monitors and TVs named after the Japanese city, Iiyama.
- IKEA – a composite of the first letters in the Swedish founder Ingvar Kamprad's name in addition to the first letters of the names of the property and the village in which he grew up: Ingvar Kamprad Elmtaryd Agunnaryd.
- IMI-Imperial Metal Industries. Split off from Imperial Chemical Industries.
- InBev – the name was created after the merger of the Belgian company Interbrew with Brazilian Ambev

- Inditex – a Spanish group named from Industria de Diseño Textil (Textile Design Industry).
- Infineon Technologies – derived from Infinity and Aeon. The name was given to Siemens's Semiconductor branch (called Siemens HL or Siemens SC/SSC) when it was spun off.
- Ingenico – electronic payment device manufacturer based in Paris and named from the French Ingenieux Compagnie (Ingenious Company).
- Intel – Robert Noyce and Gordon Moore initially incorporated their company as N M Electronics. Someone suggested Moore Noyce Electronics but it sounded too close to "more noise". Later, Integrated Electronics was proposed but it had already been taken, so they used the initial syllables (INTegrated ELectronics). To avoid potential conflicts with other companies with similar names, Intel purchased the name rights for $15,000 from a company called Intelco. (Source: Intel 15 Years Corporate Anniversary Brochure)
- Ittiam Systems – an Indian company named from the famous philosophical dictum: "I think therefore I am" (Cogito, ergo sum).
- Infosys – An Indian software major. "Information Systems"
- J2TV-from television and film production company formed by Malcolm in the Middle actor Justin Berfield and producer Jason Felts.
- JAL – from Japan Airlines
- Jat Airways – founded in 1927 as "Aeroput" (Airway in Serbian). From 1947, it was known as JAT (Jugoslovenski Aero Transport). After the break-up of the former Yugoslavia (and after Federal Republic of Yugoslavia changed its name to Serbia and Montenegro), the company kept the name, Jat, but not as an abbreviation.
- Jawa Motors-from Janeeek (the owner) and Wanderer (the motorcycle product).
- JBL – from James B Lansing, an electronics designer
- Johnson & Johnson – Originally a partnership between brothers James Wood Johnson and Edward Mead Johnson in 1885, the addition of brother Robert Wood Johnson I led to formal incorporation as Johnson & Johnson in 1887.

- JVC – Japan Victor Company (Victor Company of Japan, Ltd) was founded in 1927 as a US subsidiary, The Victor Talking Machine Company of Japan, Limited. JVC developed the VHS video cassette format.
- Kalev-after Kalev, the character from Estonian mythology and national epic *Kalevipoeg.*
- Kawasaki – from the name of its founder, Shozo Kawasaki
- KFC – short for Kentucky Fried Chicken. It is popularly believed that the company adopted the abbreviated name in 1991 to avoid the unhealthy connotations of the word 'fried'. The rumor that it was because the Commonwealth of Kentucky trademarked the name "Kentucky" is false. Commercials in the early 2000s tried to imply that the abbreviation stands for "Kitchen Fresh Chicken", but in 2007 KFC decided to return to the original "Kentucky Fried Chicken" branding (although the corporate name remained KFC).
- Kenwood Limited – named after Kenneth (Ken) Wood, who founded this kitchenware company as Woodlau Industries in the UK in 1947. It is not related to Kenwood Electronics, which started as Kasuga Radio Co in Japan in 1946 and became Trio Corporation in 1960.
- Kenworth Truck Company – Kenworth Truck Company was formed in 1923 and is named after the two principal stockholders Harry Kent and Edgar Worthington.
- Kia Motors – the name "Kia" roughly translates as "Rising from Asia" in Hanja.
- Kinko's – from the college nickname of founder, Paul Orfalea. He was called Kinko because he had curly red hair. The company was bought by FedEx for $2.4 billion in 2004.
- Kmart – Named for Sebastian S. Kresge, who opened the first Kmart in 1962 as a division of his S. S. Kresge Company. The company became Kmart Corporation in 1977. After purchasing Sears, Roebuck & Company in 2005, the merged company became Sears Holdings Corporation, with Kmart continuing as a discount store chain within the new structure.
- Kodak – Both the Kodak camera and the name were the invention of founder George Eastman. The letter "K" was a favourite with Eastman; he felt it a strong and incisive letter. He tried out various combinations of words starting and ending

with “K”. He saw three advantages in the name. It had the merits of a trademark word, would not be mis-pronounced and the name did not resemble anything in the art. There is a misconception that the name was chosen because of its similarity to the sound produced by the shutter of the camera.

- Komatsu – Japanese construction vehicle manufacturer named from the city of Komatsu, Ishikawa, where it was founded in 1917.
- Konica – it was earlier known as Konishiroku Kogaku. Konishiroku in turn is the short for Konishiya Rokubeiten which was the first name of the company established by Rokusaburo Sugiura in the 1850s.
- Korg – named from the surnames of the founders, Tsutomu Katoh and Tadashi Osanai, combined with the letters “rg” from the word organ.
- KPMG – from the last names of the founders of the firms which combined to form the cooperative: Piet Klijnveld, William Barclay Peat, James Marwick, and Reinhard Goerdeler.
- Kroger – American supermarket chain named after its founder, Barney Kroger
- KUKA – founded in 1898 in Augsburg, Germany as Keller Und Knappich Augsburg, it shortened its name to KUKA. Today, it is a manufacturer of industrial robots and automation systems.
- Kyocera – from Kyoto Ceramics, after Kyoto in Japan.
- Lada – from the name of a Slavic goddess, and used as a trading name by Russian automobile manufacturer AvtoVAZ. VAZ is derived from Volzhsky Automobilny Zavod.
- Lancôme – began in 1935, when its founder, Armand Petitjean, was exploring the ruins of a castle, Le Chateau de Lancôme (Loir-et-Cher) while vacationing in the French countryside. Petitjean’s inspiration for the company’s symbol, a rose, was the many wild roses growing around the castle.
- LCL – from *Le Credit Lyonnais.*
- Lego – combination of the Danish “leg godt”, which means to “play well”. Lego also means “I put together” in Latin, but Lego Group claims this is only a coincidence and the etymology of the word is entirely Danish. Years before the little plastic brick was invented, Lego manufactured wooden toys.

- Lenovo Group – a portmanteau of "Le-" (from former name Legend) and "novo", pseudo-Latin for "new". This Chinese company took over IBM's PC division.
- Level 3 Communications – "Level 3" is a reference to the network layer of the OSI model.
- LG – from the combination of two popular Korean brands, Lucky and Goldstar. (In Mexico, publicists explained the name change as an abbreviation to Linea Goldstar, Spanish for Goldstar Line)
- Lexmark – in the 80's, IBM wanted to spin off its printer and typewriter businesses. Their main productions facility was in Lexington, Kentucky and the code name was Lexington Marketing.
- Lionbridge – the word "localisation", which is the service this company offers, is often shortened to L10N. That is the first letter of the word and the last letter of the word, with 10 letters missing in between, hence L 10 N, which looks like lion. Bridge is the second part of the word as translation 'bridges' gap between people and markets that do not have a common language.
- Lionhead Studios – games studio named after Mark Webley's pet hamster, which died a week before the company was founded. Webley worked for Bullfrog, and co-founded Lionhead with Peter Molyneux, Tim Rance and Steve Jackson in July 1997. Microsoft bought the company in April 2006.
- Lockheed Martin – Aerospace manufacturer, a combination of Lockheed Corporation and Martin Marietta, which is a combination of Glenn L. Martin Company and American-Marietta Corporation.
- LoJack – "LoJack" (the stolen-vehicle recovery system) is a pun on the word "hijack" (to steal a vehicle).
- Longines – In 1862 the new company "Ancienne Maison Auguste Agassiz, Ernest Francillon, Successeur" was born. At that time watchmaking in the area used the skills of people working outside the "comptoir d'etablissage", often at home. In 1866 Ernest Francillon bought two plots of land on the right bank of the river Suze at the place called "Les Longines" and brought all of the watchmaking skills under one roof. This was the first "Longines factory".

- Lonsdale – boxing equipment manufacturer named after the Lonsdale belt, a boxing trophy donated by the English Lord Lonsdale.
- L'Oreal – In 1907, Eugene Schueller, a young French chemist, developed an innovative hair-colour formula. He called his improved hair dye Aureole.
- LOT – LOT Polish Airlines. "Lot" in Polish means "flight".
- Lotus Software – Mitch Kapor named his company after the Lotus Position or 'Padmasana'. Kapor used to be a teacher of Transcendental Meditation technique as taught by Maharishi Mahesh Yogi.
- Lucent Technologies – a spin-off from AT&T, it was named Lucent (meaning "luminous" or "glowing with light") because "light as a metaphor for visionary thinking reflected the company's operating and guiding business philosophy", according to the Landor Associates staff who chose the name. It was taken over by Alcatel to form Alcatel-Lucent in 2006.
- Lukoil – From the first letters of the three companies that merged to form the Russian oil giant: Langepasneftegaz, Uraineftegaz, and Kogalymneftegaz, plus the English word "oil".
- Lycos – from *Lycosidae*, the family of wolf spiders.
- Maggi – food company named after its founder, Julius Maggi. It was taken over by Nestle in 1947 and survives as a brand name.
- MAN – abbreviation for Maschinenfabrik Augsburg-Nürnberg (Augsburg-Nuremberg Machine Company). The MAN company is a German engineering works and truck manufacturer.
- Mandriva – new company formed from the merger of Mandrake Linux and Connectiva Linux
- Manhattan Associates – named from Manhattan Beach, California, where the company was founded, before it moved to Atlanta, Georgia.
- Manugistics – Manufacturing + Logistics, a supplier of supply chain optimization software.
- Manulife Financial-founded in 1887 as Manufacturing Life Insurance Company
- Mars – named after Frank C. Mars and his wife, Ethel, who started making candy in 1911. Their son, Forrest E. Mars,

joined with Bruce Murrie, the son of a Hershey executive, to form M&M Ltd (from Mars & Murrie). Forrest took over the family business after his father's death and merged the two companies in 1964. After retiring from Mars, Inc. in 1993, Forrest founded Ethel M. Chocolates, named after his mother.

- Masco Corporation – from the names of the founder Alex Manoogian, Screw and Company. Masco Screw Products Co. was founded in 1929.
- Mast-Jagermeister AG – Named for founder Wilhelm Mast and its main product, Jagermeister (German for "hunt master") liqueur.
- Mattel – a portmanteau of the founders names Harold "Matt" Matson and Elliot Handler.
- Maybach-Motorenbau GmbH-It was founded in 1909 by Wilhelm Maybach with his son Karl Maybach.
- Mazda Motor Corporation – the company was founded as Toyo Kogyo, started manufacturing Mazda brand cars in 1931, and changed its name to Mazda in 1984. The cars were supposedly named after Ahura Mazda, the chief deity of the Zoroastrians, though many think this explanation was created after the fact, to cover up what is simply a poor anglicized version of the founders name, Jujiro Matsuda. This theory is supported by the fact that the company is referred to only as "Matsuda" in Japan.
- MBNA – originally a subsidiary of Maryland National Corporation, MBNA once stood for Maryland Bank, NA (NA itself standing for National Association, a federal designation representing the bank's charter).
- McDonald's – from the name of the brothers Dick McDonald and Mac McDonald, who founded the first McDonald's restaurant in 1940.
- MCI Communications – Microwave Communications, Inc. The company later merged with Worldcom to create MCI Worldcom. The MCI was dropped in 2000 and the acquiring company changed its name to MCI when it emerged from bankruptcy in 2003.
- Mercedes – from the first name of the daughter of Emil Jellinek, who distributed cars of the early Daimler company around 1900.

- Merillat Industries – named after Orville D. Merillat, who founded the company in 1946.
- Metro-Goldwyn-Mayer (MGM) – Film studio formed from the merger of three other companies: Metro Picture Corporation, Goldwyn Pictures Corporation, and Louis B. Mayer Pictures. Goldwyn Picture Corporation in turn was named after the last names of Samuel Goldfish, and Edgar and Archibald Selwyn.
- MFI – from Mullard Furniture Industries. The original company was named after the founder's wife, whose maiden name was Mullard.
- MG Cars – from Morris Garages after co-founder William Morris. Under Chinese ownership, the company says: "We want Chinese consumers to know this brand as 'Modern Gentleman'."
- Microlins – from Microcomputers and Lins, a Brazilian city where the company was founded by Jose Carlos Semenzato
- Micron Technology – computer memory producer named after the microscopic parts of its products. It is now better known by its consumer brand name: Crucial.
- Microsoft – coined by Bill Gates to represent the company that was devoted to microcomputer software. Originally christened Micro-Soft, the '-' disappeared on 3/2/1987 with the introduction of a new corporate identity and logo. The "slash between the 'o' and 's' [in the Microsoft logo] emphasizes the "soft" part of the name and conveys motion and speed."
- Midway Games – derived from the name of an airport on the southwestern part of Chicago.
- Mincom Limited – Mincom was founded in Brisbane, Australia in 1979. Currently the largest software company in Australia and the fourth oldest ERP company globally. The company initially created software to specifically assist mining companies and the name Mining '*computing*.
- Minolta – Minolta was founded in Osaka, Japan in 1928 as Nichi-Doku Shashinki Shôten. It was not until 1934 that the name Minolta first appeared on a camera, the Minolta Vest.
- MIPRO-stands for MIcrophone PROfessionals. MIPRO is a manufactuer of wireless microphones.
- MIPS – originally stood for Microprocessor without Interlocking Pipeline Stages. When interlocks where added to a later

implementation, the name was redefined to not be an acronym but just a name. (The name also connotes computer speed, by association with the acronym for millions of instructions per second.)

- MITIE – an acronym for Managamenet Incentive Through Investment Equity
- Mitel – from Mike and Terry's Lawnmowers, after the founders Michael Cowpland and Terry Matthews, and the company's original business plan.
- MITRE – Massachusetts Institute of Technology Research Establishment (however The MITRE Corporation asserts that its name is not an acronym)
- Mitsubishi – the name Mitsubishi has two parts: mitsu means three and hishi (changing to bishi in the middle of the word) means diamond (the shape). Hence, the three diamond logo. (Note that "diamond" in this context refers only to the rhombus shape, not to the precious gem.)
- Moneris Solutions-Latin for "You *(plural)* are being protected."
- Morningstar, Inc. – The name Morningstar is taken from the last sentence in Walden, a book by Henry David Thoreau; "the sun is but a morning star"
- Motorola – Founder Paul Galvin came up with this name when his company (at the time, Galvin Manufacturing Company) started manufacturing radios for cars. Many audio equipment makers of the era used the "ola" ending for their products, most famously the "Victrola" phonograph made by the Victor Talking Machine Company. The name was meant to convey the idea of "sound" and "motion". It became so widely recognized that the company later adopted it as the company name.
- Mozilla Foundation – from the name of the web browser that preceded Netscape Navigator. When Marc Andreesen, co-founder of Netscape, created a browser to replace the Mosaic browser, it was internally named Mozilla (Mosaic-Killer, Godzilla) by Jamie Zawinski.
- MVC – from Music and Video Club, the name of a UK-based entertainment chain.
- Mustek – Taiwanese electronics manufacturer with name derived from Most Unique Scanner Technology.

- MRF – from Madras Rubber Factory, founded by K M Mammen Mappillai in 1946. He started with a toy-balloon manufacturing unit at Tiruvottiyur, Chennai (then called Madras). In 1952 he began manufacturing tread-rubber and, in 1961, tyres.
- Nabisco – formerly The National Biscuit Company, changed in 1971 to Nabisco.
- NAD Electronics-Audio equipment manufacturer named for New Acoustic Dimension.
- Napster-The service was named Napster after Fanning's hairstyle-based nickname.
- NCR Corporation – from National Cash Register.
- NEC – from Nippon Electric Company.
- Nero – Nero Burning ROM named after *Nero burning Rome* ("Rom" is the German spelling of "Rome").
- Nestle – named after its founder, Henri Nestle, who was born in Germany under the name "Nestle", which is German (actually, Swabian diminutive) for "bird's nest". The company logo is a bird's nest with a mother bird and two chicks.
- Netscape – Originally the product name of the company's web browser ("Mosaic Communications *Netscape* Web Navigator"). The company adopted the product name after the University of Illinois threatened to sue for trademark infringement over the use of the Mosaic name. Netscape is the combination of network and landscape.
- Nike – named for the Greek goddess of victory.
- Nikon – the original name was Nippon Kogaku, meaning "Japanese Optical".
- Nintendo – Nintendo is the transliteration of the company's Japanese name, *nintendou*. The first (*nin*) can be translated as to "entrusted"; *ten-dou* means "heaven".
- Nissan – the company was earlier known by the name Nippon Sangyo which means "Japan Industries".
- Nokia – started as a wood-pulp mill, the company expanded into producing rubber products in the Finnish city of Nokia. The company later adopted the city's name.
- Nortel Networks – named from Nortel (Northern Telecom) and Bay Networks. The company was originally spun off from the Bell Telephone Company of Canada Ltd in 1895 as Northern

Electric and Manufacturing, and traded as Northern Electric from 1914 to 1976.

- Novartis – after the Latin expression "novae artes" which means something like "new skills".
- Novell – Novell, Inc. was earlier Novell Data Systems co-founded by George Canova. The name was suggested by George's wife who mistakenly thought that "Novell" meant *new* in French. (Nouvelle is the feminine form of the French adjective 'Nouveau'. Nouvelle as a noun in French is 'news'.)
- OCZ – play on the word Overclockers.
- Oracle – Larry Ellison, Ed Oates and Bob Miner were working on a consulting project for the CIA. The code name for the project was Oracle. The project was designed to use the newly written SQL database language from IBM. The project was eventually terminated but they decided to finish what they started and bring it to the world. Later they changed the name of the company, Relational Software Inc., to the name of the product.
- Ornge – new name (2006) for Ontario Air Ambulance, chosen to reflect the orange colour of its aircraft. It was intended to provide a unique branding but the ornge.com misspelling was already used by an advertising portal.
- Osram – from osmium and wolfram.
- Paccar – from Pacific Car and Rail.
- PCCW – originally Pacific Century Development, the company's English name was changed from Pacific Century CyberWorks Limited to PCCW Limited on August 9, 2002. It owns Hong Kong Telecom.
- Pamida – U.S. retailer founded by Jim Witherspoon and Lee Wegener, it took its name from the first two letters of the names of Witherspoon's three sons: Patrick, Michael and David.
- Pemex – An abbreviation of the full name of the state-owned Mexican oil/gasoline company, Petróleos Mexicanos (Spanish for *Mexican Petroleum*).
- Pennzoil – formed by a merger of South Penn Oil (Penn), a former Standard Oil subsidiary, and Zapata Oil (zoil).
- Pepsi – named from the digestive enzyme pepsin.
- Petrobras – An abbreviation of the Brazilian oil company's full name, Petróleo Brasileiro (Portuguese for *Brazilian Petroleum*).

- Philco – from the Philadelphia Storage Battery Company. The pioneering U.S. radio and television manufacturer was taken over by Ford and later by Philips.
- Philips – Royal Philips Electronics was founded in 1891 by brothers Gerard (the engineer) and Anton (the entrepreneur) Philips.
- Pixar – from pixel and the co-founder's name, Alvy Ray Smith. According to the biography "The Second Coming of Steve Jobs" by Alan Deutschman, the 'el' in pixel was changed to 'ar' because 'ar' is frequently used in Spanish verbs, implying the name means "To Pix".
- PMC-Sierra – PMC from Pacific Microelectronics Centre, a research arm of BC Tel, and Sierra from the company that acquired it, Sierra Semiconductor, presumably so named because of the allure of the Sierra Nevada mountains to members of a California-based company.
- Porsche – car company named after founder Ferdinand Porsche, an Austrian automotive engineer. The family name may have originated in the Czech name "Boreš" (boresh).
- Prada – an Italian high fashion house named after the founder Mario Prada, who founded Prada in Milan 1914.
- Procter & Gamble – named after the founders, William Procter, a candlemaker, and James Gamble, a soapmaker, who pooled their resources after marrying two sisters. The company was founded in Cincinnati in 1837.
- ProfSat – Brazilian satellite-based education company, meaning Professional Sateliite.
- PRS Guitars – named after its founder, Paul Reed Smith.
- Psion – UK computer company named by its founder, South Africa-born Dr. David Potter, from Potter Scientific Instruments Or Nothing.
- Q8 – the acronym for these gas stations sounds like *Kuwait*, that is, the letter Q followed by the number 8. It is the abbreviation for Kuwait Petroleum International Limited.
- Qantas – from its original name, Queensland and Northern Territory Aerial Services.
- Qimonda – Qimonda carries different meanings and allows associations in different languages. "Qi" stands for flowing or breathing energy, and it was thought that the combination of

the English word "key" and the Latin "mundus" would be intuitively understood in the Western World as "key to the world".

- Quad – an acronym for Quality Unit Amplified Domestic. Quad Electroacoustics was founded in 1936 by Peter Walker, and was formerly called the Acoustical Manufacturing Company.
- Quark – named after an atomic particle. The word *quark* originates from Finnegans Wake by James Joyce.
- Qualcomm – Quality Communication
- QVC – Quality, Value and Convenience
- Rabobank – Raiffeisen-Boerenleenbank (Dutch for Farmers Loan Bank), a combination of the two cooperatives that merged to form the company.
- RAND – Research ANd Development.
- Raytheon – "Light of the gods". Maker of missiles such as Patriot, Maverick, Sidewinder and Tomahawk, among other military technology.
- RCA – Radio Corporation of America.
- Reckitt & Colman-named from the merger of Reckitt & Sons with J&J Colman in 1938. Colman's, best known for its mustard, was founded by Jeremiah Colman in 1814. Isaac Reckitt founded Reckitt & Sons in 1840.
- Reckitt Benckiser – consumer goods giant named from the merger of Britain's Reckitt & Colman and the Dutch company Benckiser NV in December 1999. The latter was named after its founder, Johann A. Benckiser.
- Red Hat – while at college, company founder Marc Ewing was given the Cornell lacrosse team cap (with red and white stripes) by his grandfather. People would turn to him to solve their problems and he was referred to as *that guy in the red hat.* By the time he wrote the manual of the beta version of Red Hat Linux he had lost the cap, so the manual included an appeal to readers to return his *Red Hat* if found.
- Reebok – alternate spelling of rhebok (Pelea capreolus), an African antelope.
- REO Motor Car Company – car manufacturer founded in 1904 by Ransom E. Olds, and named from its founder's initials.

Later, the rock band REO Speedwagon took its name from one of its trucks, the REO Speed Wagon.

- Repsol – name derived from Refinería de Petróleo de eScombreras Oil (Escombreras is an oil refinery in Cartagena, Spain) and chosen for its euphony when the, then, state-owned oil company was incorporated in 1986. Previously Repsol was a lubricating-oil trademark.
- Research In Motion – from the phrase "poetry in motion", which company founder Mike Lazaridis had seen used to describe a football player.
- Rickenbacker – named after co-founder Adolph Rickenbacher, with the spelling anglicised. The company started as the Electro String Instrument Corporation in 1931.
- Robeez – baby-shoe company named after the founder's son Robbie (Robert). Robeez was taken over by Stride Rite in 2006.
- Rolls-Royce – name used by Rolls-Royce plc and Rolls-Royce Motor Cars, among others. In 1884 Frederick Henry Royce started an electrical and mechanical business, making his first car, a *Royce*, in 1904. He was introduced to Charles Stewart Rolls on 4 May that year. The pair entered into a partnership in which Royce would manufacture cars to be sold exclusively by Rolls, and the cars would be called *Rolls-Royce.*
- RSA Security – formed from the first letters of the family names of its founders Ronald Rivest, Adi Shamir and Len Adleman.
- Saab – founded in 1937 in Sweden as *Svenska Aeroplan aktiebolaget* (Swedish Aeroplane Company); the last word is typically abbreviated as AB, hence Saab and Saab Automobile AB.
- Sabre – Semi-Automatic Business Research Environment.
- Saku Brewery-after the village in Saku Parish, Estonia, where the company was founded.
- Samsonite – named from the Biblical character Samson, renowned for his strength.
- Samsung – meaning *three stars* in Korean.
- Sanyo – meaning *three oceans* in Japanese.
- SAP – *SystemAnalyse und Programmentwicklung* (German for "System analysis and program development"), a company

formed by five ex-IBM employees who used to work in the 'Systems/Applications/Projects' group of IBM. Later, SAP was redefined to stand for *Systeme, Anwendungen und Produkte in der Datenverarbeitung* (Systems, Applications and Products in Data Processing).

- SAS – Scandinavian Airlines System, the flag airline carrier of Sweden, Norway and Denmark.
- SAS Institute – originally an abbreviation for Statistical Analysis System.
- Sasol – Suid-Afrikaanse Steenkool en Oli.e. (Afrikaans for *South African Coal and Oil*).
- SCB – from Standard Chartered Bank. The name Standard Chartered comes from the two original banks from which it was founded – The Chartered Bank of India, Australia and China, and The Standard Bank of British South Africa.
- SCO – from Santa Cruz Operation. The company's office was in Santa Cruz, California. It eventually formed Tarantella, Inc. and sold off its operating system division to Caldera Systems (a spin off from Novell), which is based in Utah. Caldera changed its name to The SCO Group (at which point SCO no longer stood for anything).
- Saudi Aramco – the Aramco name was derived in 1944 when California Arabian Standard Oil Company (Casoc) changed its name to Arabian American Oil Company. The Saudi government purchased the company in 1980, and changed its name to Saudi Arabian Oil Company or Saudi Aramco in 1988.
- Schick-manufacturer of shaving razors and blades, named after the inventor Jacob Schick.
- SEAT – an acronym from Sociedad Española de Automóviles de Turismo (Spanish Corporation of Touring Cars).
- Sealed Air – from the "sealed air" found in its most notable product, Bubble Wrap.
- Sega – Service Games of Japan was founded by Marty Bromley (an American) to import pinball games to Japan for use on American military bases.
- Sennheiser – named after one of its founders, Fritz Sennheiser.
- setcom – software engineering and testing for communications, an international group of companies active in the field of wireless test solutions.

- SGI – Silicon Graphics Inc.
- Sharp – Japanese consumer electronics company named from its first product, an ever-sharp pencil.
- Shell – Royal Dutch/Shell was established in 1907, when the Royal Dutch Petrol Society Plc. and the Shell Transport and Trading Company Ltd. merged their operations. The Shell Transport and Trading Company Ltd had been established at the end of the 19th century by commercial firm Samuel & Co (founded in 1830). Samuel & Co were already importing Japanese shells when they set up an oil company, so the oil company was named after the shells.
- Siemens – founded in 1847 by Werner von Siemens and Johann Georg Halske. The company was originally called *Telegraphen-Bau-Anstalt von Siemens & Halske.*
- Six Apart – company co-founders Ben and Mena Trott were born six days apart (in September 1977).
- Skanska-from Aktiebolaget Skånska Cementgjuteriet (Scanian Cement Casting Company)
- SKF – from Svenska Kullagerfabriken AB, a Swedish manufacturer founded in 1907.
- Skoda Auto – the car company was founded in 1895 and originally named Laurin & Klement after its founders, Vaclav Laurin and Vaclav Klement. It was taken over by Skoda Works, an industrial conglomerate, in 1924, and adopted the Skoda name from Emil Skoda. Skoda Auto was split off after World War II and is now part of Volkswagen.
- Skype – the original concept for the name was Sky-Peer-to-Peer, which morphed into Skyper, then Skype.
- Smart – Swatch + Mercedes + Art
- Smilebit – former Sega development studio named from what they hope to make you do (smile), and the smallest unit of computer information (bit). The company developed Jet Set Radio.
- Smeg – acronym based on the Italian towns where the original enamelling factory was located in Guastalla, Italy.
- SNK – Shin Nihon Kikaku, Japanese for *Plans for a New Japan.*
- Sony – from the Latin word 'sonus' meaning sound, and 'sonny' a slang word used by Americans to refer to a bright youngster,

"since we were sonny boys working in sound and vision", said Akio Morita. The company was founded as Tokyo Tsoshiu Kogyo KK (Tokyo Telecommunications Engineering Corporation) in 1946, and changed its name to Sony in 1958. Sony was chosen as it could be pronounced easily in many languages.

- Sorcim – "Micros" backwards. Sorcim was the original publisher of the SuperCalc spreadsheet in 1980. It was taken over by Computer Associates.
- SPAR – originally DE SPAR, from *Door Eendrachtig Samenwerken Profiteren Allen Regelmatig* (Dutch, meaning "All will benefit from united co-operation"). "De spar" in Dutch translates as "the fir tree", hence the fir tree logo. As the company expanded across Europe, the name was shortened by dropping the article, "DE".
- Sperry – company founded by Elmer Ambrose Sperry (1860–1930), originally as Sperry Gyroscope Company. Sperry took over Univac, and eventually was itself taken over by Burroughs. The merged companies became Unisys, from United Information Systems.
- Spiratone-from the last name of founders Fred Spira and Hans Spira. The company was founded as Spiratone Fine Grain Laboratories. The "tone" suffix was common in the photographic industry (an example cited by Fred Spira is Royaltone) at the time of the company's founding in the 1940s.
- Sprint – from its parent company, Southern Pacific Railroad INTernal Communications. At the time, pipelines and railroad tracks were the cheapest place to lay communications lines, as the right-of-way was already leased or owned.
- SRAM Corporation – named from its founders Scott King, Stanley Ray Day, and Sam Patterson.
- SRI International – from Stanford Research Institute, established by the trustees of Stanford University, California
- Stanley Works – name created to reflect the merger of Stanley's Bolt Manufactory of New Britain, Connecticut (founded by Frederick Trent Stanley) and the Stanley Rule and Level Company (founded by his cousin Henry Stanley).
- Starbucks – named after Starbuck, a character in Herman Melville's novel *Moby-Dick*, also a variation of Starbo; at the

time, a local mining camp north of Seattle.

- Stellent – coined from a combination of the words stellar and excellent.
- STX – pronounced as the word "sticks" because, when first founded, STX manufactured only lacrosse sticks
- Subaru – from the Japanese name for the constellation known to Westerners as Pleiades or the Seven Sisters. Subaru was formed from a merger of seven other companies, and the constellation is featured on the company's logo.
- Sun Microsystems – its founders designed their first workstation in their dorm at Stanford University, and chose the name *Stanford University Network* for their product, hoping to sell it to the college. They did not.
- SuSE – from Software und System-Entwicklung (software and system development). The company was bought by Novell for its Linux distribution.
- Suzuki – from the name of its founder, Michio Suzuki.
- Taco Bell – named after founder Glen Bell.
- Talgo – from "Tren Articulado Ligero Goicoechea-Oriol" (Spanish for "Goicoechea-Oriol Light Articulated Train"), Goicoechea and Oriol being the founders of the company.
- TAM Airlines – named from Transportes Aereos Marília (Marilia's Air Transport). Marília is a city in Sao Paulo state, Brazil.
- TAP Portugal – from "Transportes Aereos Portugueses" (Portuguese Air Transport).
- Tata Group – conglomerate named after Jamshedji Tata, considered "the father of Indian industry".
- Taxan – made-up name chosen partly because Takusan is a Japanese word for *many* or *much* and was considered propitious, but mainly because the head of the company, in the U.S. at the time, Tak Shimizu was known by everyone as Tak-san.
- TCBY – Originally, the company's name was "This Can't Be Yogurt", but a lawsuit from a competitor named "I Can't Believe It's Yogurt!" forced TCBY to create a new backronym for its initials: "The Country's Best Yogurt".
- TCL – from Today China Lion. Derived from literal translation of "ÊNåe-NyVA–ir" from Chinese to English.

- TCS – from Tata Consultancy Services, from India's Tata Group, named after founder and legendary industrialist Jamshedji Tata.
- TDK Corporation – from Tokyo Denki Kagaku (Tokyo Electronics and Chemicals).
- Tesco – founder Jack Cohen – who sold groceries in the markets of the London East End from 1919 – acquired a large shipment of tea from T. E. Stockwell. He made new labels by using the first three letters of the supplier's name and the first two letters of his surname.
- Teva Naot-outdoors shoe company is named after the modern Hebrew word for 'nature' (pronounced "tehvah")
- Texaco – from The Texas Company U.S.A.
- THX – from Tomlinson Holman Crossover, the name of the technology's inventor and the audio technology of a *crossover* amplifier. It may be a backronym, as the technology is owned by George Lucas's company, and he directed THX 1138.
- TIBCO Software – The Information Bus Company. The company was founded by Vivek Ranadive as Teknekron Software Systems in 1985.
- Tim Hortons-Canadian fast food doughnut, sandwich and coffee shop named after founder and hockey player Tim Horton. In Canada Tim Hortons is nicknamed "Tim's" and "Timmy's".
- TNT N.V. – Thomas Nationwide Transport, an Australian company which was acquired by the Dutch postal company in 1996; the postal company renamed itself TNT in 2005.
- Toshiba – named from the merger of consumer goods company Tokyo Denki (Tokyo Electric Co) and electrical firm Shibaura Seisaku-sho (Shibaura Engineering Works).
- Toyota – from the name of the founder, Sakichi Toyoda. Initially called Toyeda, it was changed after a contest for a better-sounding name. The new name was written in katakana with eight strokes, a number that is considered lucky in Japan.
- Triang – operating name for Lines Bros Ltd, which was founded by William, Walter and Arthur Edwin Lines. Three Lines make a triangle
- Tucows – an acronym for The Ultimate Collection Of Winsock Software.

- TVR – derived from the first name of the company founder TreVoR Wilkinson
- Twinings-named after founder Thomas Twining, who set up a tea-shop on the Strand in London in 1706.
- Twitter-social networking and microblogging service. The name was derived from the original idea 'Twitch', which did not bring up the right imagery.
- Ubuntu Foundation – named from a Zulu word that translates as "humanity to others".
- Umbro – Umbro was founded in 1924 by the Humphrey (Umphrey) Brothers, Harold C. and Wallace.
- Unilever – name created to reflect the merger of Margarine Unie and Lever Brothers, agreed in 1929. Lever Brothers was named after its founders, William Hesketh Lever and his brother, James.
- UNIMED – Brazilian cooperative of physicians, meaning Uniao de Medicos (Physicians' Union)
- Unisys – from United Information Systems, the new name for the company that resulted from the merging of two old mainframe computer companies, Burroughs and Sperry [Sperry Univac/Sperry Rand]. It *united* two incompatible ranges. The new-born Unisys was briefly the world's second-largest computer company, after IBM.
- Unocal Corporation – the Union Oil Company of California, founded in 1890
- UPS-United Parcel Service of America, Inc.
- UUNET – one of the industry's oldest and largest Internet Service Providers, named from UNIX-to-UNIX Network.
- Vaisala-named after founder Vilho Vaisala
- Valtra-from Valmet Tractors, where Valmet is the name of a Finnish state-owned company (originally *Valtion Metallitehtaat*- English: *State Metalworks*)
- Varig – A Brazilian airline, its name is an abbreviation of Viaçao Aerea Rio-Grandense, because it was founded in the state of Rio Grande do Sul.
- Verizon – a portmanteau of veritas (Latin for *truth*) and horizon.
- Virgin – founder Richard Branson started a magazine called Student while still at school. In his autobiography, Losing My

Virginity, Branson says that when they were starting a business to sell records by mail order, "one of the girls suggested: 'What about Virgin? We're complete virgins at business.'"

- VMware-Virtual Machine 'ware
- Vodafone – from Voice, Data, Telefone. Vodafone made the UK's first mobile call at a few minutes past midnight on 1 January 1985.
- Volkswagen – from the German for *people's car*. Ferdinand Porsche wanted to produce a car that was affordable for the masses – the *Kraft-durch-Freude-Wagen* (or "Strength-Through-Joy car", from a Nazi social organization) later became known, in English, as the *Beetle*.
- Volvo – from the Latin word *volvo*, which means "I roll". It was originally a name for a ball bearing being developed by SKF.
- Wachovia – from the Latin version of the German wachau, the name given to a region in North Carolina by German settlers because it reminded them of a river near their home in Germany. Many companies founded in or around Charlotte, North Carolina have Wachovia in their name.
- Waitrose – upmarket UK supermarket chain originally named after the founders, Wallace Waite, Arthur Rose and David Taylor. The *Taylor* was later dropped.
- Walgreens – named after founder Charles R. Walgreen, Sr.
- Wal-Mart – named after founder Sam Walton
- Wang Laboratories – from the name of the founder, An Wang, the inventor of core memory.
- Wells Fargo – From the founders of the original Wells Fargo company, Henry Wells and William G. Fargo. (When Norwest purchased Wells Fargo in 1998, it chose to retain the Wells Fargo name.)
- Wendy's – Wendy was the nickname of founder Dave Thomas' daughter Melinda.
- Weta Digital – special effects company co-founded by Lord of the Rings director Peter Jackson. 'Weta' are a group of about 70 species of insect found in New Zealand, where Weta Digital is based.
- W H Smith – founded by Henry Walton Smith and his wife Anna in London, England, in 1792. They named their small

newsagent's shop after their son William Henry Smith, who was born the same year.

- Williams-Sonoma – founded by Chuck Williams in Sonoma, California.
- Wipro – from Western India Palm Refined Oil Ltd Wipro Technologies. The company started as a modest Vanaspati and laundry soap producer and is now also an IT services giant.
- WWE – World Wrestling Entertainment, formerly World Wrestling Federation (WWF). It changed its name after a court case brought by the World Wildlife Fund (WWF), which is now called the World Wide Fund for Nature.
- Worlds of Wonder – founder Don Kingsborough wanted an eyecatching stock symbol, and Worlds Of Wonder provided WOW. The company went bankrupt in 1988.
- WPP – Global advertising and marketing company. Originally called Wire and Plastic Products.
- Xerox – named from xerography, a word derived from the Greek *xeros* (dry) and *graphos* (writing). The company was founded as The Haloid Company in 1906, launched its first XeroX copier in 1949, and changed its name to Haloid Xerox in 1958.
- Yahoo! – The word *Yahoo* was invented by Jonathan Swift and used in his book *Gulliver's Travels*. It represents a person who is repulsive in appearance and barely human. Yahoo! founders David Filo and Jerry Yang jokingly considered themselves yahoos. It's also an interjection sometimes associated with United States Southerners' and Westerners' expression of joy, as alluded to in Yahoo.com commercials that end with someone singing the word "yahoo". It is also sometime jokingly referred to by its backronym, Yet Another Hierarchical Officious Oracle.
- YKK – zipper manufacturer named from Yoshida Kogyo Kabushikikaisha (*Yoshida Company Limited*) after the founder, Tadao Yoshida. The letters YKK were stamped onto the zippers' pull tabs.
- Yakult – Official claims state that the name is derived from jahurto, an older form of jogurto, the Esperanto word for "yogurt". However, it has also been claimed that the name is derived from the fact that the product was developed from ancient Mongolian practices of culturing yak's milk in a sack

made from a yak's stomach-the combination of Yak and Culture in English giving the product name as "Yakult".

- Yoplait – from the merger of Yola and Coplait in 1965.
- Zend Technologies – a contraction derived from the names of Zeev Suraski and Andi Gutmans, the two founders.
- ZERO Corporation-Founded by Herman Zierold as Zierold Metal Corporation, it is the parent company of Zero Halliburton. In 1952, when then owner Jack Gilbert noticed that many of the company's customers mispronounced and misspelled "Zierold" as "Zero," he changed the name of the company to Zero Manufacturing.
- Zuse – pioneering German computer company named after its founder, Konrad Zuse (1910–1995). He built his first computer in his parents' living room at the end of the 1930s. Zuse was taken over by Siemens AG. The name is now supposedly echoed by SuSE (Software und System-Entwicklung: "Software and system development").

11

Commercial Evaluation

Payment Terms

Cost of Money is calculated by multiplying the applicable currency interest rate multiplied by the amount of money paid prior to the receipt of GOODS. If the money were to have remained in the buyer's account, interest would be drawn. That interest is essentially an additional cost associated with such Progress or Milestone payments.

The manufacturing location is taken into consideration during the evaluation stage primarily to calculate freight costs and regional issues which may be considered. For instance, in Europe it is common for factories to close during the month of August for Summer holiday. Labor agreements may also be taken into consideration and may be drawn into the evaluation if the particular region is known to frequent labor unions.

The manufacturing lead-time is the time from the placement of the order (or time final drawings are submitted by the Buyer to the Seller) until the goods are manufactured and prepared for delivery. Lead-times vary by commodity and can range from several days to years.

Transportation time is evaluated while comparing the delivery of goods to the Buyer's required use-date. If Goods are shipped from a remote port, with infrequent vessel transportation, the transportation time could exceed the schedule and adjustments would need to be made.

Delivery Charges-the charge for the Goods to be delivered to a stated point. Bid Validity Packing Bid Adjustments Terms and

Conditions Seller's Services Standards Organizations Financial Review Payment Currency Risk Analysis-market volatility, financial stress within the bidders Testing

Negotiating

Negotiating is a key skillset in the Purchasing field. One of the goals of Purchasing Agents is to acquire goods per the most advantageous terms of the buying entity (or simply, the "Buyer"). Purchasing Agents typically attempt to decrease costs while meeting the Buyer's other requirements such as an on-time delivery, compliance to the commercial terms and conditions (including the warranty, the transfer of risk, assignment, auditing rights, confidentiality, remedies, etc.).

Good negotiators, those with high levels of documented "cost savings", receive a premium within the industry relative to their compensation.

Depending on the employment agreement between the Purchasing Agent (Buyer) and the employer, Buyer's cost savings can result in the creation of value to the business, and may result in a flat-rate bonus, or a percentage payout to the Purchasing Agent of the documented cost savings.

Purchasing Departments, while they can be considered as a support function of the key business, are actually revenue generating departments. For example, if the company needs to buy $30 million USD of widgets and the Purchasing Department secures the widgets for $25M USD, the Purchasing Department would have saved the company $5M USD. That savings could exceed the annual budget of the department, which in effect would pay the department's overhead-the employee's salaries, computers, office space, etc.

Post-Award Administration

Post-award administration typically consists of making minor changes, additions or subtractions, that in some way change the terms of the agreement or the Seller's Scope of Supply. Such changes are often minor, but for auditing purposes must be documented into the existing agreement. Examples include increasing the quantity of a Line Item or changing the metallurgy of a particular component.

Purchasing and Procurement

Purchasing and procurement is used to denote the function of and the responsibility for procuring materials, supplies, and services.

Recently, the term "supply management" has increasingly come to describe this process as it pertains to a professional capacity. Employees who serve in this function are known as buyers, purchasing agents, or supply managers. Depending on the size of the organization, buyers may further be ranked as senior buyers or junior buyers.

History

Prior to 1900, there were few separate and distinct purchasing departments in U.S. business. Most pre-twentieth-century purchasing departments existed in the railroad industry. The first book specifically addressing institutionalized purchasing within this industry was The Handling of Railway Supplies—Their Purchase and Disposition, written by Marshall M. Kirkman in 1887.

Early in the twentieth century, several books on purchasing were published, while discussion of purchasing practices and concerns were tailored to specific industries in technical trade publications. The year 1915 saw the founding of The National Association of Purchasing Agents. This organization eventually became known as the National Association of Purchasing Management (NAPM) and is still active today under the name The Institute for Supply Management (ISM).

Harvard University offered a course in purchasing as early as 1917. Purchasing as an academic discipline was furthered with the printing of the first college textbook on the subject, authored by Howard T. Lewis of Harvard, in 1933. Early buyers were responsible for ensuring a reasonable purchase price and maintaining operations (avoiding shutdowns due to stockouts). Both World Wars brought more attention to the profession due to the shortage of materials and the alterations in the market. Still, up until the 1960s, purchasing agents were basically order-placing clerical personnel serving in a staff-support position.

In the late 1960s and early 1970s, purchasing personnel became more integrated with a materials system. As materials became a part of strategic planning, the importance of the purchasing department increased.

In the 1970s the oil embargo and the shortage of almost all basic raw materials brought much of business world's focus to the purchasing arena. The advent of just-in-time purchasing techniques in the 1980s, with its emphasis on inventory control and supplier quality, quantity, timing, and dependability, made purchasing a cornerstone of competitive strategy.

By the 1990s the term "supply chain management" had replaced the terms "purchasing," "transportation," and "operations," and purchasing had assumed a position in organizational development and management. In other words, purchasing had become responsible for acquiring the right materials, services, and technology from the right source, at the right time, in the right quantity.

Only in small firms is purchasing still viewed as a clerical position. When one notes that, on average, purchasing accounts for over half of most organizations' total monetary expenditures, it is no wonder that purchasing is marked as an increasingly pivotal position.

Factors for Purchasing

The importance of purchasing in any firm is largely determined the four factors: availability of materials, absolute dollar volume of purchases, percent of product cost represented by materials, and the types of materials purchased.

Purchasing must concern itself with whether or not the materials used by the firm are readily available in a competitive market or whether some are bought in volatile markets that are subject to shortages and price instability. If the latter condition prevails, creative analysis by top-level purchasing professionals is required.

If a firm spends a large percentage of its available capital on materials, the sheer magnitude of expense means that efficient purchasing can produce a significant savings. Even small unit savings add up quickly when purchased in large volumes. When a firm's materials costs are 40 percent or more of its product cost (or its total operating budget), small reductions in material costs can increase profit margins significantly. In this situation, efficient purchasing and purchasing management again can make or break a business.

Perhaps the most important of the four factors is the amount of control purchasing and supply personnel actually have over materials availability, quality, costs, and services. Large companies tend to use a wide range of materials, yielding a greater chance that price and service arrangements can be influenced significantly by creative purchasing performance.

Some firms, on the other hand, use a fairly small number of standard production and supply materials, from which even the most seasoned purchasing personnel produce little profit, despite creative management, pricing, and supplier selection activities.

The Role of Purchasing

There are two basic types of purchasing: purchasing for resale and purchasing for consumption or transformation. The former is generally associated with retailers and wholesalers. The latter is defined as industrial purchasing.

Purchasing can also be seen as either strategic or transactional. Also, the words "direct" and "indirect" have been used to distinguish the two types. Strategic (direct) buying involves the establishment of mutually beneficial long-term relationship relationships between buyers and suppliers. Usually strategic buying involves purchase of materials that are crucial to the support of the firm's distinctive competence. This could include raw material and components normally used in the production process. Transactional (indirect) buying involves repetitive purchases, from the same vendor, probably through a blanket purchase order. These orders could include products and services not listed on the bill of materials, such as MRO goods, but are used indirectly in producing the item.

Some experts relate that the purchasing function is responsible for determining the organization's requirements, selecting an optimal source of supply, ensuring a fair and reasonable price (for both the purchasing organization and the supplier), and establishing and maintaining mutually beneficial relationships with the most desirable suppliers. In other words, purchasing departments determine what to buy, where to buy it, how much to pay, and ensure its availability by managing the contract and maintaining strong relationships with suppliers.

In more specific terms, today's purchasing departments are responsible for:

- coordinating purchase needs with user departments
- identifying potential suppliers
- conducting market studies for material purchases
- proposal analysis
- supplier selection
- issuing purchase orders
- meeting with sales representatives
- negotiating
- contract administration
- resolving purchasing-related problems

- maintenance of purchasing records.

These functions obviously entail no insignificant amount of responsibility.

As the role of purchasing grows in importance, purchasing departments are being charged with even more responsibilities. Newer responsibilities for purchasing personnel, in addition to all purchasing functions, include participation in the development of material and service requirements and related specifications, conducting material and value-analysis studies, in bound transportation, and even management of recovery activities such as surplus and scrap salvage, as well as its implications for environmental management.

In the 1970s and 1980s purchasing fell under the rubric of "materials management." Many corporations and individual facilities employed executives who held the title "materials manager," responsible for purchasing and supply management, inventory management, receiving, stores, warehousing, materials handling, production planning, scheduling and control, and traffic/transportation. Today, the term materials management has expanded to include all activities from raw material procurement to final delivery to the customer, to management of returns; hence, the newer title supply chain management.

As purchasing personnel became even more central to the firm's operations they became known as "supply managers." As supply managers, they are active in the strategic-planning process, including such activities as securing partnering arrangements and strategic alliances with suppliers; identification of threats and opportunities in the supply environment; strategic, long-term acquisition plans; and monitoring continuous improvement in the supply chain.

A study by found that strategic purchasing enables firms to foster close working relationships with a limited number of suppliers, promotes open communication among supply chain partners, and develops a long-term strategic relationship orientation for achievement of mutual goals.

This implies that strategic purchasing plays a synergistic role in fostering value-enhancing relationships and knowledge exchange between the firm and its suppliers, thereby creating value. In addition, supply managers are heavily involved in cross-functional teams charged with determining supplier qualification and selection, as well ensuring early supplier involvement in product design and specification development.

A comprehensive list of objectives for purchasing and supply management personnel would include:

- to support the firm's operations with an uninterrupted flow of materials and services:
- to buy competitively and wisely (achieve the best combination of price, quality and service);
- to minimize inventory investment and loss;
- to develop reliable and effective supply sources;
- to develop and maintain healthy relations with active suppliers and the supplier community;
- to achieve maximum integration with other departments, while achieving and maintaining effective working relationships with them;
- to take advantage of standardization and simplification;
- to keep up with market trends;
- to train, develop and motivate professionally competent personnel;
- to avoid duplication, waste, and obsolescence;
- to analyze and report on long-range availability and costs of major purchased items;
- to continually search for new and alternative ideas, products, and materials to improve efficiency and profitability; and
- to administer the purchasing and supply management function proactively, ethically, and efficiently.

Determining Requirements

In progressive firms, purchasing has a hand in new product development. As a part of a product development team, purchasing representatives have the opportunity to help determine the optimal materials to be used in a new product, propose alternative or substitute materials, and assist in making the final decision based on cost and material availability. Purchasing representatives may also participate in a make-or-buy analysis at this point. The design stage is the point at which the vast majority of the cost of making an item can be reduced or controlled.

Whether or not purchasing had an impact on a product's design, the purchasing agent's input may certainly be needed when defining the materials-purchase specifications. Specifications are detailed explanations of what the firm intends to buy in order to get its product to market.

Generally specified is the product itself, the material from which it is to be made, the process for making it, minimum levels of quality, tolerances (a range in which a specified characteristic is acceptable, e.g., an outer diameter must be a certain size, ±25 millimeters), inspection and test standards, and a specific function the product must perform.

If the product requires a standardized component, the specifications are easily communicated by specifying a trade or brand name. However, a custom part can complicate the situation considerably; if incorrectly manufactured, such a product can severely damage a relationship, resulting in unnecessary costs and possible legal action. It is the buyer's responsibility to adequately communicate the specifications to the supplier so that there is no misunderstanding.

Supply Sourcing

Part of the sourcing decision involves determining whether to purchase a part from an outside supplier or produce the part internally. This is typically known as a make-or-buy decision. If the buyer chooses to purchase the part externally, then he must find qualified suppliers who are willing to make and sell the product to his or her firm under the specified conditions.

Buyers have a number of places to go to locate sources of supply, some obvious and some indirect. The most obvious sources would include the Yellow Pages, other purchasing departments, and direct marketing. Purchasing departments typically have a number of trade publications to which they subscribe, such as Purchasing, Iron Age, and Purchasing World, which are filled with advertisements for a multitude of suppliers. Also, being a subscriber usually puts the buyer's name on a mailing list so that flyers, postcards, and other varieties of direct marketing find their way into the purchasing department's hands.

Other sources of supply include manufacturer directories and trade registers. The best known of these is Thomas' Register of American Manufacturers, frequently referred to simply as the Thomas Register. With 125,000 trade and brand names, 151,000 U.S. and Canadian company listings, and 6,000 catalogs, it is a valuable tool for buyers. Practically every purchasing department has access to this source, either through the 34-volume book series or CD-ROMs.

Suppliers also may be found at trade exhibits, in supplier catalogs, or via recommendations from other knowledgeable sources, such as salesmen and engineers. Probably the most important and frequently used source will soon be the World Wide Web; countless firms maintain Web pages and are listed in online catalogs and directories.

Many firms find themselves in a situation where a suitable supplier cannot be found. In this situation, the firm is forced to develop a supplier. Supplier development is sometimes referred to as "reverse marketing," which entails finding the supplier with the most potential for success and providing the resources necessary for the supplier to manufacture the needed product. This could include training in production processes, quality, and management assistance, as well as providing temporary personnel, tooling, and even financing.

When the product being purchased is fairly standard and readily available, most firms choose to utilize the competitive bidding process of supplier selection. This involves little or no negotiation. A request for bids is sent to a limited number of qualified suppliers asking for a price quote for the product, given the terms and conditions of the contract. The contract generally goes to the lowest bidder. For government bid requests, the contract legally must go to the lowest bidder qualified to fulfill the contract.

Negotiation

When competitive bidding is not the appropriate mechanism for reaching the purchasing department's objectives, the buyer turns to the process of negotiation. This does not indicate a second-choice alternative, since the negotiation process is more likely to lead to a complete understanding of all issues involved between the supplier and the purchasing firm. This improved understanding can greatly reduce the number and impact of unseen problems that may arise later. A number of circumstances dictate the use of negotiation. When a thorough analysis is required to solve a difficult make-or-buy decision, or when the risks and costs involved cannot be accurately predetermined, negotiation should be used. Also, when a buyer is contracting for a portion of the seller's production capacity rather than a product, negotiation is typically appropriate.

Other circumstances where negotiation is favoured include: when early supplier involvement is employed, when tooling and setup costs represent a large percentage of the supplier's costs, when production is interrupted frequently for change orders, or when a long time is required to produce the purchased products.

If successful negotiation is to occur, the buyer must have a reasonable knowledge of what is being purchased, the process involved, and any factors that may affect cost, quality, delivery, and service. A thorough cost and/or price analysis is essential. The negotiating buyer must also know the strengths and weaknesses of the negotiating supplier, as well as his own. Also, in light of today's global marketplace, strong cultural awareness is a must. Through proper preparation and some negotiating skill, the purchasing agent should be able to secure a contract that fulfills his/her company's needs and is adequately beneficial to the supplier as well.

Supplier Management

After locating proper suppliers and securing contracts, it then falls to the purchasing function to monitor and control the suppliers' performance until the contracts are fulfilled—and beyond, if further business is to be conducted. All purchasing organizations need some vehicle for assessing supplier performance. Many firms have formal supplier-evaluation programs that effectively monitor supplier performance in a number of areas, including quality, quantity delivery, on-time delivery, early delivery (just-in-time users do not like early deliveries), cost, and intangibles. For some firms, consistent supplier performance results in certification. Supplier certification generally implies (or in some cases formally asserts) that the supplier has been a part of a formal education program, has demonstrated commitment to quality and delivery, and has proven consistency in his processes. Frequently, organizations are able to take delivery from certified suppliers and completely bypass the receiving inspection process.

The buyer is also responsible for maintaining a congenial relationship with the firm's suppliers. If the buyer is an unreasonable negotiator, and does not allow the supplier to make an adequate profit, future dealings may be endangered. The supplier may refuse to deal with the buyer in the future, or the supplier may greatly increase the price of a product the buyer could not obtain elsewhere. Also, relations can become strained when the buyer consistently asks for favoured treatment such as expediting or constantly changing a particular order's delivery schedule.

E-purchasing and E-procurement

The Internet and e-commerce is drastically changing the way purchasing is done. Internet use in buying has led to the terms "e-purchasing" or "e-procurement." Certainly, communication needed in competitive bidding, purchase order placement, order tracking, and follow-up are enhanced by the speed and ease afforded by establishing online systems. In addition, negotiation may be enhanced and reverse auctions facilitated. Reverse auctions allow buying firms to specify a requirement and receive bids from suppliers, with the lowest bid winning.

E-procurement is considered one of the characteristics of a world-class purchasing organization. The use of e-procurement technologies in some firms has resulted in reduced prices for goods and services, shortened order-processing and fulfillment cycles, reduced administrative burdens and costs, improved control over off-contract spending, and better inventory control. It allows firms to expand into trading networks and virtual corporations.

Criteria for e-purchasing include:

- Supporting complete requirements of production (direct) and non-production (indirect) purchasing through a single, internet-based, self-service system.
- Delivering a flexible catalog strategy.
- Providing tools for extensive reporting and analysis.
- Supporting strategic sourcing.
- Enhancing supply-chain collaboration and coordination with partners.

Procurement

Procurement is the acquisition of appropriate goods and/or services at the best possible total cost of ownership to meet the needs of the purchaser in terms of quality and quantity, time, and location. Corporations and public bodies often define processes intended to promote fair and open competition for their business while minimising exposure to fraud and collusion.

Overview

Almost all purchasing decisions include factors such as delivery and handling, marginal benefit, and price fluctuations. Procurement generally involves making buying decisions under conditions of scarcity. If good data is available, it is good practice to make use of economic analysis methods such as cost-benefit analysis or cost-utility analysis. An important distinction is made between analysis without risk and those with risk. Where risk is involved, either in the costs or the benefits, the concept of expected value may be employed.

Direct procurement and indirect procurement

		TYPES		
		Direct procurement	**Indirect procurement**	
		Raw material and production goods	**Maintenance, repair, and operating (MRO) supplies**	**Capital goods and services**
FEATURES	**Quantity**	Large	Low	Low
	Frequency	High	Relatively high	Low
	Value	Industry specific	Low	High
	Nature	Operational	Tactical	Strategic
	Examples	Crude oil in petroleum industry	Lubricants, spare parts	Machinery, computers

Based on the consumption purposes of the acquired goods and services, procurement activities are often split into two distinct categories. The first category being direct, production-related procurement and the second being indirect, non-production-related procurement.

Direct procurement occurs in manufacturing settings only. It encompasses all items that are part of finished products, such as raw material, components and parts. Direct procurement, which is the focus in supply chain management, directly affects the production process of manufacturing firms. In contrast, indirect procurement activities concern "operating resources" that a company purchases to enable its operations. It comprises a wide variety of goods and services, from standardised low value items like office supplies and machine lubricants to complex and costly products and services like heavy equipment and consulting services.

Procurement vs Acquisition

The US Defence Acquisition University (DAU) defines procurement as the act of buying goods and services for the government. DAU defines acquisition as the conceptualization, initiation, design, development, test, contracting, production, deployment, Logistics Support (LS), modification, and disposal of weapons and other systems, supplies, or services (including construction) to satisfy Department of Defence (DoD) needs, intended for use in or in support of military missions. Acquisition is therefore a much wider concept than procurement, covering the whole life cycle of acquired systems. Multiple acquisition models exist, one of which is provided in the following section.

Acquisition Process

The revised acquisition process for major systems in industry and defence is shown in the next figure. The process is defined by a series of phases during which technology is defined and matured into viable concepts, which are subsequently developed and readied for production, after which the systems produced are supported in the field.

The process allows for a given system to enter the process at any of the development phases. For example, a system using unproven technology would enter at the beginning stages of the process and would proceed through a lengthy period of technology maturation, while a system based on mature and proven technologies might enter directly into engineering development or, conceivably, even production. The process itself includes four phases of development:

- Concept and Technology Development: is intended to explore alternative concepts based on assessments of operational needs, technology readiness, risk, and affordability.
- Concept and Technology Development phase begins with concept exploration. During this stage, concept studies are undertaken to define alternative concepts and to provide information about capability and risk that would permit an objective comparison of competing concepts.
- System Development and Demonstration phase. This phase could be entered directly as a result of a technological opportunity and urgent user need, as well as having come through concept and technology development.
- The last, and longest, phase is the Sustainment and Disposal phase of the program. During this phase all necessary activities are accomplished to maintain and sustain the system in the field in the most cost-effective manner possible.

Procurement Systems

Another common procurement issue is the timing of purchases. Just-in-time (JIT) is a system of timing the purchases of consumables so as to keep inventory costs low. Just-in-time is commonly used by Japanese companies but widely adopted by many global manufacturers from the 1990s onwards. Typically a framework agreement setting terms and price is created between a supplier and purchaser, and specific orders are then called-off as required.

Shared Services

In order to achieve greater economies of scale, an organization's procurement functions may be joined into shared services. This combines several small procurement agents into one centralized procurement system.

Procurement Process

Procurement may also involve a bidding process i.e, Tendering. A company may want to purchase a given product or service. If the cost for that product/service is over the threshold that has been established (e.g.: Company X policy: "any product/service desired that is over $1,000 requires a bidding process"), depending on policy or legal requirements, Company X is required to state the product/ service desired and make the contract open to the bidding process. Company X may have ten submitters that state the cost of the product/ service they are willing to provide. Then, Company X will usually select the lowest bidder. If the lowest bidder is deemed incompetent to provide the desired product/service, Company X will then select the submitter who has the next best price, and is competent to provide the product/service. In the European Union there are strict rules on procurement processes that must be followed by public bodies, with contract value thresholds dictating what processes should be observed (relating to advertising the contract, the actual process etc.).

Procurement Steps

Procurement life cycle in modern businesses usually consists of seven steps:

- Information gathering: If the potential customer does not already have an established relationship with sales/marketing functions of suppliers of needed products and services (P/S), it is necessary to search for suppliers who can satisfy the requirements.
- Supplier contact: When one or more suitable suppliers have been identified, requests for quotation (RFQ), requests for proposals (RFP), requests for information (RFI) or requests for tender (RFT or ITT) may be advertised, or direct contact may be made with the suppliers.
- Background review: References for product/service quality are consulted, and any requirements for follow-up services including installation, maintenance, and warranty are investigated. Samples of the P/S being considered may be examined, or trials undertaken.
- Negotiation: Negotiations are undertaken, and price, availability, and customization possibilities are established. Delivery schedules are negotiated, and a contract to acquire the P/S is completed.

- Fulfillment: Supplier preparation, expediting, shipment, delivery, and payment for the P/S are completed, based on contract terms. Installation and training may also be included.
- Consumption, maintenance, and disposal: During this phase, the company evaluates the performance of the P/S and any accompanying service support, as they are consumed.
- Renewal: When the P/S has been consumed and/or disposed of, the contract expires, or the product or service is to be re-ordered, company experience with the P/S is reviewed. If the P/S is to be re-ordered, the company determines whether to consider other suppliers or to continue with the same supplier.

Public Procurement

Government procurement, also called public tendering or public procurement, is the procurement of goods and services on behalf of a public authority, such as a government agency. With 10 to 15% of GDP in developed countries, and up to 20% in developing countries, government procurement accounts for a substantial part of the global economy. To prevent fraud, waste, corruption or local protectionism, the law of most countries regulates government procurement more or less closely. It usually requires the procuring authority to issue public tenders if the value of the procurement exceeds a certain threshold. Government procurement is also the subject of the Agreement on Government Procurement, a plurilateral international treaty under the auspices of the WTO.

Procurement Frauds

Procurement fraud can be defined as dishonestly obtaining an advantage, avoiding an obligation or causing a loss to public property or various means during procurement process by public servants, contractors or any other person involved in the procurement.

Green Public Procurement

In Green public procurement (GPP), contracting authorities and entities take environmental issues into account when tendering for goods or services. The goal is to reduce the impact of the procurement on human health and the environment. In the European Union, the Commission has adopted its Communication on public procurement for a better environment, where proposes a political target of 50 % Green public procurement (GPP) to be reached by the Member States by the year 2010.

Haulage

Haulage may refer to:

- The business of being a haulier (UK English) or hauler (US English), also called haulage contractor, common carrier, contract carrier, or private carrier, in other words of transporting goods by road or rail for other companies or one's own company.
- The horizontal transport of ore, coal, supplies, and waste, also called cartage or drayage. The vertical transport of the same with cranes is called hoisting.
- The charges made for hauling freight on carts, drays, lorries, or trucks.

Haulage cost is the cost of loading raw ore at a mine site and transporting it to a processing plant. Haulage rights is the arrangement where one railway, supplying cars, may negotiate rates with customers located on another railway's line, the road granting haulage rights. This differs from trackage rights in that the host railway operates the trains for the other railway, where with trackage rights, the secondary railway operates trains over the host's track.

Procurement Outsourcing

Procurement outsourcing is the transfer of specified key procurement activities relating to sourcing and supplier management to a third party — perhaps to reduce overall costs or maybe to tighten the company's focus on its core competencies. Procurement categorisation and vendor management of indirect materials and services are typically the most popular outsourced activity.

Overview

Outsourced procurement teams allow companies to benefit immediately from experienced procurement specialists support & expertise. This avoids the creation of an internal team (new resources) and the required time for that team to structure itself, its processes and its expertise.

Outsourced procurement is therefore an available solution for companies who :-Have no internal competencies but want to quickly benefits from procurment action (Cost reduction, suppliers and contract management...)-Have internal procurement expertise (department) but want to outsource activity on specific area(s) like indirect materials and services.-Consider Procurement as not a non strategic/core function (which is probably a mistake) and want to have it managed by a procurement service provider-Want to develop quickly a procurement function to deliver savings, with a willingness to internally develop this function in the mid term

Procurement Categories

Procurement specialists usually split procurement activities into two parts:

1. Direct procurement. Direct categories are all goods purchased by the company which directly enter into the production process of that company. For the food industry as an example, ingredients and packaging will be the key direct procurement categories.
2. Indirect Procurement. Indirect categories are all the goods and services that are bought by the company to enable its activity. This entails a wide scope, including marketing related services (media buying, agencies), IT related services (hardware, software), HR related services (recruitment agencies, training), facilities management and office services (Telecoms, furniture, cleaning, catering, printers), or utilities (gas, electricity, water)...etc

Procurement Services Providers (PSP)

Key consulting companies offer procurement outsourcing services. They mainly focus on strategic inputs or recommendations. Specialized procurement service providers are dedicated to procurement and have developed a strong expertise in procurement and procurement outsourcing, mainly in indirect procurement. Procurement services providers will usually ask for a fixed remuneration against commitment to saving delivery. Some providers also work on incentives or performance related fees (% of savings). Apart from procurement outsourcing, PSPs will offer other services like spend analysis or opportunity assessments.

Radio-frequency Identification

Radio-frequency identification (RFID) is the use of an object (typically referred to as an RFID tag) applied to or incorporated into a product, animal, or person for the purpose of identification and tracking using radio waves. Some tags can be read from several meters away and beyond the line of sight of the reader.

Radio-frequency identification comprises interrogators (also known as readers), and tags (also known as labels). Most RFID tags contain at least two parts. One is an integrated circuit for storing and processing information, modulating and demodulating a radio-frequency (RF) signal, and other specialized functions. The second is an antenna for receiving and transmitting the signal.

There are generally three types of RFID tags: active RFID tags, which contain a battery and can transmit signals autonomously, passive RFID tags, which have no battery and require an external source to provoke signal transmission, and battery assisted passive (BAP) RFID tags, which require an external source to wake up but have significant higher forward link capability providing greater range.

There are a variety of groups defining standards and regulating the use of RFID, including: International Organization for Standardization (ISO), International Electrotechnical Commission (IEC), ASTM International, DASH7 Alliance, EPC global. (Refer to Regulation and standardization below.)

RFID has many applications; for example, it is used in enterprise supply chain management to improve the efficiency of inventory tracking and management.

History and Technology Background

In 1945 Leon Theremin invented an espionage tool for the Soviet Union which retransmitted incident radio waves with audio information. Sound waves vibrated a diaphragm which slightly altered the shape of the resonator, which modulated the reflected radio frequency. Even though this device was a covert listening device, not an identification tag, it is considered to be a predecessor of RFID technology, because it was likewise passive, being energized and activated by electromagnetic waves from an outside source.

Similar technology, such as the IFF transponder invented in the United Kingdom in 1915, was routinely used by the allies in World War II to identify aircraft as friend or foe. Transponders are still used by most powered aircraft to this day. Another early work exploring RFID is the landmark 1948 paper by Harry Stockman, titled "Communication by Means of Reflected Power" (Proceedings of the IRE, pp 1196–1204, October 1948). Stockman predicted that "... considerable research and development work has to be done before the remaining basic problems in reflected-power communication are solved, and before the field of useful applications is explored."

Mario Cardullo's U.S. Patent 3,713,148 in 1973 was the first true ancestor of modern RFID; a passive radio transponder with memory.

The initial device was passive, powered by the interrogating signal, and was demonstrated in 1971 to the New York Port Authority and other potential users and consisted of a transponder with 16 bit memory for use as a toll device. The basic Cardullo patent covers the use of RF, sound and light as transmission media. The original business plan presented to investors in 1969 showed uses in transportation (automotive vehicle identification, automatic toll system, electronic license plate, electronic manifest, vehicle routing, vehicle performance monitoring), banking (electronic check book, electronic credit card), security (personnel identification, automatic gates, surveillance) and medical (identification, patient history).

An early demonstration of reflected power (modulated backscatter) RFID tags, both passive and semi-passive, was performed by Steven Depp, Alfred Koelle, and Robert Freyman at the Los Alamos National Laboratory in 1973. The portable system operated at 915 MHz and used 12-bit tags. This technique is used by the majority of today's UHFID and microwave RFID tags.

The first patent to be associated with the abbreviation RFID was granted to Charles Walton in 1983 U.S. Patent 4,384,288. The largest deployment of active RFID is the US Department of Defence use of Savi active tags on every one of its more than a million shipping containers that travel outside of the continental United States (CONUS). The largest passive RFID deployment is the Defence Logistics Agency (DLA) deployment across 72 facilities implemented by ODIN who also performed the global roll-out for Airbus consisting of 13 projects across the globe.

Miniaturization

RFIDs are easy to conceal or incorporate in other items. For example, in 2009 researchers at Bristol University successfully glued RFID microtransponders to live ants in order to study their behavior. This trend towards increasingly miniaturized RFIDs is likely to continue as technology advances. However, the ability to read at distance is limited by the inverse-square law.

Hitachi holds the record for the smallest RFID chip, at 0.05mm x 0.05mm. The Mu chip tags are 64 times smaller than the new RFID tags. Manufacture is enabled by using the Silicon-on-Insulator (SOI) process. These "dust" sized chips can store 38-digit numbers using 128-bit Read Only Memory (ROM). A major challenge is the attachment of the antennas, thus limiting read range to only millimeters.

Potential alternatives to the radio frequencies (0.125–0.1342, 0.140–0.1485, 13.56, and 840–960 MHz) used are seen in optical RFID (or OPID) at 333 THz (900 nm), 380 THz (788 nm), 750 THz (400 nm). The awkward antennas of RFID can be replaced with photovoltaic components and IR-LEDs on the ICs.

Current Uses

RFID is becoming increasingly prevalent as the price of the technology decreases. In January 2003 Gillette announced that it ordered 500 million tags from Alien Technology. Gillette VP Dick Cantwell, now an employee of Cisco says the company paid "well under ten cents" for each tag. The Japanese HIBIKI initiative aims to reduce the price to 5 Yen (4 eurocents). And in January 2009 Envego announced a 5.9 cent tag.

Payment by Mobile Phones

Card companies are now looking for payment solutions for adding contactless payment cards to any mobile phone. A carrier solution that satisfied the industry's needs is now available, developed in partnership with CPI Card Group and First Data Corporation. Less than 3mm thick, the sub-card will withstand its environment for 2 years, protected from the elements and secured in the carrier once inserted.

Since summer 2009, two credit card companies have been working with Dallas, Texas, based Device Fidelity to develop specialized micro SD cards. When inserted into a mobile phone, the micro SD card can be both a passive tag and an RFID reader. After inserting the micro SD, a user's phone can be linked to bank accounts and used in mobile payment. Dairy Queen in conjunction with Vivotech has also begun using RFIDs on mobile phones as part of their new loyalty and rewards program. Patrons can ask to receive an RFID tag to place on their phone. After activation, the phone can receive promotions and coupons, which can be read by ViVOtech's specialized NFC devices.

Similarly, 7-Eleven has been working alongside Master Card to promote a new touch-free payment system. Those joining the trial are given a complimentary Nokia 3220 cell phone – after activation, it can be used as an RFID-capable Master Card credit card at any of 7-Eleven's worldwide chains.

Nokia's 2008 device, the 6212, has RFID capabilities also. Credit card information can be stored, and bank accounts can be directly accessed using the enabled handset. The phone, if used as a vector for mobile payment, has added security in that users would be required to enter a passcode or PIN before payment is authorized.

Transportation Payments

Governments use RFID applications for traffic management, while automotive companies use various RFID tracking solutions for product management. Many of these solutions may work together in the future, though privacy regulations prevent many initiatives from moving forward at the same pace that technology allows.

Economical alternative to car-ownership: Car-sharing

The Zipcar car-sharing service uses RFID cards for locking and unlocking cars and for member identification.

Season Parking Tickets

Following a successful pilot, Housing & Development Board (HDB) Singapore called two tenders in 2006 to implement RFID to replace the paper Season Parking Ticket (SPT). The successful tenderers have distributed RFID tags to SPT holders since March 2007. In Vietnam, Futech have auto checking ticket system apply for many building in this country.

Toll Roads

RFID is being used for E – Tolling in Motorways, Pakistan, Implemented by NADRA. In Dubai, UAE, RFID is being used for E – Tolling – Salik in Motorways, Implemented by RTA.

In Turkey, RFID has been used in the motorways and bridges as a payment system since Nov 2008; it is also used in public transportation systems in Canakkale, Izmir and Denizli.

RFID is used in Malaysia Expressways payment system. The name for the system is Touch 'n Go. As the system's name indicates, the card is designed to only function as an RFID card when the user touches it.

In Norway, all public toll roads are equipped with an RFID payment system known as Auto Pass.

In Italy, all public toll roads are equipped with an optional RFID payment system named as Telepass.

In Ireland, the eToll system uses RFID tags for payments on all road tolls, including the barrier-free M50 toll between exits 6 and 7.

In Singapore, public transportation buses and trains employ passive RFID cards known as EZ-Link cards. Traffic into crowded downtown areas is regulated by variable tolls imposed using an active tagging system combined with the use of stored-value cards (known as Cash Cards).

In Ontario, Canada, Electronic Road Pricing systems are used to collect toll payments on Highway 407.

RFID tags are used for electronic toll collection at toll booths with Georgia's Cruise Card, California's Fastrak, Colorado's E-470, Illinois' I-Pass, Oklahoma's Pikepass, the expanding eastern states' E-ZPass system (including Massachusetts's Fast Lane, Delaware, New Hampshire Turnpike, Maryland, New Jersey Turnpike, Pennsylvania Turnpike, West Virginia Turnpike, New York's Thruway system, Virginia, the Maine Turnpike, and Rhode Island's Newport Bridge); Central Florida also utilizes this technology, via its E-PASS System. E-PASS and Sunpass are mutually compatible.

Florida's Sun Pass, various systems in Texas including D/FW's NTTA Toll Tag, the Austin metro TxTag and Houston HCTRA EZ Tag (which as of early 2007 are all valid on any Texas toll road), Kansas's K-Tag, The "Cross-Israel Highway" (Highway 6), Philippines South Luzon Expressway E-Pass, Brisbane's Queensland Motorways GoVia tag (previously called E-Toll) System in Australia, Autopista del Sol (Sun's Highway), Autopista Central (Central Highway), Autopista Los Libertadores, Costanera Norte, Vespucio Norte Express and Vespucio Sur urban Highways and every forthcoming urban highway (in a "Free Flow" modality) concessioned to private investors in Chile, all toll tunnels in Hong Kong (Autotoll) and all highways in Portugal (Via Verde, the first system in the world to span the entire network of tolls), France (Liber-T system), Italy (Telepass), Spain (VIA-T), Brazil (Sem Parar-Via Facil). The tags, which are usually the active type, are read remotely as vehicles pass through the booths, and tag information is used to debit the toll amount from a prepaid account. The system helps to speed traffic through toll plazas as it records the date, time, and billing data for the RFID vehicle tag. The plaza-and queue-free 407 Express Toll Route, in the Greater Toronto Area, allows the use of a transponder (an active tag) for all billing. This eliminates the need to identify a vehicle by license plate.

Public Transit (Bus, Rail, Subway)

- Throughout Europe, and in particular in Paris (system started in 1995 by the RATP), Lyon, Bordeaux, Grenoble, Nancy and Marseilles in France, in the whole of the Portuguese highway system and in many Portuguese public car parks, Milan, Turin,

Naples and Florence in Italy, and Brussels in Belgium, RFID passes conforming to the Calypso international standard are used for public transport systems. They are also used now in Canada (Montreal), Mexico, Israel, Bogota and Pereira in Colombia, Stavanger in Norway, Luxembourg, etc.

- In South Korea, T-money cards can be used to pay for public transit. It can also be used in some stores as cash. T-money replaced Upass, first introduced for transport payments in 1996 using MIFARE technology.
- In Hong Kong, mass transit is paid for almost exclusively through the use of an RFID technology, called the Octopus Card. Originally it was launched in September 1997 exclusively for transit fare collection, but has grown to be similar to a cash card, and can still be used in vending machines, fast-food restaurants and supermarkets. The card can be recharged with cash at add-value machines or in shops, and can be read several centimetres from the reader. The same applies for Delhi Metro, the rapid transit system in New Delhi, capital city of India.
- In Shanghai the Shanghai Public Transportation Card allows the user to credit money in advance and to be debited according to the distance travelled, as determined by the check-in and check-out stations. The card can also be used to pay taxi drivers, and some shops offer card readers as well.
- The Moscow Metro, the world's second busiest, was the first system in Europe to introduce RFID smartcards in 1998.
- The Washington, D.C. Metrorail became the first U.S. urban mass-transit system to use RFID technology when it introduced the Smar Trip card in 1999.
- JR East in Japan introduced SUICa (Super Urban Intelligent Card) for transport payment service in its railway transportation service in November 2001, using Sony's FeliCa (Felicity Card) technology. The same Sony technology was used in Hong Kong's Octopus card, and Singapore's EZ-Link card.
- Since 2002, in Taipei, Taiwan the transportation system uses RFID operated cards as fare collection. The Easy Card is charged at local convenience stores and metro stations, and can be used in Metro, buses and parking lots. The uses are

planned to extend all throughout the island of Taiwan in the future.

- In the United States, the Chicago Transit Authority has offered the Chicago Card and the Chicago Card Plus for rail payments across the entire system since 2002 and for bus payments since 2005. The MBTA introduced the RFID enabled Charlie Card across Boston's subway, streetcar, and bus system in 2006, replacing the decades-old token based fare collection system.
- The New York City Metropolitan Transportation Authority conducted an RFID trial that utilized Pay Pass by Master Card. The trial primarily took place on the IRT Lexington Avenue Line with several busier stations on other lines also included. The trial ended on May 31, 2009, however the option of using Pay Pass may be reintroduced on a wider scale at a later date. The MTA is also studying the possibility of accepting Smart Link (introduced by PATH) for fare payment on the New York City Subway and Buses, and as an eventual replacement for the Metro Card.
- In the UK, operating systems for prepaying for unlimited public transport have been devised, making use of RFID technology. The design is embedded in a creditcard-like pass, that when scanned reveals details of whether the pass is valid, and for how long the pass will remain valid. The first company to implement this is the NCT company of Nottingham, where the general public affectionately refer to them as "beep cards". It has since been successfully implemented in London, where "Oyster cards" allow for pay-as-you-go travel as well as passes valid for various lengths of time and in various areas.
- In Oslo, Norway, the upcoming public transport payment is to be entirely RFID-based. The system was slated for introduction around spring 2007.
- The Transperth public transport network in Perth, Western Australia uses RFID technology its Smart Rider ticketing system, allowing passengers to "tag on" and "tag off" and be charged automatically, according to how many zones they have travelled.
- In Atlanta, MARTA (Metropolitan Atlanta Rapid Transit Authority) has transitioned its bus and rail lines from coin tokens to the new Breeze Card system which uses RFID tags

embedded in disposable paper tickets. More permanent plastic cards are available for frequent users.

- In Rio de Janeiro, “Rio Card” passes can be used in buses, ferries, trains and subway. There are two types, one you cannot recharge, the other one can be recharged if it’s been bought by the company you work for, if they provided it (only in Brazil).
- In Santiago (Chile) the subway system Metro and the recently implemented public transportation system Transantiago use an RFID card called “Bip” or “Multivia”.
- In Medellin (Colombia) the recently-implemented card system for the Metro system uses an RFID card called Civica.
- In Dubai, (United Arab Emirates) drivers through Sheikh Zayed Road and Garhoud Bridge pay tolls using RFID tags called Salik (road toll). Also Dubai has initiated a Public Transportation Card named Nol [3] (which means Fare in Arabic) for use in the metro, Bus, and Waterbus, it was introduced to service on the 9th of September 2009, the day of the official launch of the Dubai Metro.
- In San Diego, California, Metropolitan Transit Systems (MTS), North County Transit District (NCTD), and The San Diego Association Of Governments (SANDAG) use a re-writable RFID Smart Card referred to locally as the Compass Card, to store daily, weekly, or monthly passes or cash value, making the boarding of buses and trains quicker and simpler.
- In Finland, the RFID travel card system used in the Greater Helsinki region is the largest of systems in Europe that cover all modes of traffic (Busses, Trams, Commuter Train Units, Metros and Ferry Terminals) operation since 2001. RFID travel card system in Tampere has been in operation since 1995.
- In Cali (Colombia) the recently-implemented card system for the Masivo Integrado de Occidente (MIO) system uses an RFID card.
- In Dublin (Ireland) the LUAS light rail system has been using an RFID enabled ‘smart card’ system since March 2005.
- In Seattle the Orca Card was introduced in 2009 for fares on buses, ferries, light rail, a street car, and commuter trains. In Tacoma, Washington, a sticker tag is used for paying the toll of the Tacoma Narrows Bridge.

- In Osijek since 2008 public transportation (buses, trams) is controlled by RFID cards.
- In Buenos Aires (Argentina), Monedero is an RFID card used in all metro lines and, since May 2009, on some bus lines as an experimental program. The card can also be used to pay, as a debit card in some small shops and in toll roads. The Monedero card could be prepaid or linked to a credit card.
- Since 2010, bus transit in Ljubljana (Slovenia) is payable only by RFID with pre-paid city card named Urbana which can be re-filled with monthly passes or cash value on Urbanomat's scattered all over the city.

Asset Management and Retail Sales

RFID combined with mobile computing and Web technologies provide a way for organizations to identify and manage their assets. Initially introduced to major retail by Craig Patterson, Knoxville, TN. Mobile computers, with integrated RFID readers, can now deliver a complete set of tools that eliminate paperwork, give proof of identification and attendance. This approach eliminates manual data entry.

Web based management tools allow organizations to monitor their assets and make management decisions from anywhere in the world. Web based applications now mean that third parties, such as manufacturers and contractors can be granted access to update asset data, including for example, inspection history and transfer documentation online ensuring that the end user always has accurate, real-time data.

Organizations are already using RFID tags combined with a mobile asset management solution to record and monitor the location of their assets, their current status, and whether they have been maintained. RFID is being adopted for item-level retail uses. Aside from efficiency and product availability gains, the system offers a superior form of electronic article surveillance (EAS), and a superior self checkout process for consumers. The first commercial, public item-level RFID retail system installation is believed to be in May 2005 by Freedom Shopping, Inc. in North Carolina, USA.

Product Tracking

RFID use in product tracking applications begins with plant-based production processes, and then extends into post-sales configuration management policies for large buyers.

IT asset Tracking

In 2008 more than a dozen new passive UHF RFID tags emerged to be specifically mounted on metal. ODIN technologies of Reston, VA produced a Scientific Benchmark which showed vary performance of metal mount tags, with the greatest read distance being just over 25 feet in real-world conditions.

At the same time new integrated circuits (ICs) were introduced by Alien, Impinj and NXP (formerly Philips) which proved much better performance and the IT Asset Tracking application exploded.

The largest adopter to date appear to be Bank of America and Wells Fargo – each with more than 100,000 assets across more than a dozen data centres.

- High-frequency RFID or HFID/HighFID tags are used in library book or bookstore tracking, jewelry tracking, pallet tracking, building access control, airline baggage tracking, and apparel and pharmaceutical items tracking. High-frequency tags are widely used in identification badges, replacing earlier magnetic stripe cards. These badges need only be held within a certain distance of the reader to authenticate the holder. The American Express Blue credit card now includes a HighFID tag. In Feb 2008, Emirates Airline started a trial of RFID baggage tracing at London and Dubai airports.
- BGN has launched two fully automated Smartstores that combine item-level RFID tagging and SOA to deliver an integrated supply chain, from warehouse to consumer.
- UHF, Ultra-HighFID or UHFID tags are commonly used commercially in case, pallet, and shipping container tracking, and truck and trailer tracking in shipping yards.
- In May 2007, Bear River Supply began utilizing Intelleflex Corporation's ultrahigh-frequency identification (UHFID) tags to help monitor their agricultural equipment.
- In Colombia, "Federation National de Cafeterias" uses an RFID solution to trace the coffee.
- Purdue Pharma currently uses RFID to track shipments of the painkiller Oxy Contin.
- In Berlin, Germany, the Berliner Wasserbetriebe (water treatment facility) Uses RFID systems from Psion Teklogix and Elektronik system-und-Logistik-GmbH (ESG) to identify and track its 60,000 assets.

Transportation and Logistics:

- Logistics and transportation are major areas of implementation for RFID technology. For example, yard management, shipping and freight and distribution centres are some areas where RFID tracking technology is used. Transportation companies around the world value RFID technology due to its impact on the business value and efficiency.
- The North American railroad industry operates an automatic equipment identification system based on RFID. Locomotives and rolling stock are equipped with two passive RFID tags (one mounted on each side of the equipment); the data encoded on each tag identifies the equipment owner, car number, type of equipment, number of axles, etc. The equipment owner and car number can be used to derive further data about the physical characteristics of the equipment from the Association of American Railroads' car inventory database and the railroad's own database indicating the lading, origin, destination, etc. of the commodities being carried.
- Aerospace applications that incorporate RFID technology are being incorporated into Network Centric Product Support architecture. This technology serves to help facilitate more efficient logistics support for systems maintenance on-board commercial aircraft.
- Baggages passing through the Hong Kong International Airport are individually tagged with "HKIA" RFID tags as they navigate the airport's baggage handling system, which improves efficiency and reduces misplaced items.

Animal Identification

RFID tags for animals represent one of the oldest uses of RFID technology. Originally meant for large ranches and rough terrain, since the outbreak of Mad Cow Disease, RFID has become crucial in animal identification management.

An implantable variety of RFID tags or transponders can also be used for animal identification. The transponders are more well-known as passive RFID technology, or simply "Chips" on animals.

RFID Tracking and Tracing for Meatpackers

The Canadian Cattle Identification Agency began using RFID tags as a replacement for barcode tags. The tags are required to identify a bovine's herd of origin and this is used for tracing when a packing plant condemns a carcass. Currently CCIA tags are used in Wisconsin and by US farmers on a voluntary basis. The USDA is currently developing its own program.

Inventory Systems

An advanced automatic identification technology such as the Auto-ID Labs system based on the Radio Frequency Identification (RFID) technology has significant value for inventory systems. Notably, the technology provides an accurate knowledge of the current inventory. In an academic study performed at Wal-Mart, RFID reduced Out-of-Stocks by 30 percent for products selling between 0.1 and 15 units a day. Other benefits of using RFID include the reduction of labor costs, the simplification of business processes, and the reduction of inventory inaccuracies.

In 2004, Boeing integrated the use of RFID technology to help reduce maintenance and inventory costs on the Boeing 787 Dreamliner. With the high costs of aircraft parts, RFID technology allowed Boeing to keep track of inventory despite the unique sizes, shapes and environmental concerns. During the first six months after integration, the company was able to save $29,000 in labor alone.

Wal-Mart Mandate

In January 2005, Wal-Mart required its top 100 suppliers to apply RFID labels to all shipments. To meet this requirement, vendors use RFID printer/encoders to label cases and pallets that require EPC tags for Wal-Mart. These smart labels are produced by embedding RFID inlays inside the label material, and then printing bar code and other visible information on the surface of the label.

In October 2005 the University of Arkansas' Information Technology Research Institute released a report on its preliminary study of the impact of RFID on reducing retail out-of-stocks and concluded that RFID reduced OOS by 16% over non-RFID based stores.

Two years later the Wall Street Journal published an article titled" Wal-Mart's Radio-Tracked Inventory Hits Static." The articles stated that the RFID plan set forth by Wal-Mart was "showing signs of fizzling" due to a lack of progress by Wal-Mart executives to introduce the technology to its stores and to the non-existent incentives for suppliers.

In October 2007 Wal-Mart announced new focus areas for its RFID implementation:

1) Shipments going to Sam's Club
2) Promotional displays and products going to Wal-Mart stores
3) tests to see RFID's impact in improving category management in select areas.

Another Wal-Mart division, Sam's Club, has also moved in this direction. It sent letters dated Jan. 7, 2008 to its suppliers, stating that by Jan. 31, 2008, every full single-item pallet shipped to its distribution centre in DeSoto, Texas, or directly to one of its stores served by that DC, must bear an EPC Gen 2 RFID tag. Suppliers failing to comply will be charged a service fee. However, in January 2009 Sam's Club drastically lowered the penalty for failure to tag pallets from $2 a pallet to just 12 cents a pallet. The 12 cents a pallet is what Wal-Mart estimated it would cost Sam's to do the tagging itself. Sam's also announced that pallet-level tagging is expected to be introduced throughout the entire chain in 2010 while the deadline for tagging individual items was "under review."

In February 2009 Procter & Gamble stated it was ending its promotional program with Wal-Mart after Procter & Gamble "validated" benefits of the RFID program in merchandising and promotional displays. This implied Wal-Mart was not acting on the information to improve store execution.

Department of Defence Mandate

The DoD requirements for RFID tags on packages is prescribed in the Defence Federal Acquisition Regulations Supplements (DFARS) 252.211-7006. Positioning of the tag needs to be completed in accordance with the clause and definitions in MIL STD 129 and as of 1 March 2007, EPC Global tags must comply with EPC global Class 1 Generation 2 specification.

Promotion Tracking

Manufacturers of products sold through retailers promote their products by offering discounts for a limited period on products sold to retailers with the expectation that the retailers will pass on the savings to their customers. However, retailers typically engage in forward buying, purchasing more product during the discount period than they intend to sell during the promotion period. Some retailers engage in a form of arbitrage, reselling discounted product to other retailers, a practice known as diverting. To combat this practice, manufacturers are exploring the use of RFID tags on promoted merchandise so that they can track exactly which product has sold through the supply chain at fully discounted prices.

Libraries

Among the many uses of RFID technology is its deployment in libraries. This technology has slowly begun to replace the traditional barcodes on library items (books, CDs, DVDs, etc.). The RFID tag can contain identifying information, such as a book's title or material type, without having to be pointed to a separate database (but this is rare in North America). The information is read by an RFID reader, which replaces the standard barcode reader commonly found at a library's circulation desk. The RFID tag found on library materials typically measures 50×50 mm in North America and 50×75 mm in Europe. It may replace or be added to the barcode, offering a different means of inventory management by the staff and self service by the borrowers. It can also act as a security device, taking the place of the more traditional electromagnetic security strip And not only the books, but also the membership cards could be fitted with an RFID tag.

While there is some debate as to when and where RFID in libraries first began, it was first proposed in the late 1990s as a technology that would enhance workflow in the library setting. Singapore was certainly one of the first to introduce RFID in libraries and Rockefeller University in New York may have been the first academic library in the United States to utilize this technology, whereas Farmington Community Library in Michigan may have been the first public institution, both of which began using RFID in 1999. In Europe, the first public library to use RFID was the one in Hoogezand-Sappemeer, the Netherlands, in 2001, where borrowers were given an option. To their surprise, 70% used the RFID option and quickly adapted, including elderly people.

Worldwide, in absolute numbers, RFID is used most in the United States (with its 300 million inhabitants), followed by the United Kingdom and Japan. It is estimated that over 30 million library items worldwide now contain RFID tags, including some in the Vatican Library in Rome. At the time of 2010, the largest RFID implementation in academic library is the University of Hong Kong Libraries which have over 1.20 million library items contain RFID tags; whereas the largest implementation for public institution has been installed in Seattle Public Library in the United States.

RFID has many library applications that can be highly beneficial, particularly for circulation staff. Since RFID tags can be read through an item, there is no need to open a book cover or DVD case to scan an item. This could reduce repetitive-motion injuries. Where the books have a barcode on the outside, there is still the advantage that borrowers can scan an entire pile of books in one go, instead of one at a time. Since RFID tags can also be read while an item is in motion, using RFID readers to check-in returned items while on a conveyor belt reduces staff time. But, as with barcode, this can all be done by the borrowers themselves, meaning they might never again need the assistance of staff.

Next to these readers with a fixed location there are also portable ones (for librarians, but in the future possibly also for borrowers, possibly even their own general-purpose readers). With these, inventories could be done on a whole shelf of materials within seconds, without a book ever having to be taken off the shelf. In Umea, Sweden, RFID is being used to assist visually impaired people in borrowing audiobooks. In Malaysia, Smart Shelves are used to pinpoint the exact location of books in Multimedia University Library, Cyberjaya. In the Netherlands, handheld readers are being introduced for this purpose.

The Dutch Union of Public Libraries ('Vereniging van Openbare Bibliotheken') is working on the concept of an interactive 'context library', where borrowers get a reader/headphones-set, which leads them to the desired section of the library (using triangulation methods, rather like GPS) and which they can use to read information from books on the shelves with the desired level of detail (e.g. a section read out loud), coming from the book's tag itself or a database elsewhere, and get tips on alternatives, based on the borrowers' preferences, thus creating a more personalised version of the library. This may also lead them to sections of the library they might not otherwise visit. Borrowers could also use the system to exchange experiences (such as grading books).

However, as of 2008 this technology remains too costly for many smaller libraries, and the conversion period has been estimated at 11 months for an average-size library. A 2004 Dutch estimate was that a library which lends 100,000 books per year should plan on a cost of €50,000 (borrow-and return-stations: 12,500 each, detection porches 10,000 each; tags 0.36 each). RFID taking a large burden off staff could also mean that fewer staff will be needed, resulting in some of them getting fired, but that has so far not happened in North America where recent surveys have not returned a single library that cut staff because of adding RFID. In fact, library budgets are being reduced for personnel and increased for infrastructure, making it necessary for libraries to add automation to compensate for the reduced staff size. Also, the tasks that RFID takes over are largely not the primary tasks of librarians. A finding in the Netherlands is that borrowers are pleased with the fact that staff are now more available for answering questions.

A concern surrounding RFID in libraries that has received considerable publicity is the issue of privacy. Because RFID tags can-depending on the RFID transmitter & reader-be scanned and read from up to 350 feet or 100 m (e.g. Smart Label RFID's), and because RFID utilizes an assortment of frequencies (both depending on the type of tag, though), there is some concern over whether sensitive information could be collected from an unwilling source. However, library RFID tags do not contain any patron information, and the tags used in the majority of libraries use a frequency only readable from approximately ten feet. Also, libraries have always had to keep records of who has borrowed what, so in that sense there is nothing new. However, many libraries destroy these records once an item has been returned. RFID would complicate or nullify this respect of readers' privacy. Further, another non-library agency could potentially record the RFID tags of every person leaving the library without the library administrator's knowledge or consent. One simple option is to let the book transmit a code that has meaning only in conjunction with the library's database. Another step further is to give the book a new code every time it is returned. And if in the future readers become ubiquitous (and possibly networked), then stolen books could be traced even outside the library. Tag removal could be made difficult if the tags are so small that they fit invisibly inside a (random) page, possibly put there by the publisher.

Human Identification

The success of various animal identification uses since the early 1990s has spurred RFID research into various human tracking alternatives. Some vendors place them in .clothing.

Passports

The first RFID passports ("E-passport") were issued by Malaysia in 1998. In addition to information also contained on the visual data page of the passport, Malaysian e-passports record the travel history (time, date, and place) of entries and exits from the country.

Other countries that insert RFID in passports include Norway (2005), Japan (March 1, 2006), most EU countries (around 2006) including Spain, Ireland and UK, Australia, Hong Kong and the United States (2007), Serbia (July 2008), Republic of Korea (August 2008), Taiwan (December 2008), Albania (January 2009), The Philippines (August 2009).

Standards for RFID passports are determined by the International Civil Aviation Organization (ICAO), and are contained in ICAO Document 9303, Part 1, Volumes 1 and 2 (6th edition, 2006). ICAO refers to the ISO/IEC 14443 RFID chips in e-passports as "contactless integrated circuits". ICAO standards provide for e-passports to be identifiable by a standard e-passport logo on the front cover.

In 2006, RFID tags were included in new US passports. The US produced 10 million passports in 2005, and it has been estimated that 13 million will be produced in 2006. The chips inlays produced by Smartrac will store the same information that is printed within the passport and will also include a digital picture of the owner. The US State Department initially stated the chips could only be read from a distance of 10 cm (4 in), but after widespread criticism and a clear demonstration that special equipment can read the test passports from 10 meters (33 ft) away, the passports were designed to incorporate a thin metal lining to make it more difficult for unauthorized readers to "skim" information when the passport is closed.

The department will also implement Basic Access Control (BAC), which functions as a Personal Identification Number (PIN) in the form of characters printed on the passport data page. Before a passport's tag can be read, this PIN must be entered into an RFID reader. The BAC also enables the encryption of any communication between the chip and interrogator.

Security expert Bruce Schneier has suggested that a mugger operating near an airport could target victims who have arrived from wealthy countries, or a terrorist could design an improvised explosive device which functioned when approached by persons from a particular country if passengers did not put their cards in an area close to their body (high liquid and saline content) or in a foil-lined wallet. Some other European Union countries are also planning to add fingerprints and other biometric data, while some have already done so.

Schools and Universities

School authorities in the Japanese city of Osaka are now chipping children's clothing, back packs, and student IDs in a primary school. A school in Doncaster, England is piloting a monitoring system designed to keep tabs on pupils by tracking radio chips in their uniforms. St. Charles Sixth Form College in West London, England, started September, 2008, is using an RFID card system to check in and out of the main gate, to both track attendance and prevent unauthorized entrance. As is Whitcliffe Mount School in Cleckheaton, England which uses RFID to track pupils and staff in and out of the building via a specially designed cards.

In the Philippines, some schools already use RFID in IDs for borrowing books and also gates in those particular schools have RFID ID scanners for buying items at a school shop and canteen, library and also to sign in and sign out for student and teacher's attendance. These schools are Claret School of Quezon City, Colegio de San Juan de Letran, San Beda College and other private Schools.

Social Retailing

When customers enter a dressing room, the mirror reflects their image and also images of the apparel item being worn by celebrities on an interactive display. A webcam also projects an image of the consumer wearing the item on the website for everyone to see. This creates an interaction between the consumers inside the store and their social network outside the store. The technology in this system is an RFID interrogator antenna in the dressing room and Electronic Product Code RFID tags on the apparel item.

Race Timing

Many forms of RFID race timing have been in use for timing races of different types since the early 1990s. The practice began with pigeon racing, introduced by a company called deister electronic Gmbh of Barsinghausen, Germany. It is used for registering race start and end timings for animals or individuals in large running races or multi-sport races where it is impossible to get accurate stopwatch readings for every entrant.

In the race, the racers wear passive or active tags that are read by antennae placed alongside the track or on mats across the track. UHF based tags instead of low or high frequency last-generation tags provide accurate readings with specially designed antennas. Rush error, lap count errors and accidents at start time are avoided since anyone can start and finish any time without being in a batch mode.

Bibliography

Albarran, Alan B. and Gregory G. Pitts: *The Radio Broadcasting Industry*, Boston, Allyn and Bacon, 2001.

Allman, Paul: *Careers in Video and Digital Video*, New York: Rosen, 2001.

Armstrong, G. & Kotler, P., : *Marketing: An Introduction*. New Jersey: Pearson Education Inc., 2005.

Assael, H. : *Consumer Behaviour and Marketing Action*, USA: PWS-Kent, 1992.

Brunt, Paul: *Market Research in Travel and Tourism*, Oxford, Butterworth Heinemann, 1997.

Carl H. : *Internet Distribution of European Travel and Tourism Services*, Research Centre of Bornholm, Denmark, 1999.

Cukier, J. : *Tourism Employment in Bali: Trends and Implications*, London: Thompson, 1996.

David L: *International Tourism Policy, New York*, Van Nostrand and Reinhold, 1990.

Donald E. : *Public Personnel Management: Contexts and Strategies*, Upper Saddle River, NJ: Prentice Hall, 1998.

Douglas C: *Practical Tourism Forecasting*, Oxford, Butterworth Heinemann, 1996.

Eberts, Marjorie: *Careers in Travel, Tourism, and Hospitality*, Lincolnwood, VGM Career Horizons, 1997.

Fesenmaier D., Klein, S. : *Information & Communication Technologies in Tourism*, Springer-Verlag, Wien-New York, 2000.

Graham M S: *Language of Tourism*, The, Wallingford, CAB International, 1996.

Harrison, Lyndon: *Tourism Means Jobs*, Chester, Lyndon Harrison, 1996.

Ireland, Lewis: *Quality Management for Projects and Programs*, Upper Darby, PMI, 1991.

Judi Radice: *Restaurant & Food Graphics*, Glen Cove, PBC International, 1994.

Karski, A: *Urban Tourism* - A Key to Urban Regeneration?, 1990.

Kotler, Philip: *Marketing for Hospitality and Tourism*: New Jersey, Prentice-Hall, 1998.

Kotler, Philipl: *Marketing Places: Attracting Investment, Industry & Tourism etc*, New York, free press, 1993.

Leivadi, S: *Sociology of Tourism, The: Theoretical And Empirical Investigations*, London, Retailed, 1996.

Lucas, Rosemary E.: *Managing Employee Relations in the Hotel and Catering Industry*, London, Cassell, 1995.

Madhukar Manoj : *Hospitality Industries in Next Millennium*, Rajat, Delhi, 2001.

Margaret Wade: *Medieval Travellers: The Rich and Restless*, London, Hamish Hamilton, 1982.

Morrell, J. : *Employment in Tourism*, London: British Tourist Authority, 1985.

Nancy, N.: *Choosing a Career in Hotels, Motels, and Resorts*, New York, Rosen Pub. Group, 1997.

Pearce, Douglas: *Tourism Today: A Geographical Analysis*, Harlow, Longman, 1995.

Sabharwal Rajiv : *Tourism and Hospitality Management in Liberalised Era*, Pacific, Delhi, 2011.

Shrivastava Atul : *Modern Hospitality and Tourism Management*, Centrum Press, Delhi, 2010.

Slinn, Judy A: *Tourism: Management of Facilities*, London, Pitman: M & E, 1993.

Smith, V.L. : *Hosts and Guests: The Anthropology of Tourism*, Oxford: Blackwell, 1978.

Tribe, John *Corporate Strategy for Tourism, London*, International Thomson Business Press, 1997.

Var, Turgut: *Tourism Planning*, London, Retailed, 2002.

Index

N

O

P

R

S

T

V

❑❑❑